MATHS IN ACTION

National 3
Lifeskills

M Armstrong
H Brown
M Brown
R Howat
G Marra
G Meikle
E Mullan
R Murray
K Nisbet
J Thomson

Series editor: E Mullan

OXFORD

UNIVERSITY PRESS

OXFORD
UNIVERSITY PRESS

Great Clarendon Street, Oxford, OX2 6DP, United Kingdom

Oxford University Press is a department of the University of Oxford.
It furthers the University's objective of excellence in research, scholarship,
and education by publishing worldwide. Oxford is a registered trade mark of
Oxford University Press in the UK and in certain other countries.

British Library Cataloguing in Publication Data
Data available

978-1-4085-2377-3

1 3 5 7 9 10 8 6 4 2

Printed in China

Contents

Introduction   v

1 Whole numbers   1
1.1   Adding and subtracting   2
1.2   Multiplication   4
1.3   Division   5
1.4   Rounding   7
1.5   More number work   9

2 Decimals   12
2.1   Rounding to the nearest unit   13
2.2   Adding and subtracting
      decimals   15
2.3   Multiplying decimals   17
2.4   Division of decimals   18
2.5   Multiplying and dividing by 10
      and 100   20
2.6   Add, subtract, multiply or
      divide   21
2.7   Rounding in context, and
      remainders   23

3 Positive and negative numbers   26
3.1   Below zero   27
3.2   Other uses for negative
      numbers   31

4 Buying, selling and bills   37
4.1   Money calculations   38
4.2   Bills and discounts   41
4.3   Gas and electricity bills   44
4.4   Profit and loss   46

5 Extra charges, Value Added Tax and
      borrowing   50
5.1   Calculating percentages   51
5.2   Extra charges   53

5.3   Value Added Tax (VAT)   55
5.4   Loans and Hire Purchase (HP) 57

6 Tables   62
6.1   Tables in everyday use   63
6.2   Ready reckoners and distance
      charts   68

7 Reading graphs   72
7.1   Bar graphs   74
7.2   Line graphs   76
7.3   Pie charts   78

8 Length   82
8.1   Estimating length   83
8.2   Using millimetres   84
8.3   Changing to a smaller unit   86
8.4   Changing to a bigger unit   88
8.5   Perimeter   90

9 Managing time   94
9.1   The 12-and 24-hour clock   95
9.2   Units of time   98
9.3   Duration   99
9.4   Planning ahead   101

10 Speed, distance and time   106
10.1 Speed – how fast?   107
10.2 Distance – how far?   110
10.3 Time – how long?   112
10.4 Timetables   115

11 2-D shapes   119
11.1 Triangles   120
11.2 Quadrilaterals   123
11.3 Working with circles   127

12 Handling data 130
12.1 Frequency tables 131
12.2 Averages 135
12.3 What's the chance? 139

13 Earnings 145
13.1 Wages and salaries 146
13.2 Hourly rates 148
13.3 Piecework 150
13.4 Commission 152
13.5 Take-home pay 154
13.6 Benefits and the
       Universal Credit 157

14 Proportion 161
14.1 Rates 162
14.2 Best buys 165
14.3 Proportion 166
14.4 Scales, models and maps 168

15 Perimeter and area 172
15.1 Perimeter 173
15.2 Estimating an area 175
15.3 Area of rectangles 178
15.4 Area and perimeter
       problems 180

16 Volume and weight 184
16.1 Volumes of cuboids 185
16.2 A formula and units 187
16.3 Capacity and litres 189
16.4 Volume and weight
       connection 191

17 Fractions and percentages 195
17.1 Fraction values 196
17.2 Percentages 199

18 Scale drawings 205
18.1 The mariner's compass 206
18.2 Bearings 209
18.3 Scales 210
18.4 Scale drawings 213
18.5 Giving directions 216
18.6 Enlargements and
       reductions 218

19 Patterns and formulae 222
19.1 Patterns 223
19.2 Counting numbers 225
19.3 Finding the rule 228
19.4 Formulae 230

20 Percentages and money 234
20.1 Calculating percentages 235
20.2 Calculating percentages 237
20.3 Simple interest 239
20.4 Loans 241

21 Tiling and symmetry 244
21.1 Mirror symmetry 244
21.2 Tilings 247
21.3 Coordinates with symmetry
       and tilings 249

22 Statistics 253
22.1 Pictograms 255
22.2 Bar charts 257
22.3 Spotting trends and making
       comparisons 259
22.4 Probability 262

Acknowledgements

Introduction

This book has been created especially to cater for the needs of the student attempting the National 3 Lifeskills course. It is important that a student sees the relevance of a subject in order to learn it effectively.

With that in mind, wherever possible, real-life scenarios from daily living, the workplace and a variety of school subjects have been chosen to give questions a context. Inevitably, these contexts do get simplified as other factors not relevant to the occasion are omitted. In some cases we may have altered material facts slightly in order to make the scenarios mathematically accessible to students.

Each chapter is structured in the same way and begins with a problem associated with a real-life situation. Although some students may be able to attempt this already, it will prove to be a challenge to most, as they are unlikely to have the necessary skills and experience to solve the problem fully. It should therefore act as an introductory stimulus for bringing into play the strategies for problem solving that students are already familiar with, while perhaps also showing the shortcomings of these for the task in hand. By the time students have worked through the chapter, they should be able to complete the problem successfully, and when the problem is reintroduced at the end of the chapter, they should appreciate how their skills have expanded.

There follows a feature called 'What you need to know', which contains a few questions that students should be able to tackle using their current knowledge. It is important that students are comfortable with each of these, because the questions exercise the very skills required to get the most from the chapter.

Exposition of the new skills is accompanied by worked examples, which the student is encouraged to mimic in the laying out of their own solutions.

The level of difficulty of questions is indicated in the following ways:

Questions essential to the successful completion of the course are contained in the A exercises. If students can do these, they are on target for success.

A student wishing to take Maths further into National 4/National 4 Lifeskills should also be able to handle the strategies needed to complete the B exercises that have a green-tinted background and are more challenging.

At the end of each chapter there is a section called 'Preparation for assessment'. If a student cannot do one of these questions they should perhaps revisit the corresponding section in the chapter or ask the teacher for help. This section culminates with a revisit to the introductory question, which by now should be totally accessible. This will act to bring the class together again if students have been working at different levels.

Throughout the book, various icons have been used to identify particular features: indicate the most appropriate mode of tackling a problem. As part of the assessment measures students' numerate abilities without the aid of a calculator, it is essential that the parts marked 'non-calculator' are indeed done without a calculator.

indicates a topic suitable for class discussion. This device is used when, as a topic starts, we are aware that students may have different educational experiences as they advanced through S1 to S3 following the CfE. A class discussion will help to make the necessary knowledge base the same for the whole group.

 indicates a question for which some research or investigative work would enrich the student's experience.

 indicates where a puzzle has been added also for the sake of enrichment. These puzzles can always be taken further.

Opportunities exist, especially in the area of finance, for exploiting the power of the spreadsheet. The use of IT should be thoroughly explored.

Statistics is to be seen as a practical subject, and, as well as the exercises provided, investigative surveys leading to a written report would be beneficial. This too is made more pertinent and enjoyable through the use of IT.

Finally, a convention is followed throughout the series whereby the decimal point is placed mid-line, e.g. when writing '3 point 14' we would write 3·14 and not 3.14. The latter style is used in spreadsheets, however.

In Britain we often use the 'point on the line' to act as a less conspicuous multiplication sign than '×'. This is especially useful in algebra:

e.g. When $x = 6$ then $3x + 2 = 3.6 + 2 = 18 + 2 = 20$

In conclusion, maths is everywhere, it's relevant, it *is* essential, and it can be enjoyed.

1 Whole numbers

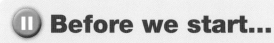

⏸ Before we start...

The Romans recorded their numbers using letters.
They did their calculations on a special abacus.
The first setting represents zero.

The second setting shows DCCLXXXVII.
What number is that?

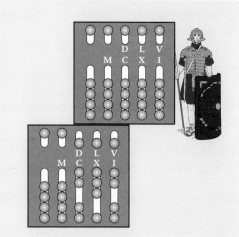

▶ What you need to know

1 a On a hill walk, I climbed two thousand,
   four hundred and fifteen feet.
   Write this in figures.

   b The height of Goat Fell is 2867 feet.
   Write this in words.

2 a Put these numbers in order, starting with the smallest.
   5041   5107   4513   5042   4527

   b Put these numbers in order, starting with the largest.
   1775   1814   1504   1498   1841

3 Calculate:

   a 27 + 62   b 26 + 18   c 73 + 66   d 94 − 58

   e 74 − 35   f 418 + 214   g 876 − 524   h 325 − 188.

4 Calculate:

   a 23 × 10   b 125 × 10   c 50 ÷ 10   d 470 ÷ 10.

5 Calculate:

   a 49 × 100   b 21 × 100   c 371 × 100   d 1200 ÷ 100   e 9400 ÷ 100.

6 A box of salt weighs 350 g. What would 10 boxes weigh?

7 A garden path is made from eight slabs laid in a line. It is 416 centimetres long.
   What is the length of one slab?

1.1 Adding and subtracting

Example 1

Add 3475 and 2387.

Th H T U		Th H T U		Th H T U		Th H T U
3 4 7 5		3 4 7 5		3 4 7 5		3 4 7 5
+ 2 3 8 ₁7	⟶	+ 2 3 ₁8 7	⟶	+ 2 3 8 7	⟶	+ 2 3 8 7
2		6 2		8 6 2		5 8 6 2

Add the units
$5 + 7 = 12$

Add the tens
$8 + 7 + 1 = 16$

Add the hundreds
$3 + 4 + 1 = 8$

Add the thousands
$2 + 3 = 5$

Example 2

Subtract 2567 from 7385.

Th H T U		Th H T U		Th H T U		Th H T U
7 3 8 5		7 3 ⁷8 ¹5		7 3 ⁷8 ¹5		⁶7 ¹3 8 5
− 2 5 6 7	⟶	− 2 5 6 7	⟶	− 2 5 6 7	⟶	− 2 5 6 7
		8		1 8		4 8 1 8

$5 − 7 = ?$

$15 − 7 = 8$

$7 − 6 = 1$

$3 − 5 = ?$
so $13 − 5 = 8$
and $6 − 2 = 4$

Exercise 1.1A

1 Calculate:

   a 426 + 517   b 741 + 175   c 578 + 294

   d 2513 + 765   e 5367 + 297   f 5958 + 696.

2 Calculate:

   a 3516 + 2473   b 4747 + 2159   c 3284 + 6285

   d 7365 + 1589   e 3942 + 2856   f 2857 + 4435.

3 Calculate:

   a 854 − 423   b 621 − 208   c 625 − 350

   d 9624 − 716   e 4623 − 258   f 6043 − 376.

4 A tanker delivers petrol to garages. It fills up with 225 barrels of petrol.

   By noon it had delivered 158 barrels to garages.

   How many barrels of petrol does it have left?

5 A bag held 756 grams of sugar. Georgina used 59 grams to make a cake.

   What weight of sugar was left in the bag?

6   The average height of a man in the UK is 177 cm.

In Indonesia the average height of a man is 158 cm.

What is the difference in their heights?

7   Two paintings were sold at an auction.

One was sold for £960 and the other for £279.

How much more expensive was the first painting?

Exercise 1.1B

1   How much will a new car cost if I trade in my old car?

ONLY
£9559

£2998 OFF
for trade in

2   An electrician has 4000 cm of cable.

He uses 1756 cm re-wiring a flat.

How much cable has he left?

3   In a recent census there were 1826 people counted in the village of Newbiggins.

There were 914 males in the village. How many females were counted?

4   Michael earned £2487 a month.

He was given a pay rise of £198 a month.

What is his new monthly wage?

5   Jackie kept a log of the distance she travelled weekly.

At the beginning the milometer read 8159 miles.

In the first week she drove 785 miles. In the second week she drove 814 miles.

What did the milometer read at the end of the two weeks?

6   The population of Scotland in the census of 2011 was 5295 thousand.

This was a rise of 233 thousand on the previous census of 2001.

What was the population of Scotland in 2001?

7   A company was drilling for oil which was 3000 m down.

On the first day they got down 356 m. On the second day they drilled a further 389 m.

How far do they still have to drill to reach the target of 3000 m?

1.2 Multiplication

Example

Calculate 457×3

$$
\begin{array}{r}
457 \\
\times \ _23 \\
\hline
1
\end{array}
$$
$3 \times 7 = 21$

$$
\begin{array}{r}
457 \\
\times _1 \ 3 \\
\hline
71
\end{array}
$$
$3 \times 5 + 2 = 17$

$$
\begin{array}{r}
457 \\
\times \ \ 3 \\
\hline
1371
\end{array}
$$
$3 \times 4 + 1 = 13$

Exercise 1.2A

1 Calculate:

a 38×6 b 125×5 c 397×2

d 480×3 e 917×8 f 214×9

g 1226×7 h 2174×4 i 5102×6

2 A trestle table is 225 cm in length. Eight are placed in a row for a banquet.
How long is the row?

3 A can of cola holds 250 ml of liquid.
How much cola is there in a pack of eight cans?

4 At the wind farm, each turbine has an output of 255 kilowatts.
There are eight turbines.
What is the total output from the wind farm?

5 At Christmas, the school took 78 students to a pantomime. Eight teachers went to supervise.
The theatre charged £5 each for the students and £14 each for the teachers.
a What was the total charge for the students?
b How much was charged for the whole party?

6 Bed and breakfast at a country inn costs £24 per person per night.
How much would it cost two people staying 4 nights?

7 Bryan grew tulips and sunflowers in his garden.
On average his tulips were 37 cm tall. His average sunflower was four times bigger.
What is the average height of his sunflowers?

Exercise 1.2B

1 A staircase has 14 steps. Each step has a rise of 195 mm.
a How much will you rise when you climb: **i** 10 steps   **ii** 4 steps?
b How much will you rise when you climb all 14 steps?

2 A can of juice weighs 280 g. They are sold in boxes of 12.

  a How much will the weight be of: **i** 10 cans **ii** 2 cans?

  b If the box itself weighs 50 g, what will the box of 12 cans weigh?

3 Practising for the marathon, Helen ran 15 miles each day for the month of July (31 days). How many miles is this in total?

4 The computer department orders 18 laptops at £429 each. What is the total cost?

5 Edinburgh Castle, on average, attracted 3579 visitors every day in 2013. How many visitors was this over the year?

6 Kenneth borrowed £7000.

The bank he borrowed it from asked him to pay £356 a month for 24 months.

  a How much did he pay?

  b How much more than the £7000 is this?

7 The highest point of the Eildon Hills in the Scottish Borders is 422 m. Mount Everest is roughly 21 times as big.

  a What is the height of Everest?

  b What is the difference in height between Everest and the Eildons?

1.3 Division

Example

Calculate $952 \div 7$.

$$\begin{array}{r} 1 \\ 7\overline{)9\,{}^2 5\ 2} \end{array}$$
$9 \div 7 = 1\ r\ 2$

$$\begin{array}{r} 1\ 3 \\ 7\overline{)9\,{}^2 5\,{}^4 2} \end{array}$$
$25 \div 7 = 3\ r\ 4$

$$\begin{array}{r} 1\ 3\ 6 \\ 7\overline{)9\,{}^2 5\,{}^4 2} \end{array}$$
$42 \div 7 = 6$

Exercise 1.3A

1 Calculate:

  a $78 \div 3$
  b $128 \div 4$
  c $335 \div 5$
  d $4902 \div 6$

  e $2296 \div 7$
  f $3136 \div 8$
  g $4608 \div 9$
  h $6936 \div 8$.

2 A fence round a playing field is 588 m long. The fence forms a square.

  a How long is each side?

  b The fence is made up of sections which are 7 m long. How many sections are needed?

3   Six identical boxes of nails were made up to give to the joiners on the building site.
    The total weight of nails used was 9912 g.
    What weight of nails was in one box?

4   Before 1971, the half-crown was a coin in use.
    Eight half-crowns were needed to make £1.
    An archaeologist found a hoard of them in an old safe.
    There were 1568 of them.
    How many pounds (£1) was this?

5   Robert has 9 months to save the £2772 he needs for his holiday abroad.
    He saves the same amount each month.
    a   How much should he save a month?
    b   This can be broken down into four equal weekly payments.
        How much should he save a week?

7   Since 14 = 2 × 7, we can divide by 14 by dividing by 2 and then by 7.
    a   Calculate 4564 ÷ 14.
    b   Calculate 6804 ÷ 21. (Hint: 21 = 3 × 7.)
    c   Calculate 9456 ÷ 24.

Exercise 1.3B

1   The river Nile is 6650 km long. This is roughly 38 times the length of the River Clyde.
    How long is the River Clyde?

2   An astronomer took notes of the two moons of Mars, Phobos and Deimos.
    a   Phobos moved 61 304 km in 8 hours.
        How far does it travel in 1 hour?
    b   Deimos travelled 151 001 km in 31 hours.
        How far does it travel in 1 hour?

3   An adult grey seal weighs 238 kg.
    As a new-born pup, it only weighed 14 kg.
    a   How much heavier is the adult?
    b   How many times heavier is the adult now than
        it was as a pup?

4   The area of Northern Ireland is approximately 13 825 km².
    Lough Neagh is in Northern Ireland and is the largest loch in the UK.
    Northern Ireland is 35 times the size of Lough Neagh.
    What is the area of Lough Neagh?

5 **A** When a number is divisible by 3, the sum of its digits is divisible by 3.

Example 1: Can 726 be divided by 3?

The digits add to give 15. ($7 + 2 + 6 = 15$)

15 is divisible by 3 so 726 is divisible by 3.

Example 2: Can 12 835 be divided by 3?

$1 + 2 + 8 + 3 + 5 = 19$ ... the digits add to give 19.

19 does not divide by 3 so 12 835 is not divisible by 3.

  a Which of these numbers is divisible by 3?

  i 891   **ii** 372   **iii** 9456   **iv** 4172   **v** 3027   **vi** 9659

  b Find two 5-digit numbers which are divisible by 3.

  c If we add two numbers that can be divided by 3, is the result divisible by 3?

B When a number is divisible by 4, the last 2 digits of the number will be divisible by 4.

Example 1: Can 3732 be divided by 4 exactly?

The last 2 digits are 32. $32 \div 4 = 8$ ... with no remainder.

So 3732 can be divided by 4 exactly.

  a Which of these numbers can be divided by 4?

  i 5736   **ii** 8526   **iii** 2004   **iv** 1994   **v** 2013

  b Find out about the rule that lets you decide whether a year is a leap year or not.

1.4 Rounding

Example 1

Round 57 to the nearest 10.

50 51 52 53 54 55 56 **57** 58 59 60

57 lies between 50 and 60.

It is closer to 60.

We say $57 = 60$ to the nearest 10.

Example 2

Round 285 to the nearest 10.

280 281 282 283 284 **285** 286 287 288 289 290

285 lies exactly midway between 280 and 290.

We always round **up** when this happens.

So, $285 = 290$ to the nearest 10.

You can use rounding to estimate the answers to problems.

This lets you check the answer given by your calculator.

7

Example 3

Calculate 562 + 3861 and check your answer by rounding to the nearest 100.

The calculator gives 4423.

Round each number to the nearest 100.

The numbers in the sum round to 600 + 3900 = 4500.

4500 is fairly close to 4423 ... the calculator is probably right.

Exercise 1.4A

1 Round these numbers to the nearest 10:

    a 77   **b** 83   **c** 91   **d** 35   **e** 63

    f 581   **g** 618   **h** 729   **i** 815   **j** 796.

2 Round these numbers to the nearest 100:

    a 742   **b** 872   **c** 395   **d** 750   **e** 811

    f 625   **g** 2545   **h** 1356   **i** 2907   **j** 1950.

3 **a** Round these numbers to the nearest 10:

      i 412   **ii** 728   **iii** 418   **iv** 825.

    b Using your rounded numbers from part **a**, give estimates for these sums:

      i 412 + 728   **ii** 418 − 412   **iii** 825 + 418   **iv** 825 − 728.

    c Round the same numbers to the nearest 100 and give other estimates for the same sums.

    d Work out the actual answers to the sums in part **b**.

    e Which estimates give the closest answers?

4 **a** Round these numbers to the nearest 100:

      i 3560   **ii** 4492   **iii** 9550   **iv** 2050.

    b Using the rounded answers from part **a**, give estimates for these sums:

      i 3558 ÷ 6   **ii** 4491 ÷ 9   **iii** 9550 × 8   **iv** 2050 × 7.

    c Work out the actual answers for the sums in part **b** using a calculator.

Exercise 1.4B

1 Travelling on the bus between Edinburgh and Glasgow we spotted a wire horse sculpture.

    The satnav on our phone said we had travelled 65 km from Edinburgh.

    The bus route between Edinburgh and Glasgow is 76 km.

    a What distance have we still to go to reach Glasgow?

    b Estimate what fraction of the journey still has to be made.

2 Seven friends each pay £623 for a holiday in The Highlands.

Estimate how many hundreds of pounds the holiday will cost in total.

3 From Glasgow to London is a journey of 404 miles and will take 6 hours, according to a website.

Estimate what the website thinks is the number of miles you drive in one hour.

4 A few puzzles. Find the missing numbers.

a
```
  ● 9 ●
+ 7 ● 8
-------
● 3 1 5
```

b
```
  ● 4 ●
+ 2 ● 5
-------
  5 7 0
```

c
```
  7 1 ●
- ● ● 5
-------
  1 1 6
```

d
```
  ● ● 1 ●
-   3 7 9
---------
    7 ● 9
```

e
```
  ● 5 2
×     ●
-------
● 9 1 2
```

f
```
  ● 5 ●
×     7
-------
● 7 ● 9
```

g
```
      7 4
  ●)3 7 ●
```

h
```
      6 ●
  ●)5 ● 8
```

1.5 More number work

Remember to estimate before calculating.

1 John was studying the story of coal. He found that it was formed in the Carboniferous era, which started 359 million years ago and ended 299 million years ago.

For how long did the Carboniferous era last?

2 The four faces of this pyramid have a total area of 348 m².

a What is the area of one face?

b The stone costs £120 for a square metre.

To multiply by 120, you can:
first multiply by 2
then multiply the answer by 6
then multiply the answer by 10.

How much does it cost for stone for one face of the pyramid?

3 James earned £2547 in January. He earned £3579 in February.

How much more did he earn in February?

4 In 2012, Felix Baumgartner flew to an altitude of 39 045 m in a balloon and then jumped out.

He reached a speed of 1344 km per hour.

He free fell for 36 529 m before opening his parachute.

a How high was he when he opened his chute?

b He reached a speed which was 12 times the legal limit in Britain.

Calculate the legal limit in Britain.

5 In roman numerals, I = 1, V = 5, X = 10, L = 50, C = 100, D = 500, M = 1000.

What is the value of: **a** MMXIII **b** MMDCCCLXXVII?

Exercise 1.5B

1 A ferry makes the trip between an island and the mainland. The distance is 15 miles.

a What distance is travelled there and back again?

b The ferry makes 6 such return trips each day, Monday to Saturday.

It only makes 4 return trips on a Sunday.

How many trips does it make in a week?

c What distance does it travel in a week?

2 In 2013, Nik Wallenda crossed the Grand Canyon on a tightrope.

The rope was 374 m long, and it took him 22 minutes to make the crossing.

How far was he travelling per minute?

3 Hampden Park football stadium is allowed to hold a crowd of 52 063 people.

However, in 1937, the regulations were not as tight.
The record crowd then was 149 415 people for a Scotland v. England match.

a How many people above the modern safety limit is this?

b James says the record crowd is roughly 2 times the modern limit but
Sati says it is closer to 3 times. Who is correct?

4 From Land's End to John O'Groats by bike is 1407 km.

The Cycling Club intend to do it in 12 days by cycling 117 km a day.

Will this be enough?

5 From Edinburgh to Perth by road is a distance of 69 km.

From Perth to Thurso is 354 km.

a What is the total distance from Edinburgh to Thurso?

b Three drivers share the distance equally.
How far does each driver go?

c The first driver does his whole share of the driving straight away.
How far from Perth is he when they change drivers?

Preparation for assessment

1 Calculate:

  a 571 + 399   b 398 + 617   c 926 − 257   d 724 − 536.

2 Calculate:

  a 375 × 6   b 299 × 9   c 715 × 8   d 247 × 7.

3 Calculate:

  a 364 ÷ 4   b 906 ÷ 6   c 819 ÷ 9   d 4354 ÷ 7.

4 Round these numbers to the nearest: i 10   ii 100.

  a 178   b 845   c 6545   d 3819

5 Estimate the answers by rounding first:

  a 274 + 1927   b 8145 − 499   c 143 × 7   d 143 ÷ 7   e 1522 ÷ 8.

6 During a charity drive, three classes collected pennies.

  1A collected 2541 pennies, 1B collected 2799 pennies and 1C collected 3582 pennies.

  How many pennies were collected altogether?

7 Seven cars are parked bumper-to-bumper in the car factory storage area.

  Each car was 485 cm in length.

  What was the length of the queue formed?

8 The Coast-to-Coast Walk goes from St Bees to Robin Hood's Bay ... a distance of 293 km.

  a In 1991, the route was run in just under 40 hours.
     Estimate how far the runner travelled each hour.

  b For charity Ted intends to do the walk from St Bees to
     Robin Hood's Bay and back again to St Bees.

     After he had walked 350 km, how far had he still got to go?

9 Remember Roman numerals?

  The Romans recorded their numbers using letters.

  They did their calculations on a special abacus.

  The first setting represents zero.

  The second setting shows DCCLXXXVII.

  What number is that?

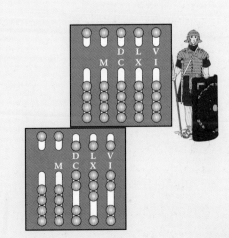

2 Decimals

 Before we start...

The 'Loch Eck', a car ferry, can **just** carry 18 cars of length 4·4 metres when they are parked nose-to-tail in **two** rows on the car deck.

Each car has to pay £42.

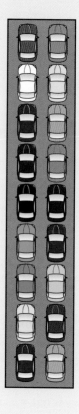

a How much money will the ferry company take in from a ferry-load of cars?

b What is the length of the car deck?

c Vans are 5·7 m in length. They can fit two rows of vans on the deck. If they had a ferry-load of vans, what should they charge each van to take in the same amount of money as a ferry-load of cars?

What you need to know

1 Write down the answer to:

   a 9×5 **b** 7×8 **c** 8×6 **d** 5×7 **e** 6×6

   f $63 \div 9$ **g** $49 \div 7$ **h** $42 \div 7$ **i** $45 \div 5$ **j** $56 \div 8$.

2 State the value of:

   a 5×10 **b** 8×100 **c** 12×1000 **d** 25×100

   e $450 \div 10$ **f** $7900 \div 10$ **g** $3200 \div 100$ **h** $400 \div 100$.

3 Round these numbers to the nearest: **i** 10   **ii** 100.

   a 6753   **b** 3083   **c** 4875   **d** 8995   **e** 4005

4 A length of wood is 180 cm. It has to be cut into 9 equal bits. How long will each bit be?

5 Calculate:

    a 14×5 **b** 25×6 **c** $68 \div 4$ **d** $84 \div 7$.

6 In the number 34·56, the 3 represents 3 tens …

    What do the following represent?

    a The 4.   **b** The 5.   **c** The 6.

2.1 Rounding to the nearest unit

When rounding to the nearest unit, look at the first digit after the decimal point.

- If it is a 4 or less, round down.
- If it is a 5 or more, round up.

Example 1

a Round 7·3 to the nearest whole unit.

b Round 11·52 to the nearest unit.

a The first digit after the point is a 3.   … a 4 or less, **round down**
So 7·3 rounds to 7.

b The digit after the point is 5.   … a 5 or more, **round up**
So 11·52 rounds to 12.

Example 2

On a ferry, one car and a driver are charged £41·90. A passenger is charged £14·40.

a Round each charge to the nearest pound.

b Use your answer to estimate the cost of taking a car, driver and passenger on the ferry.

a £41·90 rounds to £42. Note the first digit after the point was 5 or bigger.
£14·40 rounds to £14. Note the first digit after the point was 4 or less.

b As an estimate the total cost is £42 + £14 = £56.

Exercise 2.1A

1 Round these numbers to the nearest whole unit.

    a 12·7   **b** 24·5   **c** 13·4   **d** 16·8   **e** 84·1

    f 77·6   **g** 59·9   **h** 85·2   **i** 99·3   **j** 99·5

2 An oystercatcher had a beak of 7·7 cm.

Its height was measured as 18·7 cm.

The width of its wing was 11·5 cm.

The wing length was 16·5 cm.

Round each size to the nearest centimetre.

3 Round each weight to the nearest kilogram.

a   12·7 kg   b   37·5 kg   c   29·9 kg

d   91·3 kg   e   79·5 kg

4 a   Round each number to the nearest pound.

i   £16·70   ii   £36·50   iii   £52·67

iv   £49·95   v   £99·49

b   Using the rounded numbers in part **a**, work out estimates for these sums:

i   16·70 + 36·50   ii   36·50 + 49·95

iii 49·95 − 16·70   iv 36·50 − 16·70.

Whenever you use a calculator you should estimate what your answer
is likely to be using this method.

Exercise 2.1B

1 Round each of these to the nearest whole number:

a   13·34   b   84·57   c   81·79   d   42·85

e   77·49   f   39·52   g   748·77   h   899·62.

2 Round these weights to the nearest kilogram:

a   2·47 kg   b   6·96 kg   c   5·94 kg   d   1·52 kg

e   23·49 kg   f   57·81 kg   g   74·49 kg   h   9·99 kg.

3 Sam and his father went for a trip on the *Waverley*.

His dad paid £27·78 for himself and £14·49 for Sam.

a   Round each amount to the nearest whole pound.

b   Using these rounded amounts, estimate how much the trip cost.

4 Susan measured the lengths of the five walls of her classroom.

They measured 6·24 m, 5·81 m, 5·93 m, 3·39 m and 4·58 m.

a   Round each length to the nearest metre.

b   Find an estimate for the distance round the edge of the room.

2.2 Adding and subtracting decimals

When adding or subtracting decimal numbers keep the points in a column.

This will make sure the right digits line up.

Example 1

Add 6·9 and 3·3.

```
  T U   t
    6 · 9
+   3 · 3
  ─────────
  1 0 · 2
```

Note: adding 9 and 3 gives 12 ... so we put the 2 in the tenths column and carry 1 into the units column.

We then add 6 and 3 and 1 to get 10.

Example 2

Find the difference between 8·2 and 3·9.

```
  T U   t              T U    t
    8 · 2                7 · ¹2
−   3 · 9      ⟹    −    3 · 9
  ─────────           ─────────
      ·                  4 · 3
```

Note: we can't take 9 from 2
... so we change 8 units and 2 tenths to 7 units and 12 tenths ... and we can take 9 from 12.

Exercise 2.2A

1 Add: **a** 5·7 and 4·2   **b** 8·5 and 3·7   **c** 7·1 and 5·7   **d** 9·7 and 4·6.

2 Copy and complete these sums:

a $\begin{array}{r} 6·7 \\ + 9·8 \\ \hline \\ \hline \end{array}$ **b** $\begin{array}{r} 10·8 \\ + \;\; 9·5 \\ \hline \\ \hline \end{array}$ **c** $\begin{array}{r} 14·2 \\ + 11·8 \\ \hline \\ \hline \end{array}$ **d** $\begin{array}{r} 22·5 \\ + 17·9 \\ \hline \\ \hline \end{array}$

3 Find the difference between:

a 8·6 and 2·4   **b** 7·6 and 4·5

c 8·1 and 3·8   **d** 7·5 and 2·6.

4 **a** $\begin{array}{r} 8·4 \\ - 5·2 \\ \hline \\ \hline \end{array}$ **b** $\begin{array}{r} 9·2 \\ - 1·9 \\ \hline \\ \hline \end{array}$ **c** $\begin{array}{r} 7·7 \\ - 2·8 \\ \hline \\ \hline \end{array}$ **d** $\begin{array}{r} 5·8 \\ - 3·9 \\ \hline \\ \hline \end{array}$

e $\begin{array}{r} 12·3 \\ - \;\; 3·9 \\ \hline \\ \hline \end{array}$ **f** $\begin{array}{r} 25·8 \\ - \;\; 6·1 \\ \hline \\ \hline \end{array}$ **g** $\begin{array}{r} 38·9 \\ - \;\; 7·5 \\ \hline \\ \hline \end{array}$ **h** $\begin{array}{r} 52·4 \\ - \;\; 9·6 \\ \hline \\ \hline \end{array}$

5 Add: **a** 3·42, 7·66 and 1·45   **b** 24·6, 18·5 and 6·7.

6 In a nature survey a red and a grey squirrel were weighed.

The red weighed 271·6 g and the grey weighed 502·4 g.

What was their difference in weight?

7 Joe keeps a record of his hill walks.

On his last three, he walked for 13·7 km, 20·8 km and 23·2 km.

How far has he walked in total on these walks?

Example 3

Find the sum of 16·4 and 3·75.

```
  T  U   t  h
  1  6 · 4  0        Note: use the points to line up the digits ...
+    3 · 7  5        if a place has no digit, imagine it as a zero.
  2  0 · 1  5
```

Example 4

Subtract 4·69 from 12·9.

```
  T  U   t  h
  1  2 · 9  0        Note: use the points to line up the digits ...
−    4 · 6  9        if a place has no digit, imagine it as a zero.
     8 · 2  1
```

Exercise 2.2B

1 Calculate:

    a 36·2 + 3·81   **b** 65·12 + 2·6   **c** 5·7 + 12·94

    d 14·8 + 12·37   **e** 2·9 + 21·54   **f** 2·65 + 32·9.

2 Calculate:

    a 3·14 − 1·7   **b** 4·7 − 1·32   **c** 24·6 − 3·27

    d 18·14 − 14·6   **e** 25·37 − 3·7   **f** 52·3 − 3·26.

In each of questions 3−7, estimate your answer first ... by rounding.

3 Mr Drum weighs 76·32 kg and his wife weighs 57·49 kg.

What is the difference between their weights?

4 Two rugby players are weighed before a match.

The first player weighs 59·25 kg and the other 1·72 kg more.

How much does the second player weigh?

5 A transport lorry weighs 10·87 tonnes when empty.

When fully laden, it weighs 39·91 tonnes.

How heavy is its load?

6 A builder buys three neighbouring plots of land.

The areas of the plots are 12·67 square metres, 21·35 square metres and 18·55 square metres.

What is the total area he has for building?

7 A petrol tank can hold 54·25 litres when full.

There were only 12·96 litres in the tank.

How much needs to be added to the tank to fill it?

2.3 Multiplying decimals

Example 1

Multiply 23·6 by 4.

```
  H  T  U  ·  t
     2  3  ·  6
×           4
        2  4
     1  2
  0  8
     9  4  ·  4
```

Multiply the 6 by 4 ... and start your answer under the 6.
Multiply the 3 by 4 ... and start your answer under the 3.
Multiply the 2 by 4 ... and start your answer under the 2.
Add your answers.

Example 2

Find the product of 75·36 and 8.

```
  H  T  U  ·  t  h
     7  5  ·  3  6
×              8
           4  8
        2  4
     4  0
  5  6
  6  0  2  ·  8  8
```

Multiply the 6 by 8 ... and start your answer under the 6.
Multiply the 3 by 8 ... and start your answer under the 3.
Multiply the 5 by 8 ... and start your answer under the 5.
Multiply the 7 by 8 ... and start your answer under the 7.
Add your answers.

Exercise 2.3B

1 Calculate:

  a 9·2 × 3   **b** 4·5 × 7   **c** 8·9 × 4   **d** 1·7 × 5

  e 5·26 × 7   **f** 7·54 × 8   **g** 6·27 × 6   **h** 8·63 × 9.

2 A plumber has eight pieces of piping each measuring 3·85 m in length.
What is the total length of piping that he has?

3 Seven friends go to the cinema. The cost for one ticket is £8·65.
How much do they pay altogether?

4 A ferry can just carry a row of seven cars on its deck. Each car is of length 4·6 m.
If they are parked bumper-to-bumper, what is the length of the deck?

5 These five cygnets are a week old and each weighs 592·4 grams.
Calculate the total weight of the cygnets.

Exercise 2.3B

1 Find the value of each product.

a 26·36 × 5	**b** 81·18 × 4	**c** 56·82 × 9	**d** 79·99 × 6
e 31·6 × 7	**f** 271·2 × 3	**g** 317·1 × 8	**h** 989·8 × 2

2 Malcolm pays £1·96 each day on buses to and from school.
How much does he pay in a week when he goes to school Monday to Friday?

3 On a breezy day a wind turbine generates 1·76 units of electricity
an hour.

    a How much would it generate in 6 hours?

    b How much would eight such turbines generate in this time?

4 Mary has an MP3 player. She knows a typical three-minute song
needs 4·56 MB of memory.
She's been told that the new album of her favourite group will
need nine times that amount of memory.
How much memory will it need?

2.4 Division of decimals

Example 1

Divide 7·71 by 3.

$$
\begin{array}{r} 2\cdot \\ 3\overline{)7\cdot{}^17\ 1} \end{array}
$$
7 ÷ 3 = 2 r 1

➠

$$
\begin{array}{r} 2\cdot5 \\ 3\overline{)7\cdot{}^17{}^21} \end{array}
$$
17 ÷ 3 = 5 r 2

➠

$$
\begin{array}{r} 2\cdot5\ 7 \\ 3\overline{)7\cdot{}^17{}^21} \end{array}
$$
21 ÷ 3 = 7

Example 2

Divide 83·52 by 6.

$$
\begin{array}{r}
1 \\
6\overline{)8^23\cdot5\ 2}
\end{array}
\qquad
\begin{array}{r}
1\ 3\cdot \\
6\overline{)8^23\cdot{}^55\ 2}
\end{array}
\qquad
\begin{array}{r}
1\ 3\cdot\ 9 \\
6\overline{)8^23\cdot{}^55^12}
\end{array}
\qquad
\begin{array}{r}
1\ 3\cdot\ 9\ 2 \\
6\overline{)8^23\cdot{}^55^12}
\end{array}
$$

$8 \div 6 = 1\,r\,2$ $23 \div 6 = 3\,r\,5$ $55 \div 6 = 9\,r\,1$ $12 \div 6 = 2$

Exercise 2.4A

1 Copy and complete these divisions:

    a $4\overline{)31\cdot2}$ **b** $3\overline{)9\cdot57}$ **c** $5\overline{)22\cdot80}$ **d** $6\overline{)7\cdot98}$

2 Calculate:

    a $6\cdot56 \div 4$ **b** $8\cdot73 \div 3$ **c** $18\cdot25 \div 5$ **d** $25\cdot32 \div 6$

    e $56\cdot76 \div 4$ **f** $23\cdot82 \div 3$ **g** $47\cdot16 \div 6$ **h** $39\cdot34 \div 7.$

3 A stretch limo is 10·26 m long. The makers claim it is the length of three Mini Coopers.

    What is the length of a Mini Cooper?

4 A sports shop has 246·75 metres of rope which it cuts into seven bits of equal length to sell to climbers.

    How long is each bit of rope?

Exercise 2.4B

1 Divide 13 by 4. (Hint: write 13 as 13·0.)

2 Calculate:

    a $36\cdot6 \div 5$ **b** $111 \div 6$ **c** $19 \div 5.$

3 Five friends dined out at the local restaurant. They chose to share the bill equally.

    It came to £133·05 in total.

    a How much did they each pay?

    b Peter paid with two £20 notes. What change did he get?

4 The car deck of a ferry is 38·7 m long.

    The operator says it can hold a row of nine cars parked bumper-to-bumper.

    If all the cars are the same length, what is the length of a car?

5 Gavin completed a road race in 124·8 minutes.

The race was 8 laps of a course. Each lap took Gavin the same amount of time.

Calculate the time Gavin took for each lap.

6 In the garden centre they used 7·5 kg of compost when potting up six plants.
Each plant was given the same amount of compost.

What weight of compost did each get?

2.5 Multiplying and dividing by 10 and 100

When multiplying by 10, the point appears to move 1 place to the right.

When multiplying by 100, the point appears to move 2 places to the right.

Example 1

Multiply 3·782 by: **a** 10 **b** 100.

a 3·782 × 10 = 37·82   ... the point seems to move 1 place to the right.

b 3·782 × 100 = 378·2   ... the point seems to move 2 places to the right.

When dividing by 10, the point appears to move 1 place to the left.

When dividing by 100, the point appears to move 2 places to the left.

Example 2

Divide 539·6 by: **a** 10   **b** 100.

a 539·6 ÷ 10 = 53·96   ... the point appears to move 1 place to the left.

b 539·6 ÷ 100 = 5·396   ... the point appears to move 2 places to the left.

Exercise 2.5A

1 Multiply each number by 10:

    a 3·64   **b** 21·72   **c** 54·3   **d** 916·4.

2 Multiply these numbers by 100:

    a 3·916   **b** 12·485   **c** 18·05   **d** 276·27.

3 Divide each number by 10:

    a 47·5   **b** 32·6   **c** 4·3   **d** 7·9

    e 17·0   **f** 27   **g** 0·36   **h** 0·01.

4 Divide these numbers by 100:

    a 279·3   **b** 741·9   **c** 59·3   **d** 66·8

    e 7·71   **f** 8·04   **g** 1·01   **h** 0·5.

5 Jamie works in the supermarket. They ask him to re-price items.

They take a tenth off the marked price.

What is the discount on items marked:

    a £24·50   **b** £3·60   **c** £124?

Exercise 2.5B

1 Calculate:

    a £7·99 × 10   **b** £0·53 × 100   **c** 12·45 m ÷ 10

    d 6·5 m × 100   **e** 0·6 litre ÷ 10   **f** 19·4 tonnes × 10.

2 There are 10 millimetres in a centimetre.

To turn millimetres into centimetres we divide by 10.

Turn the following sizes into centimetres:

    a 123 mm   **b** 75 mm   **c** 9 mm   **d** 12 cm 8 mm.

3 There are 100 cm in a metre.

To turn metres into centimetres we multiply by 100.

    a How many centimetres are in: **i** 4·64 m   **ii** 32·25 m   **iii** 3·5 m?

    b How would you turn centimetres into metres?

    c How many metres are in: **i** 529 cm   **ii** 635 cm   **iii** 81 cm   **iv** 5 cm?

4 To divide by 20 we can divide by 2 and then divide our answer by 10.

    a Divide each of the following by 20: **i** £248   **ii** £368   **iii** £96.

    b A box of 20 mobile phones costs the shop £2600.

        How much does each phone cost?

2.6 Add, subtract, multiply or divide

You may use a calculator but ... remember to estimate your answer before calculating it.

Exercise 2.6A

1 A path uses 18 slabs to get from the door to the gate.

Each slab has an area of 840 cm^2.

What is the area of the path?

2 Petra ordered 8 bags of compost.

The total weight of the bags was 178·8 kg.

What was the weight of one bag of compost?

3 Mary has a small paper round. She gets £12·45 each week from the shopkeeper.

How much will she get over 48 weeks?

4 A car ferry charges £39·65 for a car and its driver. It charges £15·20 for a passenger.

    a What is the total cost of a car with a driver and passenger?

    b What is the cost of the car alone, assuming that £15·20 of the £39·65 is for the driver?

5 Sam wanted to weigh his dog but it wouldn't stand on the bathroom scales itself.

He weighed himself at 75·7 kg. He picked up the dog and weighed him and the dog together ... 95·1 kg.

What was the weight of his dog?

Exercise 2.6B

1 **a** Each of the sides of this 50p piece is 12·25 mm long.

      What is the total length of all of the sides?

    b A 20p piece measures 67·2 mm all round.

      What is the length of one side of a 20p piece?

    c What is the difference between the distance round the two coins?

2 Margaret is going into town to see a film.

The bus will cost £1·20 each way and the cinema will cost £4·60.

How much change will she have from £10?

3 A parking bay has spaces for six vehicles.

Each space is 2·56 m wide.

How wide is the parking bay?

4 An electrician has to put in six extra wires in a theatre.
Each wire has to be 23·47 m.

How much wire does he need in total?

5 In a school, a corridor is 25·6 m long. It gives access to a book cupboard, an office and a classroom.

The classroom is 14·4 m long. The cupboard and the office are the same length.

How long is the office?

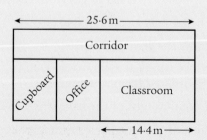

2.7 Rounding in context and remainders

Sometimes the normal rules of rounding have to be ignored because of the story line.

Example 1

A taxi can carry four people.

How many journeys will it need to make to transport 33 people?

$33 \div 4 = 8.25$ ... we would normally round this down to 8.

If the taxi makes 8 journeys then it will carry $8 \times 4 = 32$ people ... it will leave 1 person behind.

So the taxi needs to make 9 journeys.

Example 2

A box can hold 6 cakes.

Jemima makes 51 cakes and puts them into boxes.

a How many boxes can she fill?   **b** How many extra cakes are there?

a $51 \div 6 = 8.5$ ... we would normally round this up to 9.

   If she wants to fill 9 boxes she needs $6 \times 9 = 54$ cakes.

   She can only *fill* 8 boxes.

b $8 \times 6 = 48$ ... she uses 48 cakes.

   So $51 - 48 = 3$, she has 3 cakes left over.

Exercise 2.7A

1 The farmer collects 129 eggs. He puts them in boxes of six.

   a How many boxes will he fill?   **b** How many will be left over?

2 A ferry can carry 18 vehicles across the river at a time.

   There are 313 cars booked in to use the ferry.

   a How many journeys will it need to make to carry 313 vehicles across?

   b If all the journeys take a full load except for the last one, how many vehicles are in the last load?

3 Builders use a hoist to raise materials to the floor on which they are working.

   The hoist can lift 1·25 tonnes.

   How many times must it be used to raise 12·3 tonnes of materials?

4 A stretch of land is to be used for car parking.

   The minimum width needed for a car, to allow for people getting in and out of their vehicles, is 2·4 metres.

   The stretch is 28·5 m long.

   How many cars can be parked in the stretch?

Exercise 2.7B

1 Faisal is making shelves. Each shelf is to be 1·8 m long.

He has a plank of wood 10 m long.

  a How many shelves can he get from the plank?

  b How many metres are left unused?

2 Seven people are in a lottery syndicate. They win £12 000 and share it equally between them.

They each take an exact number of pounds and agree to send the rest to charity.

  a How much does each winner get?

  b What amount gets sent to charity?

3 Four friends are travelling to London, a distance of 405 miles.

They set off and agree to stop every 85 miles and change drivers.

  a How many times do they change drivers?

  b How far does the last driver have to drive during the journey? (Be careful!)

4 Michael has a debt of £394. He pays off the same amount each week.

  a What size must the repayment be to make sure the debt is paid off by the sixth payment?

  b How much will he have overpaid?

Preparation for assessment

1 Calculate:

  a $42.84 + 7.42$ **b** $241.56 - 27.41$ **c** 32.7×6

  d $4.67 + 21.9$ **e** $37.2 - 1.79$ **f** $292.6 \div 7.$

2 Calculate:

  a 79.37×10 **b** $129.6 \div 100$ **c** 2.55×100

  d $12.7 \div 10$ **e** $1.01 \div 10$ **f** $9.34 \div 100.$

3 Round each number to the nearest whole number.

  a 84·49   **b** 321·2   **c** 825·5

  d 8·63   **e** 99·59

4 A transporter carries nine cars. Each car weighs 948·3 kg.

What is the weight of the total load on the transporter?

5 A six-pack of Fizzy Juice costs £7·62.

   a What is the cost of one can?

   b They are also sold in eight-packs.

     What should be the cost of an 8-pack?

6 A minibus holds 12 passengers.

There are 43 people to be transported.

   a How many full bus loads will this make?

   b How many passengers will be in the last trip, if all the other trips were full bus loads?

7 The local cinema runs the following offer:

'If a teacher accompanies 10 students, the teacher is not charged.'

An entry ticket costs £7·50.

What is the total cost of entry for Mr McKenna and 10 students?

8 On a building site a small hoist is used to raise the bricks up to the bricklayers.

The hoist can raise 150 kg at a time safely.

A brick weighs 2·75 kg. A workman loads 60 bricks onto the hoist.

Can the hoist lift the load safely? (Show your working.)

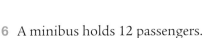

9 Remember the 'Loch Eck' car ferry can **just** carry 18 cars of length 4·4 metres when they are parked nose-to-tail in **two** rows on the car deck.

Each car has to pay £42.

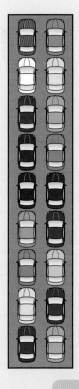

   a How much money will the ferry company take in from a ferry-load of cars?

   b What is the length of the car deck?

   c Vans are 5·7 m in length. They can fit two rows of vans on the deck.

     If they had a ferry-load of vans, what should they charge each van to take in the same amount of money as a ferry-load of cars?

3 Positive and negative numbers

⏸ Before we start...

We measure temperature most often using a thermometer with a Celsius (°C) scale.

Many old cookery books use a Fahrenheit (°F) scale.

We can switch from °F to °C using the number machine:

a Use the machine to convert the following temperatures to degrees Celsius.

i 212 °F   **ii** 68 °F   **iii** 23 °F

b The lit-up part of the Moon reaches temperatures of 257 °F.

The dark side gets as cold as −247 °F.

i Convert both temperatures to degrees Celsius.

ii What is the difference between these two temperatures on the Celsius scale?

▶ What you need to know

1 Some temperatures were noted one January in places around the world.

Alice Springs	35 °C	Fuzhou	19 °C
Bahrain	20 °C	Glasgow	2 °C
Chicago	1 °C	Hong Kong	18 °C
Darwin	32 °C	Ibiza	14 °C
Edinburgh	0 °C	Jakarta	29 °C

a List the temperatures, warmest first.

b How many degrees warmer was Bahrain than:

i Ibiza   **ii** Glasgow?

c How many degrees colder was Chicago than:

i Alice Springs   **ii** Jakarta?

2 In an old cookbook from 1970 there is a list of cheesy recipes for the oven.
Each comes with a temperature setting:

Potato Galette	20–30 mins	400 °F
Cheese Pizza	30 mins	425 °F
Vegetable Layers	1–1·5 hours	350 °F
Macaroni and Cheesy Mushroom	10–15 mins	450 °F

a Sort the temperatures in order, coldest first.

b What is the difference in temperature between the hottest and the coldest settings?

c Convert each temperature to Celsius, rounding your answers to the nearest degree.

3.1 Below zero

When the **Celsius scale** was developed, it was set so that:
- water turns to ice at 0 °C ... the freezing point of water
- water turns to steam at 100 °C ... the boiling point of water.

In winter, it can get colder than the freezing point of water ... colder than 0 °C.

We show this by using a negative sign (−).

The weatherman talks of 2 degrees of frost ... we write −2 °C ... which means 2 degrees below zero.

Numbers get smaller going to the left.

Example 1

Which is larger, −2 or −5?

Since −2 is to the right of −5 on the line, then −2 is larger than −5.

Exercise 3.1A

1 How would we write:

a six degrees below zero   **b** four degrees below zero

c twenty degrees above zero   **d** seventeen degrees below zero?

2 Which temperature is higher?

a 8 °C or 2 °C   **b** 5 °C or 0 °C   **c** −7 °C or 7 °C

d −3 °C or 0 °C   **e** 9 °C or −12 °C   **f** −5 °C or −6 °C

g −25 °C or −14 °C **h** 0 °C or −8 °C

3 Write down the temperature that is 2 °C warmer than:

a 7 °C　　**b** −1 °C　**c** −5 °C　**d** 0 °C　　**e** −2 °C.

4 Write down the temperature that is 3 °C lower than:

a 5 °C　　**b** 3 °C　　**c** −1 °C　**d** −6 °C　**e** −5 °C.

5 At the school, outdoor temperatures were measured throughout the day.

Time (o'clock)	9	10	11	12	1	2	3	4
Temperature (°C)	−4	−3	−1	0	−2	−2	−5	−7

a Between what times was the temperature:
　i rising　　**ii** falling?

b What was:
　i the warmest temperature recorded
　ii the coldest temperature recorded?

c Was it warmer at 9 a.m. or 4 p.m.?

d What was the temperature difference between 10 a.m. and 3 p.m.?

6 In Scotland, ice is never really safe to walk on.

However, in shallow pools, it is sometimes used for skating and curling when it is 10 cm thick and the temperature stays below zero.

Here are some cases where the temperature is rising steadily.

Continue the pattern to decide when the ice is not safe to use (when the temperature goes above 0 °C).

a −4 °C, −3 °C, −2 °C, ...　　　　**b** −12 °C, −10 °C, −8 °C, ...

c −25 °C, −20 °C, −15 °C, ...　　　**d** −17 °C, −12 °C, −7 °C, ...

7 **a** Write down the temperatures shown on these Celsius thermometers:

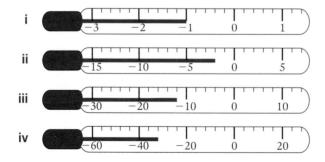

b What will each thermometer read if it gets 4 degrees warmer?

c What will each read if it gets 5 degrees colder?

Exercise 3.1B

1 a When Yanqun checked the temperature one morning in November it was −7 °C.

By midday, the temperature had risen by 8 degrees.

What was the temperature at midday?

b When Yanqun woke up on Christmas Day, the temperature was −5 °C and it had been snowing.

She was delighted that it was a white Christmas.

By 2 o'clock the temperature had risen by 7 degrees. Why might Yanqun be disappointed?

c In April, Yanqun went to bed with the temperature at 3 °C.

During the night, the temperature dropped by 10 °C.

How many degrees of frost were there?

2 Nuuk is on the west coast of Greenland.

The table shows its average temperature each month throughout the year.

Month	Jan	Feb	Mar	Apr	May	Jun	Jul	Aug	Sep	Oct	Nov	Dec
Temperature (°C)	−7.4	−7.8	−8.0	−3.8	0.6	3.9	6.5	6.1	3.5	−0.7	−3.7	−6.2

a What is the difference between the January and the April average temperature?

b How much warmer is August than:
   i May
   ii March?

c Name:
   i the coldest month
   ii the warmest month.

d Calculate the range of the average monthly temperatures.

3 A confectioner makes a variety of sweets by heating up sugar.

Different sweets need different temperatures.

Fudge: 118 °C   Toffee: 140 °C

Caramel: 170 °C   Tablet: 120 °C

a Arrange the temperatures in order, coolest first.

b Each sweet cools to room temperature (20 °C) before being eaten.

By how much does each sweet drop in temperature?

c They can be stored in the freezer at −5 °C.

What is the drop in temperature from the cooking temperature to the freezer?

4 On 1st January, the weather station at Paisley recorded the temperature every two hours.

The graph shows the results.

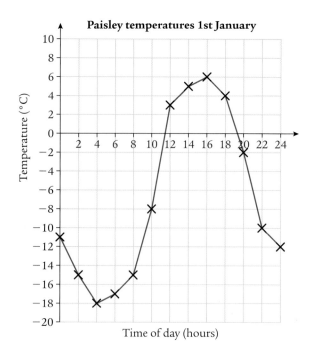

Paisley temperatures 1st January

a **i** What was the coldest temperature measured in Paisley on 1st January?

    ii At what time was it recorded?

b Between what two times was the temperature above zero. Give your answers to the nearest hour.

c Between what hours was the temperature rising?

d What was the temperature at:

    i 10 a.m.   **ii** 10 p.m.?

5 The table shows the record temperatures for the different parts of the UK in December.

Record December temperatures (°C)

	Maximum		Minimum	
	Highest	Lowest	Highest	Lowest
Scotland	18·3	−15·9	12·5	−27·2
Wales	18·0	−7·8	15·0	−22·7
England	17·7	−9·0	13·7	−25·2
N. Ireland	16·0	−11·3	14·3	−18·7

One December the maximum temperature to be measured in Scotland was 18·3 °C.

However, in another December, the maximum temperature was −15·9 °C.

a What is the difference between the 'best' and 'worst' maximum temperatures in Scotland?

b Which part of the UK holds the record for the lowest minimum temperature?

c What is the coldest temperature measured in England in December?

d What is the difference between Wales's lowest maximum and lowest minimum temperatures?

3.2 Other uses for negative numbers

Heights

Heights are measured from sea level.

Example 1

The highest point on the Sleeping Warrior in Arran is 721 m **above** sea level.

The stretch of water that runs beside Arran is called the Kilbrannan Sound.
It is about 75 metres deep.

Measuring from sea level, we could say that it was **−75 m high**.

What is the difference between these heights?

From the top of the ridge we go 721 m to sea level and then a further 75 m to get to
the bottom of the Kilbrannan Sound ... a total height difference of 721 + 75 = 796 m.

Above or below average

Golf scores can be recorded by noting how many strokes above or below the average
(par) you take to sink the ball at each hole.

A score of −2 would mean 2 below par. A score of 1 would mean 1 above par.

Example 2

George played nine holes and recorded his scores as
−2, −1, 0, −1, 1, 1, −1, 0, 1.

What was his total score?

The **below par** scores add up to −5. The **above par** scores add up to 3.

So altogether, he has ended up 2 below par. His total score is −2.

Exercise 3.2A

1   Some places on land are below sea-level.
   • The Danakil Depression in Ethiopia is at a height of −125 m.
   • The Dead Sea in Israel is −413 m, the lowest point on dry land.
   • Jericho, at −258 m, is the lowest city in the world.
   • The Caspian Sea in Russia is −28 m.

- Lake Eyre in Australia is −15 m.
- The Fens in England are at −4 m.
- Death Valley, USA, −86 m.
- New Orleans, USA, −2 m.

a What is the difference in height between:
  i Jericho and the Fens
  ii The Caspian Sea and the Danakil Depression
  iii New Orleans and the Dead Sea?

b The top of Ben Nevis is the highest point in the UK at 1344 m.

   What is the difference in height between it and i Death Valley   ii Lake Eyre?

2 Cehi 2 is the deepest cave in Slovenia. The height above sea level of its bottom is −1502 metres.

The tallest structure in the world is the Burj Khalifa at 828 m above sea level.

a What is the difference in height between the bottom of the cave and the top of the building?

b A newspaper article said that the cave was twice as deep as the building was high. Is this true?

c How high above sea level would the top of the building have been if they had built it by the Dead Sea?

3 Martin and Freda play nine holes of golf.

Their scores are shown.

Hole	1	2	3	4	5	6	7	8	9
Martin	−2	−1	−3	0	2	4	−1	1	0
Freda	0	−1	2	−1	−2	1	0	1	−1

In golf, the lower the score the better.

a Which was: i Martin's best hole   ii Freda's best hole?

b What was Martin's overall score?

c i Who won?   ii By how much?

4 At a sweet factory a machine fills boxes with sweets.

Each box should have 40 sweets in it.

A checker picks boxes at random and counts the contents.

He would record a box with 43 sweets as +3 and he would record a box with 38 sweets as −2.

a How would he record a box with:

  i 30 sweets   ii 40 sweets   iii 39 sweets   iv 34 sweets?

b He records a sample of 5 boxes as −2, −3, 4, −1, 0.

   How many sweets were in the 5 boxes altogether?

Money matters

In business, negative numbers can be used to show a loss.

In banking they can be used to show a debt.

Example 3

In an Enterprise scheme, a class bought memory sticks for £8 each and sold them for £12.

They bought screen wipes for 20p and sold them for 12p.

Describe how the students fared with:

a the memory sticks

b the screen wipes.

Use + to show a profit and − to show a loss.

a 12 − 8 = 4 ... since they sold the memory sticks for **more** than they bought them, the students made a **profit**.

For each sale they made +£4.

b 20 − 12 = 8 ... since they sold the screen wipes for **less** than they bought them, the students made a **loss**.

For each sale they made −8 pence.

Example 4

Tom had £50 in the bank.

He put in a further £20. This is called a **deposit**.

He then made a debit card payment for £100. This is a **withdrawal**.

Complete the table to show his bank balance.

In bank	£50
Deposited	
Withdrawn	
Balance	

When completed, the table looks like this:

In bank	£50
Deposited	£20
Withdrawn	−£100
Balance	−£30

Money put in (deposited) is positive. Money withdrawn is negative.

Money owed (in Tom's case, −£30) is negative.

Exercise 3.2B

1   Calculate the profit or loss for each of the following.
    Use a negative sign to show a loss.

    a A pen bought for £5 and sold for £3.

    b A DVD bought for £18 and sold for £12.

    c A poster bought for £15 and sold for £19.

    d A folder bought for 22p and sold for 16p.

    e A T-shirt bought for £25 and sold for £30.

    f A book bought for £15 and sold for £15.

2   In each case, calculate the profit or loss, using a negative sign to show the loss.

    a A shop bought 100 pens for £15 and sold them for 12 pence each.

    b The furniture store bought 4 cushions for £100 and sold them at £30 each.

    c The café bought in 20 ready-meals for £240 and sold them at £20 each.

    d The sweet shop bought 200 chocolate bars for £10 and sold them at 40p each.

3   Asif had £75 in the bank when he paid a bill for £90.

    What would his bank balance be after paying the bill?

4   Sarah kept a note of her money matters in January.

	IN (£)	OUT (£)
Balance at start of January	300	
Hire purchase payment		−25
Electricity		−150
Birthday gift	25	
Holiday payment		−125
Totals		
Balance at end January		

    a What were her total outgoings that month?

    b What was her balance at the end of January?

5   The table shows the profit or loss made each month by *Classic Online Cinema Club*.
    The figures are rounded to the nearest £100.

Month	Jan	Feb	Mar	Apr	May	Jun	Jul	Aug	Sep	Oct	Nov	Dec
Profit (£)	500	−200	−200	400	300	−200	−100	−400	100	100	0	500

    a In which months did the business make a loss?

    b How was the business doing in the first half of the year?

    c January, February, March is known as the first quarter of the year. April, May, June is the second
    quarter, and so on. In which quarter did the business make a loss?

    d How did the company perform over the year?

Preparation for assessment

1 Which temperature is higher:

   a $3\,°C$ or $-16\,°C$ b $-35\,°C$ or $-29\,°C$?

2 Write down the temperature that is $5\,°C$ higher than:

   a $-5\,°C$ b $-6\,°C$ c $-20\,°C$.

3 The weather map gives the temperatures in degrees Celsius of some places in mainland Scotland on a winter morning.

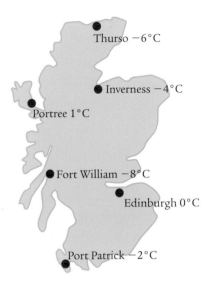

Thurso $-6\,°C$

Inverness $-4\,°C$

Portree $1\,°C$

Fort William $-8\,°C$

Edinburgh $0\,°C$

Port Patrick $-2\,°C$

   a Arrange these places in order, putting the coldest first:

      i Fort William, Inverness, Edinburgh

      ii Portree, Port Patrick, Thurso.

   b How many degrees colder than Port Patrick is Fort William?

   c How many degrees warmer than Thurso is Edinburgh?

   d The next day the temperature of Fort William rose $5\,°C$ and Portree dropped $5\,°C$.

      i Which place is now warmer?   ii By how much?

4 On the banks of the Clyde there are two neighbouring features.

The Glasgow Tower, whose height has been given as $127\,m$.

The Rotunda, which is an opening to a Victorian Clyde tunnel that has a vertical shaft whose depth is approximately $-23\,m$.

   a Explain what the numbers $127\,m$ and $-23\,m$ mean.

   b What is the vertical distance from the top of the tower to the bottom of the shaft?

5 The Dalbhui Tower is a seasonal tourist attraction, which only opens between May and October.

The table shows the profits made by the Tower each month.

Month	May	June	July	August	September	October
Profit (£)	-200	-100	900	700	-300	-600

   a What do the negative numbers represent?

   b What happened to the profits between:

      i June and July   ii September and October?

   c If the tower were to be closed for one extra month in the year, which month would you chose?

6 Remember that we measure temperature most often using a thermometer with a Celsius (°C) scale.

Many old cookery books use a Fahrenheit (°F) scale.

We can switch from °F to °C using the number machine:

a Use the machine to convert the following temperatures to degrees Celsius.

   i 212 °F   ii 68 °F   iii 23 °F

b The lit-up part of the Moon reaches temperatures of 257 °F.

The dark side gets as cold as −247 °F.

   i Convert both temperatures to degrees Celsius.

   ii What is the difference between these two temperatures on the Celsius scale?

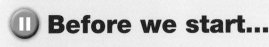
⏸ Before we start...

Class 3A made 8 chocolate cakes to sell at the school fair.

The 8 cakes cost £14 in total to make.

All 8 cakes were sold at the fair.

a How much money was obtained from the sale of the cakes?

b Did the cakes make a profit or loss?

c How much profit or loss was made?

d Was the profit or loss greater than 50% of the cost price? Explain your answer.

CHOCOLATE CAKES
£2·50 each

▶ What you need to know

1 Calculate:

a
£
7·36
+ 5·57
————

b
£
12·37
− 9·54
————

c
£
62·75
+ 28·49
————

d
£
41·23
− 8·52
————

e
£
28·43
− 18·65
————

2 Calculate:

a £2·78 + £3·14

b £17·58 − £4·83

c £37·62 + £55·38

d £85·20 − £28·15

3 **a** Sanjay buys a cabbage for 83p. How much change does he get from £1?

b Mel buys a birthday card for £2·65. What change does she get from £5?

c Sinita's train ticket costs £11·59. How much change does she get from £20?

4 Calculate:

a 3·85 × 10   **b** 4·02 × 100   **c** 35·1 ÷ 10   **d** 202·9 ÷ 100

5 a An ice cream costs £1·25. Calculate the cost of three ice creams.

b Three calculators cost £15·90. What is the cost of one of the calculators?

c Charlie's return flight to Pisa costs him £187·65. His hotel bill was £341·25.

  i What is the total cost of the hotel and the flight?

  ii How much more does the hotel cost than the flight?

6 These calculators are displaying amounts of money.
Write down the amounts shown on each in pounds and pence.

a `7.18`   **b** `12.8`   **c** `0.27`   **d** `20.6`

4.1 Money calculations

When doing calculations with money, look for quick methods.

Example 1

Calculate £5·99 + £7·99.

£5·99 is £6 − 1p, £7·99 = £8 − 1p.

So, £5·99 + £7·99 = £6 + £8 − 1p − 1p = £14 − 2p = £13·98.

Example 2

Add £7·40 + £5·83 + £4·60.

Sometimes changing the order makes the calculation easier.

Since £7·40 + £4·60 = £12.

Then £12 + £5·83 = £17·83.

Example 3

Calculate £6·99 × 4.

£6·99 is 1p less than £7.

£7 × 4 = £28.

1p × 4 = 4p.

So £6·99 × 4 = £28 − 4p = £27·96.

Example 4

What is £27 ÷ 6?

Dividing by 6 is the same as dividing by 3, then dividing the answer by 2.

£27 ÷ 3 = £9.

Then £9 ÷ 2 = £4·50.

So, £27 ÷ 6 = £4·50.

Example 5

Calculate   **a** £5·99 × 10   **b** £26·00 ÷ 10.

a   £5·99 × 10 = £59·90.   To **multiply by 10** ... move the point **one place to the right**.

b   £26·00 ÷ 10 = £2·60.   To **divide by 10** ... move the point **one place to the left**.

Exercise 4.1A

1 Calculate:

   a £2 + £3·99   **b** £4·35 + £8   **c** £6·99 + 99p   **d** £3·99 + £4·99.

2 Calculate:

   a £6 − £5·99   **b** £9 − £3·99   **c** £12 − £8·95   **d** £32 − £8·90.

3 Calculate:

   a 10p + 95p + 90p   **b** £6·37 + £5·90 + £11·10

   c £36 + £69 + £64   **d** £23·99 + £59·99.

4 Calculate:

   a £3·99 × 2   **b** £5·99 × 5   **c** £6·49 × 4   **d** £7·95 × 3.

5 Calculate:

   a £7 ÷ 2   **b** £11·20 ÷ 2   **c** £15 ÷ 4   **d** £8·40 ÷ 3.

6 Calculate:

   a £2·10 × 10   **b** £0·72 × 10   **c** £36·70 × 10   **d** £18·45 × 10.

7 Calculate:

   a £48·00 ÷ 10   **b** £36·00 ÷ 10   **c** £382·00 ÷ 10   **d** £0·70 ÷ 10.

8 Gwen pays £5·99 for a pair of earrings with a £10 note.
   How much change is she given?

9 Mr Clarke takes his young son golfing.

    a How much does he pay for the two tickets?

    b What change is he given if he pays with a £20 note?

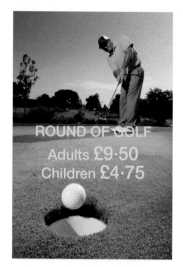

ROUND OF GOLF
Adults £9·50
Children £4·75

10 Joe earns £5·85 an hour working in a supermarket.

    How much is he paid for working:

    a 3 hours   **b** 5 hours   **c** 10 hours?

11 Four oranges cost £1·56.

    What is the cost of one orange?

12 Asel is learning to drive.

    A course of 10 lessons costs £190.

    Calculate the cost of each lesson.

13 Sue paid £83·99 for a pair of curtains, £17·99 for a curtain rail and £6·99 for a packet of curtain hooks.

    a How much did she spend altogether?

    b What was the difference in price between the curtains and the curtain rail?

Example 6

Calculate: **a** £13·50 × 100   **b** £365·00 ÷ 100.

a £13·50 × 100 = £1350.   To **multiply by 100** ... move the point **two places to the right**.

b £365·00 ÷ 100 = £3·65.   To **divide by 100** ... move the point **two places to the left**.

Exercise 4.1B

1 Calculate:

    a £6·42 × 100   **b** £38·95 × 100   **c** £80·00 ÷ 100   **d** £517·00 ÷ 100.

2 **a** 100 plastic rulers cost £37.

       Calculate the cost of one plastic ruler.

    b A ball-point pen costs 18p.

       Calculate the cost of:

       i 10 ball-point pens   **ii** 100 ball-point pens.

3 Rhona filled her petrol tank with 100 litres of petrol from Gary's Garage.

   a How much did she have to pay?

   b How much would 100 litres of diesel cost?

   c How much cheaper is 100 litres of petrol than 100 litres of diesel?

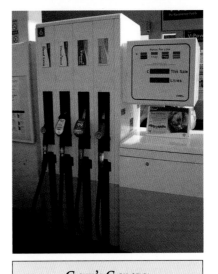

4 The school gardening club is given £50 to buy plants for the flower bed at the entrance to the school.

    | *Gary's Garage:* |
    Petrol – £1·47 a litre
    Diesel – £1·53 a litre

They buy geraniums for £18·25, marigolds for £14·95 and blue lobelia for £8·50.

   a How much did they spend?

   b How much of the £50 is left?

5 Which is cheaper and by how much:

10 calculators at £3·85 each or 8 calculators at £5·10 each?

6 Chris pays £189·95 for Bed and Breakfast for five nights.

How much does each night cost?

7 Sophie works weekends in a supermarket. She earns £68·45 each weekend.

She saves her earnings for four weeks and then buys a racing bike for £199·99.

How much of her earnings will Sophie have left?

8 Six coconuts cost £8·10.

Calculate the cost of:

   a 1 coconut   **b** 8 coconuts   **c** 10 coconuts.

4.2 Bills and discounts

Example 1

Find the total cost of this bill: bread (£1·20), 6 eggs (£1·75), jar of coffee (£4·49).

Keep the decimal points in line.

Bread	£1·20
6 eggs	£1·75
Coffee	£4·49
Total	£7·44

41

Example 2

The normal price of a snow shovel is £16·99.

In a sale there is a discount of £5 on the shovel.

What is the cost of the snow shovel in the sale?

Cost = £16·99 − £5   The 'discount' means that the snow shovel is £5 cheaper than normal.
If one price has pence, it is a good idea to show the pence in the other price so we can line up the points more easily.

$$
\begin{array}{r}
16\cdot99 \\
-5\cdot00 \\
\hline
11\cdot99
\end{array}
$$

Cost of snow shovel in the sale is £11·99.

Exercise 4.2A

1 Jessie buys nail varnish for £6·99 and a bottle of nail varnish remover for £2·50.

   a How much is the total bill?

   b What change is she given from £10?

2 Paul buys a shirt.

   The normal price is £25. A discount of £6·50 is offered.

   How much does Paul pay for the shirt?

3 Ali has his car serviced.

   Parts cost £83·26, labour is £127·48.

   a Calculate the total bill.

   b There is a special discount of £15 for bills over £100.

   How much does Ali pay for the service?

4 Wilma was given a £10 gift card for a digital music store.

   To download one track costs £0·89.

   a How much did it cost Wilma to download ten tracks?

   b How much was left on her gift card?

5 Mrs Scott calls a roofer to replace some missing tiles on her roof.

   The labour costs are £32·25. The cost of materials is £16·38.

   a What is the total bill?

   b Mrs Scott gives the roofer £50. How much change does she get?

6 The Thomson family had their bedrooms decorated.
The bill is shown.

   Work out the total cost.

Paula the Painter	
Paint	£72·50
Wallpaper	£186·99
Labour	£485·00

7 Diarmad downloads four books on to his e-book reader.

The titles and their costs are shown.

How much in total was Diarmad charged?

Where Eagles Dared	**£2 · 65**
To Mars and Back	**£3 · 99**
Rapper Hits	**£7 · 50**
Tall Stories	**£2 · 99**

8 Copy and complete these supermarket bills.

a

2 bottles of cola at £1.65 per bottle	£...
5 choc ices at 85p per choc ice	£...
6 packets of crisps at 45p a packet	£...
Total	£...

b

3 tins of tuna at 0.89 a tin	£...
4 packs of yoghurt at £2·15 a pack	£...
5 pears at 0.39 each	£...
Total	£...

Exercise 4.2B

1 Tom and Betty take their daughter to the safari park.

There is a discount of £4·50 on each adult ticket.
There is a discount of £2·75 on a child's ticket.

a With the discount:
   i what is the price of an adult ticket
   ii what is the price of a child's ticket?

b Calculate the total cost of the three tickets with
the discount.

The Jungle Safari Park
Adults **£12**
Children **£8.50**

2 **a** A tracksuit normally costs £89·50.

> **SPORTIES HALF PRICE SUPER SALE**
>
> 50% Discount On All Items

What does it cost in the Super Sale?

b A Sporties tennis racquet usually costs £36·80.

What does it cost in the Super Sale?

3 Emma and her four friends hire a stretch limousine to take them
to their school Prom.

The limousine costs £95.

a How much would each girl have to pay?

b The hire firm gives the girls a discount of £25.

How much should each girl pay with the discount?

4 Emma has her hair done at *Curl-Up and Dye*.

Her bill is shown.

a Calculate the total cost.

b Because Emma is a student, she gets a discount of
10%. How much does she have to pay?

> ### *Curl-Up and Dye*
>
> | | |
> |---|---|
> | *Cut and blow-dry* | *£36·75* |
> | *Colouring* | *£27·65* |
> | *Ladies hair up* | *£35·50* |

4.3 Gas and electricity bills

Customers are charged for the amount of gas or electricity they use.

Value Added Tax (VAT) is added to the bill. The tax gets sent to the government.

Example 1

Calculate what must be paid if the cost of gas used is £124·36 and there is £6·22 VAT to pay.

Cost of gas used	£124·36
VAT	£6·22
Total bill	£130·58

Sometimes there is a regular charge for being connected.

This charge is called the **standing charge**. It is a fixed amount which is added to a customer's bill.

It is payable even if the customer uses no gas or electricity.

Example 2

James uses £87·35 worth of electricity. There is a standing charge of £9·42.

a Calculate how much this is in total.

b He also has to pay £4·84 VAT. What was his total bill?

a
Cost of electricity	£87·35
Standing charge	£9·42
Total electricity and charges	£96·77

b
VAT	£4·84
Total bill	£101·61

Exercise 4.3A

1 Calculate these gas bills:

a
Cost of gas	£72·00
VAT	£ 3·60
Total bill	£

b
Cost of gas	£92·80
VAT	£ 4·64
Total bill	£

c
Cost of gas	£107·32
VAT	£ 5·37
Total bill	£

2 Find the missing entries for these electricity bills:

a
Cost of electricity	£78·40
Standing charge	£ 7·60
Total electricity and charges	£
VAT	£ 4·30
Total bill	£

b
Cost of electricity	£53·26
Standing charge	£ 8·76
Total electricity and charges	£
VAT	£ 3·10
Total bill	£

3 **a** Who pays more for their gas, Mrs Reid or Mr Wright?

   b How much more?

GAS BILL Mrs B. Reid		*GAS BILL* Mr R. Wright	
Cost of gas used	£97·38	Cost of gas used	£107·42
Standing charge	£ 8·64	Standing charge	£ 3·73
Total gas and charges	£	Total gas and charges	£
VAT	£ 5·30	VAT	£ 5·56
Total bill	£	Total bill	£

The VAT on gas and electricity is 5% of the cost of the fuel.

To calculate 5% of an amount, first find 10% of the amount and then divide your answer by 2.

$10\% = \frac{1}{10}$. To find $\frac{1}{10}$ of an amount, divide by 10.

Example 3

Find 5% of £74·00:

a without a calculator   **b** with a calculator.

a 10% of £74·00 = £74·00 ÷ 10 = £7·40.
   So 5% of £74 = £7·40 ÷ 2 = £3·70.

b Key in: 5 ÷ 1 0 0 × 7 4 =
   which gives 3·7.
   The answer is £3·70.

Example 4

Moira received her gas bill. She had used 120 units of gas at 67·52p per unit.

She had to pay VAT at 5%.

Complete her bill.

Gas Bill M. Smith The B.E.S.T. Gas Company		
Cost of gas:	120 units of gas at 67·52p per unit	£81·02
VAT:	5% of the cost of gas	£ 4·05
	Total bill	£85·07

Exercise 4.3B

1 Calculate 10% of each amount:

   a £36·00   **b** £87·00   **c** £37·40   **d** £29·10   **e** £93.

2 Calculate 5% of each amount:

   a £80·00   **b** £7·00   **c** £43·00   **d** £56·20   **e** £24.

3 Find the VAT, at 5%, to be paid on these fuel bills:

    a £30·00   **b** £70   **c** £32·40   **d** £79·40   **e** £120.

4 Copy and complete these gas bills:

    a Cost of gas £50·00   **b** Cost of gas £92·00   **c** Cost of gas £66·20

       VAT at 5% £ _____   VAT at 5% £ _____   VAT at 5% £ _____

       Total bill £ _____   Total bill £ _____   Total bill £ _____

5 **Use a calculator** to complete these bills:

    a Cost of gas £149·60   **b** Cost of gas £173·20   **c** Cost of gas £267·80

       VAT at 5% £ _____   VAT at 5% £ _____   VAT at 5% £ _____

       Total bill £ _____   Total bill £ _____   Total bill £ _____

6 The Young family received its gas bill for last month.

Use a calculator to find the amounts which should appear in place of A and B. Give your answers to the nearest penny, where appropriate.

Gas Bill T. Young   Energy Plus – the Energy Company

Cost of gas: 140 units of gas at 64·75p per unit   £ A

VAT: 5% of the cost of gas   £ 4·53

                                 Total bill   £ B

7 Here is the Scott family's electricity bill. Calculate the values of C, D and E.

Electricity Bill A. Scott   **The Power Company**

Cost of electricity: 365 units at 31·7p per unit   £ C

VAT: 5% of the cost of electricity   £ D

                                Total bill   £ E

4.4 Profit and loss

When an item is sold for more than it cost, a **profit** is made.

When an item is sold for less than it cost, a **loss** is made.

Example 1

A shopkeeper buys a tent for £48·50. She sells it for £74·99.

Calculate the profit.

Cost price = £48·50, selling price = £74·99.

Profit = selling price − cost price

     = £74·99 − £48·50 = £26·49

Example 2

Danny bought a car for £1750. He sold it six months later for £1375.

Calculate the loss Danny made on the car.

Cost price = £1750, selling price = £1375.

Loss = cost price − selling price

= £1750 − £1375 = £375

Example 3

Millie bought a coffee table at a car-boot sale for £12·50.

She cleaned and polished it, then sold it for a profit of £8·75.

Calculate the selling price.

Selling price = cost price + profit

= £12·50 + £8·75 = £21·25

Exercise 4.4A

1 At lunchtime the school cafeteria is always busy.

Work out the profit on each item sold.

a Apple juice (bought for 50p, sold for 75p).

b Cola (bought for 45p, sold for 60p).

c Bananas (bought for 18p, sold for 25p).

d Apples (bought for 12p, sold for 25p).

e Crisps (bought for 38p, sold for 50p).

f Bar of chocolate (bought for 27p, sold for 45p).

2 To sell all its stock quickly a store reduces its prices.

Calculate the profit or loss on each item:

a printers (bought for £54, sold for £50)

b black ink cartridges (bought for £12·50, sold for £9·99)

c coloured ink cartridges (bought for £13·25, sold for £10·99)

d reams of paper (bought for £2·65, sold for £2·99)

e memory pens (bought for £7·99, sold for £6·50).

3 Calculate the selling price of each of these scooters.

a **Pro Scooter**

Cost price £79

Profit £30·95

b **SkillTrixx Scooter**

Cost price £82·50

Loss £7·51

c **Stunt Scooter**

Cost price £89·99

Profit £14

4 A dealer buys five electric guitars. Each one cost her £125.

She sells each of the guitars for £169.

   a How much profit does she make on each guitar?

   b Calculate her total profit.

5 The school Art Club made Christmas cards. The materials they used cost £37.

The Club sold 80 cards at 40p each, 45 cards at 50p each and 32 cards at 60p each.

Calculate the profit made by the Art Club.

Example 4

The cost price of an e-book reader is £90. It is sold at a loss of 10%.

a How much is the loss?

b What is the selling price?

   a $10\% = \frac{1}{10}$. Loss = 10% of £90 = £90 ÷ 10 = £9.

   b Selling price = £90 − £9 = £81.

Exercise 4.4B

1 A shop sells furniture. It makes a profit of 10% on each of these three items.

Calculate the profit on each item.

   a Dining table   **b** Dining chair   **c** Settee

      Cost price £250   Cost price £35·00   Cost price £1490

2 A shoe shop has a sale to clear old stock. It makes a loss of 5% on each item.

What loss is made on each of these?

   a Ankle boots   **b** Casual mid boots   **c** Biker long boots

      Cost price £58   Cost price £64·80   Cost price £87·60

3 The manager of the local garden centre buys 100 geranium plants for £90.
He sells them for £1·75 each.

Calculate the total profit made on the geraniums.

4 Mary helped to organise a disco. The cost of hiring a hall and printing the tickets was £132·50.

She sold 50 tickets at £3·50 each. Calculate Mary's profit or loss.

Preparation for assessment

1 A pair of trousers normally costs £39·50.

  Simon, who works in the store, is given a £15 discount.

  How much does Simon pay for the trousers?

2 Karen purchased some items for her new flat.

Copy and complete her bill.

Dekor's Store

Metal folding table	£79·95
Sparkle mirror	£119·00
Pencil pleat curtains	£199·99
Total cost	_____

3 Gregor buys a football jersey for £39·99, shorts for £23·50 and a pair of football socks for £3.

a Calculate the total cost.

b Because the total is more than £50, Gregor is given a discount of £7·50.

Calculate how much he has to pay.

4 Copy and complete the Wilson's electricity bill.

The High Energy Company	R. Wilson
Cost of electricity	£70·36
Standing charge	£ 8·42
Total electricity/charges	£ ____
VAT	£ 3·94
Total bill	£ ____

5 India buys cartons of ice cream for 35p and sells them for 80p.

a What is the profit on one carton?
She sells 100 cartons of ice cream.

b What is the profit on 100 cartons?
At the end of the day, she sells the last 50 cartons of ice cream at 30p each.

c Calculate the loss she made on these 50 cartons.

6 Remember Class 3A made 8 chocolate cakes to sell at the school fair.
The 8 cakes cost £14 in total to make.
All 8 cakes were sold at the fair.

a How much money was obtained from the sale of the cakes?

b Did the cakes make a profit or loss?

c How much profit or loss was made?

d Was the profit or loss greater than 50% of the cost price?
Explain your answer.

CHOCOLATE CAKES
£2·50 each

5 Extra charges, Value Added Tax and borrowing

 Before we start...

Sandy bought his ticket for the pop concert.

He expected it to cost him £35, but there were extra charges!

One of these charges was **Value Added Tax (VAT)** at 20% of the ticket price.

a How much was Sandy charged for VAT?

Also there was a **booking fee** of £3·50 and a **credit card charge** of 2% of the total transaction, because he was paying by credit card.

b Calculate the credit card charge.

c What was the total price Sandy paid for his ticket?

Pop Concert
3 JUNE
Tickets **£35** (excluding VAT)
Book your ticket online NOW at
www.ticketpop.uk.net

 What you need to know

Do not use a calculator for questions 1 to 7.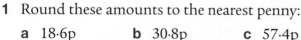

1 Round these amounts to the nearest penny:

   a 18·6p   **b** 30·8p   **c** 57·4p   **d** 19·2p   **e** 40·5p.

2 Calculate:

   a £6·47 + 99p   **b** £7·82 + £5·18   **c** £9·70 + £2·69 + £2·30.

3 Calculate:

   a £8·50 × 10   **b** £63·25 × 100   **c** £3·60 ÷ 10   **d** £485·00 ÷ 100.

4 A supermarket sells 100 carrier bags for £5.
How much does each bag cost?

5 Calculate:

   a £32 × 2   **b** £46 × 5   **c** £6·50 × 4   **d** £8·27 × 3.

6 In Ann's class, 53% of the students are girls.

What percentage are boys?

7 Match the percentages with the decimal fractions below.

100%   25%   50%   10%   1%   5%

0·1   1·0   0·25   0·05   0·01   0·5

8 Mr and Mrs Kidd take their three children to the Safari Park.

Calculate the total cost of their tickets.

Bonnyside Safari Park	
Adult	£18·50
Child	£9·75

9 Find 50% of each of these amounts:

a £4·00   **b** £27·00   **c** £6·38   **d** £34·52.

10 Find 25% of each of these amounts (your answers to question **9** may help):

a £4·00   **b** £27·00   **c** £6·38   **d** £34·52.

5.1 Calculating percentages

1% means '1 per hundred' or '1 hundredth'.

Therefore, $1\% = \frac{1}{100} = 0\cdot01$. So to find 1% of an amount we divide by 100.

Example 1

Find 1% of £36·00.

£36·00 ÷ 100 = £0·36   To divide by 100, move the point 2 places to the left.

Example 2

Calculate 8% of £14.

Method 1: 1% of £14 = £14·00 ÷ 100 = £0·14 or 14p.

2% of £14 = 14p × 2 = 28p   2% = 1% × 2

4% of £14 = 28p × 2 = 56p   4% = 2% × 2

8% of £14 = 56p × 2 = £1·12   8% = 4% × 2

Method 2: 8% of £14 = $\frac{8}{100} \times$ £14·00

= 0·08 × £14

= £1·12

51

Exercise 5.1A

1 Calculate:

    a £1·00 ÷ 100   **b** £3·00 ÷ 100   **c** £15·00 ÷ 100   **d** £475·00 ÷ 100.

2 Calculate 1% of each of these amounts:

    a £5·00   **b** £7·00   **c** £40·00   **d** £56·00   **e** £840·00.

3 Calculate: **a** 1% of £3   **b** 2% of £3.

4 Calculate: **a** 1% of £20   **b** 2% of £20   **c** 4% of £20   **d** 8% of £20.

5 Calculate: **a** 1% of £16   **b** 2% of £16   **c** 4% of £16   **d** 8% of £16.

6 Calculate: **a** 1% of £700   **b** 2% of £700   **c** 4% of £700   **d** 8% of £700.

7 Masamba earns £200 a week working in his local supermarket.

    He is given a 2% pay rise.

    a How much is his pay rise?

    b How much now is his weekly pay?

Percentages, decimals and common fractions

$50\% = 0.5 = \frac{1}{2}$.

$25\% = 0.25 = \frac{1}{4}$.

Example 3

a Calculate 50% of £26.

b Calculate 25% of £26.

a 50% of £26 $= \frac{1}{2}$ of £26 = £13.

b 25% of £26 $= \frac{1}{4}$ of £26 = £6·50.

Exercise 5.1B

1 Calculate 50% of:

    a £14   **b** £68   **c** £37   **d** 80p   **e** £4·84.

2 Calculate 25% of:

    a £14   **b** £68   **c** £8   **d** 20p   **e** £8·48.

3 Find 10% of:

    a £120   **b** £16   **c** £5·40   **d** £17·30   **e** 60p.

4 Find 5% of:

    a £120   **b** £16   **c** £5·40   **d** £17·30   **e** 60p.

5 Copy and complete the table.

	1%	2%	4%	8%
£5	5p	10p		
£12				
£30	30p			
£86				

6 Which would you rather have: 25% of £18 or 10% of £48?
Explain your answer.

7 a Calculate 50% of £672.

b Calculate 25% of £672.

c How much did Neema pay for the
£672 television in the sale?

MASSIVE SALE
£672 TV reduced by 75% !!!

5.2 Extra charges

Dan's **weekly** train ticket costs £38·65.

He pays an extra £2·70 **per day** to park his car at the station.

Dan travels by train five days each week.
What is his total weekly cost?

Total cost = £38·65 + £2·70 × 5

= £38·65 + £13·50 = £52·15

Exercise 5.2A

1 Anwar is a waiter. His weekly wage is £236·50. One week he earned
an extra £28·75 in tips.

How much did Anwar earn in total that week?

2 Gregor bought a pair of football boots online.
They cost £42·75. The charge for postage and packing was £3·99.
What was the total charge for the football boots?

3 Sara flies to Lanzarote. Her return ticket cost £169.
She booked her seat for an extra charge of £15 per flight.
How much did Sara have to pay altogether?

4 Kate bought a secondhand car for £3650.

She had to pay an extra £573 to insure the car and another £58 for road tax.

How much did she pay in total?

5 Xiu needs a new bedroom carpet. She buys one for £389·45.

She has several extra charges to pay:

Underlay   £94·68
Delivery   £25
Fitting   £45

   a What is the total of the extra charges?

   b How much altogether did the carpet cost?

Example 2

Max's basic holiday insurance costs £28·60.

Because he is going to paraglide, there is an extra charge of 50% on his insurance.

Calculate:

a the extra charge

b the total cost of Max's insurance.

a Extra charge = 50% of £28·60

               = $\frac{1}{2}$ of £28·60

               = £14·30

b Total cost = £28·60 + £14·30 = £42·90.

Exercise 5.2B

1 When paying for a holiday with Continental Tours, there is an extra charge for paying by credit card.

The extra charge is 1% of the cost of the holiday.

Calculate the extra charge on holidays costing:

   a £90   **b** £200   **c** £570   **d** £1200   **e** £1699.

2 In the Dine with Style restaurant, a 10% service charge is added to the bill.

Calculate the service charge to be added to these bills:

   a £30 - **b** £70   **c** £64·30 **d** £108   **e** £42·21.

3 A country in the eurozone adds a government tax of 5% to the price of restaurant meals.

How much tax is added to the prices of these meals?

   a 100 euros **b** 40 euros   **c** 35 euros   **d** 52 euros   **e** 120 euros

4 The prices of different heights of Christmas tree are shown.

If a tree is sprayed to keep its needles from falling, the cost increases by 10%.

How much does it cost in total for a sprayed tree with a height of:

   a   4 feet   b   5 feet   c   6 feet?

Height (feet)	4	5	6
Cost	£20	£28	£36

5 The A to Z taxi firm charges £25 to take passengers from Bo'ness to the airport.

   a   An extra charge of 2% of the fare is made for each suitcase it carries.
   How much does it cost passengers going to the airport with:

      i   1 suitcase   ii   2 suitcases   iii   3 suitcases?

   b   Between the hours of 10 p.m. and 7 a.m. the £25 charge is increased by 10%.
   Calculate the night-time charge.

5.3 Value Added Tax (VAT)

Teachers, police, nurses, doctors, civil servants, local authority workers, fire brigades, schools, hospitals ... all have to be paid for. To do so, the government and local authorities raise money from taxes.

One of these taxes, introduced by the government, is **Value Added Tax** (VAT).

We pay VAT on most goods and services we buy.

Example 1

Greg's car was serviced by his local garage.

The service cost £168·45. Added to this is VAT of £33·69.

What is the cost of the service, including VAT?

Cost of service, including VAT = £168·45 + £33·69 = £202·14.

Example 2

Calculate the price of the bicycle before VAT is added.

Price of bicycle before VAT = £141·60 − £23·60 = £118.

Bicycle £141·60 including VAT (VAT is £23·60)

Exercise 5.3A

1 To remove a tall tree from a garden costs £250. £50 VAT is added to the bill.

What is the total cost of removing the tree?

2 A plumber's bill is £85·62 + VAT. The VAT is £17·12.

What is the total to be paid to the plumber?

3 Melanie went shopping.

Calculate the cost of each item she bought, including VAT.

a Ankle boots: £42·00 + VAT of £8·40.

b Skinny jeans: £36·40 + VAT of £7·28.

c Sunglasses: £17·89 + VAT of £3·58.

4 Kali buys wallpaper priced at £7·84 + VAT for each roll. The VAT to be paid is £1·57.

a What is the total cost of a roll of wallpaper?

b Kali needs five rolls of the wallpaper. How much is her total bill?

5 Copy and complete the table.

Item	Price before VAT	VAT	Price including VAT
Tablet PC	£259·99	£52	
Skateboard	£18·50		£22·20
3-D TV		£61	£365·99
Laptop	£895·95		£1075·14
Denim jeans		£5·80	£34·79

Calculating VAT

On most goods and services the VAT rate is 20%. (On gas and electricity the VAT rate is 5%.)

The government can change the VAT rate from time to time.

Example 3

The price of a wristwatch before VAT is added is £24·60.

The rate of VAT is 20%.

a Calculate the amount of VAT to be paid.

b What is the total cost including VAT?

a 10% of £24·60 = £2·46   Move the point 1 place to the left.

20% of £24·60 = 2 × £2·46   20% = 2 × 10%

         = £4·92

b Total cost = £24·60 + £4·92 = £29·52.

Exercise 5.3B

1 Calculate 20% of each amount:

    a £10   **b** £15   **c** £42   **d** £87   **e** £123.

2 Calculate the VAT at 20% to be added to the price of these items.

    a A garage bill of £114·50.

    b A vet's bill of £43·50.

    c A pram at £389.

3 Calculate the VAT at 20% on these items:

a

E-book Reader
£87·59

b

Garden Shed
£309·99

4 For a long time, the rate of VAT in the UK was 17·5%.

To calculate 17·5% of an amount of money looks very difficult. But is it?

Example: Find 17·5% of £30.

17·5% = 10% + 5% + 2·5%

10% of £30 = £3·00	A tenth of 100%
5% of £30 = £1·50	A half of 10%
2·5% of £30 = £0·75	A half of 5%
17·5% of £30 = £5·25	10% + 5% + 2·5%

Without using a calculator, find 17·5% of:

a £80 b £70 c £250 d £640.

5.4 Loans and Hire Purchase (HP)

Bonnie wants to buy a secondhand motorbike.

She borrows the money from her bank.

They charge her for borrowing the money.

The amount Bonnie pays back depends on how much she borrows
and how long she takes to repay it.

		Amount borrowed				
		£500	**£1000**	**£1500**	**£2000**	**£3000**
Time to repay	6 months	£98	£196	£294	£392	£588
	12 months	£54	£108	£162	£216	£324
	18 months	£38	£76	£114	£152	£228
	24 months	£29	£58	**£87**	£116	£174

Bonnie borrows £1500 and arranges to make 24 monthly payments.

a How much will her monthly payments be?

b Calculate the total of her payments.

c How much more than £1500 does Bonnie pay for the motorbike?

a From the table her monthly payments are £87.   Row 4, column 3.

b Total of payments = £87 × 24 = £2088.

c Cost of loan = £2088 − £1500 = £588.

Hire Purchase (HP)

Goods can be bought by making a set of equal payments, usually each month or each week.

You can take the item away at the first payment, but it doesn't belong to you until the last payment is made.

This is called buying on **hire purchase** (**HP**).

Example 2

Davina wants to buy a television for her bedroom.

She can pay cash or buy it on hire purchase.

How much more does it cost to buy the television through hire purchase?

The cost of buying on HP = £35 × 6 = £210.

The difference between the HP price and the cash price = £210 − £189 = £21.

Cash Price £189

Six monthly payments of £35

Exercise 5.4A

Use the table from Example 1 to help you answer the following questions.

1 Find the monthly payments for each of these loans:

    a £500 repaid over 12 months

    b £2000 repaid over 18 months

    c £3000 repaid over 24 months.

2 Dan borrows £1000 to pay for double glazing.

    He pays it back over 18 months.

    a What are his monthly payments?

    b How much will he pay altogether?

    c How much more than £1000 is this?

3 The Frasers borrow £1500 to have their garden landscaped.

   a How much are the monthly payments if they pay it back over:

      i 12 months   **ii** 18 months?

   b Calculate the total amount they will pay over:

      i 12 months   **ii** 18 months.

   c How much more will it cost them to pay over 18 months rather than 12 months?

4 Cheryl buys a pair of binoculars.

   She pays for them over six months. Each month she pays £18.

   How much does Cheryl pay altogether?

5 Calculate the total price paid on hire purchase for each of these items.

   a Tablet PC   *10 monthly payments of £18.*

   b Mobile Phone   *6 monthly payments of £16.*

   c Digital Camera *12 monthly payments of £14.*

6 Steve buys a games console on HP.

   a How much does he pay altogether?

   b Calculate the difference between the HP price and the cash price.

Cash Price £429

HP TERMS
12 monthly payments of £41

Deposits

Sometimes you have to pay money at the beginning of a hire purchase agreement.

This payment is called a **deposit**.

Example 3

Amir buys this go-kart on HP.

a Calculate the deposit.

b What is the total cost of the monthly payments?

c How much does he pay altogether?

d Calculate the difference between the HP price and the cash price.

Go-Kart
Cash Price **£375**

HP TERMS
DEPOSIT 10%
+ 9 monthly payments of **£42**

a Deposit = 10% of £375 = £37·50.

b Monthly payments = £42 × 9 = £378.

c Total payment = £378 + £37·50 = £415·50.

d Difference between HP price and cash price = £415·50 − £375 = £40·50.

Exercise 5.4B

1 Jack buys a skateboard on hire purchase.
   - Cash price: £49·95
   - HP terms: £15 deposit and 3 monthly payments of £13

   a What is the total of the monthly payments?

   b How much does he pay altogether?
      (Hint: total monthly payments + deposit.)

   c Calculate the difference between the HP price and the cash price.

2 Ann buys a printer for her computer.
   - Cash price: £76·00
   - HP terms: £20 deposit and 6 monthly payments of £11

   a What is the total of the monthly payments?

   b How much does she pay altogether?
      (Hint: total monthly payments + deposit.)

   c Calculate the difference between the HP price and the cash price.

3 A quad bike is for sale at a cash price of £344·90.
   The HP terms are:
   - deposit − 10% of cash price
   - plus 20 monthly payments of £17.

   a Calculate the deposit.

   b What is the total of the monthly payments?

   c What is the total cost of the bike on HP?

   d Calculate the difference between the HP price and the cash price.

4 The Boyd family are buying a tent.
   The cash price is £189·99.
   The HP terms are:
   - deposit − 10% of cash price
   - plus 12 monthly payments of £16·50.

   a Calculate the deposit.

   b What is the total of the monthly payments?

   c What is the total cost of the tent on HP?

   d Calculate the difference between the HP price and the cash price.

Preparation for assessment

1 Find:

   a   1% of £60   b   2% of £60   c   4% of £60   d   8% of £60.

2 Calculate: a   10% of £29   b   5% of £29.

3 Calculate: a   50% of £56   b   25% of £56.

4 Janice ordered a football strip online for £62·75. Next-Day delivery costs her £4·99.
   How much does she pay in total?

5 A bracelet costs Wendy £8·75 plus VAT of £1·75.
   How much does she pay for the bracelet altogether?

6 The rate of VAT is 20%.
   Tennis shoes are priced at £54 plus VAT.

   a   Calculate the VAT to be paid on the tennis shoes.

   b   How much do the shoes cost altogether?

7 The cash price of a set of golf clubs is £165.
   Barry buys a set on HP:
   • deposit £45
   • plus 6 monthly payments of £22·50.

   a   What is the total of the monthly payments?

   b   How much does he pay altogether?

   c   Calculate the difference between the HP price and the cash price.

8 Two friends buy a tandem bike on HP.
   The cash price is £999·99. The HP terms are:
   • deposit − 10% of cash price
   • plus 10 monthly payments of £105.

   a   Calculate the deposit.

   b   What is the total cost of the monthly payments?

   c   How much will the tandem cost them altogether?

9 Remember Sandy bought his ticket for the pop concert. He expected it to cost him £35, but there were extra charges!
   One of these charges was **Value Added Tax (VAT)** at 20% of the ticket price.

   a   How much was Sandy charged for VAT?

   Also there was a **booking fee** of £3·50 and a **credit card charge** of 2% of the total transaction, because he was paying by credit card.

   b   Calculate the credit card charge.

   c   What was the total price Sandy paid for his ticket?

Pop Concert
3 JUNE
Tickets £35 (excluding VAT)
Book your ticket online NOW at
www.ticketpop.uk.net

6 Tables

Before we start...

The table below is a **ready reckoner** that converts miles to kilometres.

Miles	1	2	3	4	5	6	7	8	9	10	20	30	40	50
Kilometres	1·6	3·2	4·8	6·4	8·0	9·7	11·3	12·9	14·5	16·1	32·2	48·3	64·4	80·5

a Write down the number of kilometres in:

   i 6 miles   ii 10 miles   iii 40 miles.

b Write down the number of km in:

   i 8 miles   ii 18 miles   iii 50 miles

   iv 25 miles   v 100 miles.

c Estimate the number of miles in:

   i 10 km   ii 30 km   iii 100 km.

What you need to know

1 The table shows some species of animal that are in danger of becoming extinct.

Animal	Estimated number	Continent
Amur leopard	30	Asia
Javan rhino	50	Asia
Mountain gorilla	850	Africa
Sumatran elephant	2500	Asia
Black rhino	4800	Africa

a How many mountain gorillas are there according to the table?

b On which continent are the black rhinos?

c Which animals are to be found in Asia?

2 Kafi and Sean are collecting information on the world's largest cities according to population.

They organise the information into a table.

The table shows the five largest cities in alphabetical order.

City	Country	Population
Istanbul	Turkey	13 855 000
Karachi	Pakistan	12 991 000
Moscow	Russia	11 978 000
Mumbai	India	12 478 000
Shanghai	China	17 836 000

Use the table to answer these questions.

a In what country is Mumbai?

b What is the population of Karachi?

c i Which city has the largest population in the world?

   ii What country is it in?

6.1 Tables in everyday use

This table is familiar to road users.

It gives the approximate distances needed to stop a car travelling at different speeds.

Notes: (1) **total stopping distance** = **thinking distance** + **braking distance.**
     (2) the speed is measured in miles per hour (mph) and the distances in metres.

Speed (mph)	20	30	40	50	60	70
Thinking distance (metres)	6	9	12	15	18	21
Braking distance (metres)	6	14	24	38	54	75
Total stopping distance (metres)	12	23	36	53	72	96

Exercise 6.1A

1 From the table above, check that the **total stopping distance** for a speed of 40 mph is 36 metres.

a What is the total stopping distance for a car travelling at 30 mph?

b For a car travelling at 60 mph, what is:

   i the thinking distance

   ii the braking distance

   iii the total stopping distance?

c Suggest what the thinking distance for a car travelling at 80 mph would be.

2   The table compares some gas and electric oven settings.
    (The comparison is only approximate.)

Heat of oven	Gas setting	Electricity
Very Cool	1	140 °C
Cool	2	150 °C
Warm	3	170 °C
Moderate	4	180 °C
Fairly Hot	5	190 °C
Hot	7	220 °C
Very Hot	8	230 °C

a   What temperature would you get at gas mark 7?

b   Gina wants her oven to be fairly hot. What setting should she use on:
    i a gas oven   ii an electric oven?

c   What is the difference in temperature between:
    i gas marks 2 and 3   ii gas marks 1 and 8?

d   By how much does the temperature of the oven rise as we switch from
    a **warm** to a **hot** setting?

3   The table lets you switch between four different systems for measuring ladies shoe sizes. (The
    Japanese system is based on the length of the foot in centimetres.)

Ladies shoe sizes													
British	2	2.5	3	3.5	4	4.5	5	5.5	6	6.5	7	7.5	8
European	34	35	35.5	36	37	37.5	38	38.5	39	39.5	40	41	42
American	4.5	5	5.5	6	6.5	7	7.5	8	8.5	9	9.5	10	10.5
Japanese (cm)	21.5	22	22.5	23	23	23.5	24	24	24.5	25	25.5	26	26.5

a   Jen's shoe size is a British size 5. What is her shoe size in America?

b   Una bought a size 39.5 shoe in Paris. What is her British shoe size?

c   Susie's foot is 22.5 cm long. What size of shoe does she buy in Scotland?

4   The **Beaufort Scale** is used to describe the strength of the wind.

Strength	Speed (mph)	Description	Effect
0	Less than 1	Calm	Smoke rises vertically
1	1−3	Light air	Smoke drifts
3	8−12	Gentle breeze	Light flags extended
5	19−24	Fresh breeze	Small trees in leaf begin to sway
7	32−38	High wind	Effort to walk against wind
9	47−54	Strong gale	Slight structural damage
11	64−72	Violent storm	Widespread damage
12	More than 73	Hurricane	Devastation

a A wind of strength 3 has a speed between 8 mph and 12 mph.
 What is the speed of a wind:
 i of strength 7   **ii** of strength 11   **iii** described as a strong gale?

b A weather report gives the wind speed as 10 mph.
 i What is the strength of the wind and how would you describe it?
 ii What effect would you expect to see?

c A storm has a strength of 10. Trees are uprooted.
 Describe the speed of the storm.

5 The Highland View Hotel advertises as shown below.

a Mr Bowie spends one night at the Highland View Hotel.
 How much does it cost?

b Mr and Mrs Box spend a fortnight at the hotel.
 How much does it cost them?

c Mr and Mrs Chang and their 10-year-old
 twins spend seven nights at the Highland
 View Hotel.
 What was the total bill for the family?

d A group of friends (all adults) spent
 one night at the hotel.
 Their hotel bill was £390.
 How many friends were there?

The Highland View Hotel *****		
Full Board	*Relax with breathtaking views!*	
	Adult prices per person	Child prices (up to 14 years of age)
1 night	£78	£42
2 nights	£142	£80
7 nights	£410	£230
14 nights	£710	£390

e John and Mary and their children stayed for two nights at the hotel.
 All the children were under 14. The total bill was £604.
 How many children do John and Mary have?

6 Prices for admission to a zoo are shown in the table:

	Adult	Child 3–15 years	Child (under 3)	Concession
Price	£14·50	£10·45	FREE	£12·25

a Mr and Mrs Mills are going with their children Zak (aged 5) and
 Zoe (aged 2).
 Calculate how much in total it will cost them to go in to the zoo.

Family tickets are available.

Family Ticket	2 Adults 2 Children	2 Adults 3 Children	1 Adult 2 Children	1 Adult 3 Children
Price	£45·00	£54·50	£31·50	£41·25

b The Gupta family of two adults and three children (all over 3)
 are going to the zoo.
 How much will it cost them if:
 i they don't buy a family ticket
 ii they do buy a family ticket?

c How much do the Guptas save with a family ticket?

d How much does a family of one adult and two children, both over 3, save with a family ticket?

Buying in bulk

The cost of an item sometimes depends on how many of the items you buy.

Example 1

Using the table, how much would it cost for:

a 6 canes   **b** 12 canes?

a If you buy 6 canes, you pay 14p each.

Cost: 14p × 6 = 84p.

b If you buy 12 canes, you pay 12p each.

Cost: 12p × 12 = 144p = £1·44.

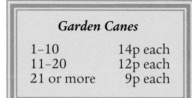

Garden Canes	
1–10	14p each
11–20	12p each
21 or more	9p each

Exercise 6.1B

1 Using the table from Example 1, calculate the cost of:

     a 8 canes   **b** 15 canes   **c** 24 canes   **d** 30 canes.

2 Mr Tait is ordering jotters for his classes. The table shows the prices per jotter.

     a What is the total cost of: **i** 50 plain jotters
       ii 100 plain jotters   **iii** 300 plain jotters?

     b Mr Tait orders: 150 plain jotters, 250 lined jotters
       and 200 squared jotters.
       What is the total cost of his order?

Jotters	1−99	100−199	200+
Plain	11p	10p	9p
Lined	12p	11p	10p
Squared	13p	12p	11p

     c What is the cost of: **i** 100 lined jotters   **ii** 95 lined jotters?

     d **i** What do you notice about your answers to part **c**?
       ii What would you do if you wanted to buy 95 lined jotters?

3 Several breeds of dog in Britain are at risk of extinction.
The table shows the number of pups born and registered with the Kennel Club
in 2002, 2005 and 2011.

Breed	Group	Registration year		
		2002	2005	2011
Bull terrier (miniature)	Terrier	278	275	216
Collie (smooth)	Pastoral	85	72	75
English setter	Gundog	568	450	234
Toy terrier (black)	Toy	56	103	95
Otterhound	Hound	54	50	38

     a Which breeds decreased steadily in number from 2002, through 2005, to 2011?

     b By how many has the Otterhound decreased between 2002 and 2011?

     c By how many has the English setter decreased between 2005 and 2011?

     d **i** Which breed had more pups registered in 2011 than in 2002?
       ii How many more?

4 The table lists some handy measures for liquids.

Unit	... is roughly	Millilitres
1 teaspoon	$\frac{1}{3}$ tablespoon	5
1 dessertspoon	2 teaspoons	10
1 tablespoon	3 teaspoons	15
1 cup	16 tablespoons	285
1 pint	2 cups	570
1 quart	2 pints	1136
1 litre	$3\frac{1}{2}$ cups	1000
1 gallon	4 quarts	4560

a   How many teaspoons hold the same quantity of liquid as a tablespoon?

b   How many tablespoons hold the same quantity of liquid as a cupful?

c   How many cupfuls are roughly the same as 2 litres?

d   Four cupfuls is roughly the same as how many: i pints   ii millilitres?

e   Use the table to help you describe how you could measure out:

   i 300 ml   ii 250 ml.

5 The cost of placing an advert in *The Daily News* is given in the table.

Words	Less than 11	11 to 20	21 to 30	31 or more
Price	30p per word	25p per word	20p per word	15p per word

> **PRINTER.** As good as new. £50.
> Telephone 2324256 for details.

a   i Check that the advert above has 10 words.
      (Note: *£50* and *2324256* each count as a word.)

   ii Now calculate the cost of placing the advert in the paper.

b   Work out the cost of placing these adverts in *The Daily News*.
   Words with a hyphen count as two words.

   i
> **SECOND-HAND SUPERMINI** for sale.
> 2012 MOT certificate. Four new tyres.
> 38,000 miles Taxed till June £2500. Tel.
> 6999250 Mobile no. 77034160

   ii
> **FOR SALE:** 2 bedroom semi-detached
> house. Gas central heating, double-glazed
> throughout. Garage. Large, well-kept
> garden. Close to shops, school and
> railway station. Needs some modernising.
> Price negotiable. Phone 20202043 to
> arrange a time to view.

c   You have a TV for sale.
   i Make up your advert for *The Daily News*.
   ii Work out the cost of your advert.

6.2 Ready reckoners and distance charts

A **ready reckoner** is a table made up to save you having to do repeated calculations.

Example 1

This ready reckoner lets you check the cost of the petrol you have put in your petrol tank.

Petrol (litres)	1	2	3	4	5	6	7	8	9	10	20	30	40
Cost (£)	1·42	2·84	4·26	5·68	7·10	8·52	9·94	11·36	12·78	14·20	28·40	42·60	56·80

a What is the cost of 8 litres of petrol?

b Calculate the price of 32 litres of petrol.

a Look along the 'litres' row until you get to '8'. Look directly below to find the cost ... £11·36.
   So the cost of 8 litres is £11·36.

b Cost of 32 litres = cost of 30 litres + cost of 2 litres.
   $\qquad$ = £42·60 + £2·84 $\qquad$ From the table.
   $\qquad$ = £45·44

Exercise 6.2A

1 **a** Using the ready reckoner from Example 1, write down the cost of:
   i 6 litres of petrol **ii** 9 litres of petrol **iii** 20 litres of petrol.

   b Work out the cost of:
   i 12 litres **ii** 35 litres **iii** 50 litres **iv** 90 litres.

2 Sophie works part-time in the supermarket. She is paid £6·72 an hour.

   Sophie has a ready reckoner to help her work out her weekly wage.

Hours	1	2	3	4	5	6	7	8	9	10	20
Wage (£)	6·72	13·44	20·16	26·88	33·60	40·32	47·04	53·76	60·48	67·20	134·40

   a Calculate how much Sophie earns in a week where she works:
   i 7 hours **ii** 9 hours **iii** 20 hours.

   b Work out how much she earns for:
   i 14 hours **ii** 15 hours **iii** 27 hours **iv** 32 hours **v** 35 hours.

   c How many hours must Sophie work to earn £127·68?

3 This ready reckoner gives the cost of Regal floor tiles. They are sold in boxes of five.

Boxes	1	2	3	4	5	6	7	8	9	10	20	30
Price (£)	9·25	18·50	27·75	37·00	46·25	55·50	64·75	74·00	83·25	92·50	185·00	277·50

   a What is the cost of: **i** 5 boxes **ii** 20 boxes?

   b Calculate the cost of: **i** 15 boxes **ii** 24 boxes **iii** 50 boxes.

   c The floor of the local library is being recovered with Regal floor tiles.
   Charles estimates that approximately 375 tiles are required.
   i How many boxes of tiles are needed? (Remember, each box contains 5 tiles.)
   ii How much will they cost?

Distance charts

Distances between towns can be read easily from a **distance chart**.

Example 2

The chart shows the distances in miles between five Ayrshire towns.

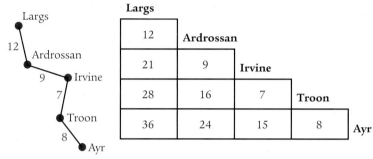

Largs				
12	**Ardrossan**			
21	9	**Irvine**		
28	16	7	**Troon**	
36	24	15	8	**Ayr**

What is the distance between Ardrossan and Troon?

To find the distance between Ardrossan and Troon, look where the *Ardrossan column* crosses the *Troon row*.

They are **16 miles** apart.

Check that the distances on the map agree with the distances in the table.

Largs				
12	**Ardrossan**			
21	9	**Irvine**		
28	16	7	**Troon**	
36	24	15	8	**Ayr**

1 The distance chart gives the distances, in miles, between six Scottish towns.

a Write down the distance in miles between:
   i Aberdeen and Ayr
   ii Aberdeen and Perth
   iii Edinburgh and Inverness.

b Shirley drives from Ayr to Edinburgh and then on to Perth.
   i What is the distance from Ayr to Edinburgh?
   ii What is the distance from Edinburgh to Perth?
   iii What is the total distance Shirley travelled?

c Tony leaves his home in Perth and drives to a meeting in Inverness. He then drives across to Aberdeen.

   How far did Tony drive?

d The sketch map shows the positions of the six places from the distance chart.
   i Copy the sketch map.
   ii Add the distances from place to place.

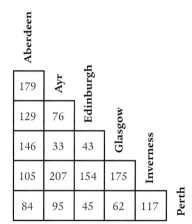

Aberdeen					
179	Ayr				
129	76	Edinburgh			
146	33	43	Glasgow		
105	207	154	175	Inverness	
84	95	45	62	117	Perth

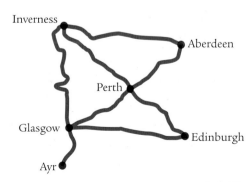

2 The sketch map shows five towns. The distances between them are given in miles.

   a Copy the table.

   b Use the distances on the map to help you fill in the table.

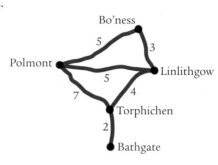

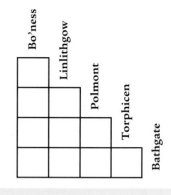

3 This ready reckoner converts euros (€) to pounds (£), working to the nearest 10 cents.

€ to £	0·00	0·10	0·20	0·30	0·40	0·50	0·60	0·70	0·80	0·90
1	0·85	0·94	1·02	1·11	1·19	1·28	1·36	1·45	1·53	1·62
2	1·70	1·79	1·87	1·96	2·04	2·13	2·21	2·30	2·38	2·47
3	2·55	2·64	2·72	2·81	2·89	2·98	3·06	3·15	3·23	3·32
4	3·40	3·49	3·57	3·66	3·74	3·83	3·91	4·00	4·08	4·17
5	4·25	4·34	4·42	4·51	4·59	4·68	4·76	4·85	4·93	5·02
6	5·10	5·19	5·27	5·36	5·44	5·53	5·61	5·70	5·78	5·87
7	5·95	6·04	6·12	6·21	6·29	6·38	6·46	6·55	6·63	6·72
8	6·80	6·89	6·97	7·06	7·14	7·23	7·31	7·40	7·48	7·57
9	7·65	7·74	7·82	7·91	7·99	8·08	8·16	8·25	8·33	8·42
10	8·50	8·59	8·67	8·76	8·84	8·93	9·01	9·10	9·18	9·27
20	17·00	17·09	17·17	17·26	17·34	17·43	17·51	17·60	17·68	17·77
30	25·50	25·59	25·67	25·76	25·84	25·93	26·01	26·10	26·18	26·27
40	34·00	34·09	34·17	34·26	34·34	34·43	34·51	34·60	34·68	34·77
50	42·50	42·59	42·67	42·76	42·84	42·93	43·01	43·10	43·18	43·27

Notes: €3·20 is found where the '3' row and column '0·20' cross ... £2·72. €35·80 = €30·00 + €5·80.

   a How many pounds do you get for:

     i €2·00   **ii** €5·50   **iii** €4·30   **iv** €8·60   **v** €30?

   b Work out how many pounds are worth:

     i €11·00   **ii** €14·50   **iii** €18·70   **iv** €46·50   **v** €80·00.

   c How many euros do you get for:

     i £34·68   **ii** £42·67   **iii** £8·25?

Preparation for assessment

1 The table allows you to buy the correct size of man's casual shirt or top.

Size	Small	Medium	Large	X Large	XX Large
Neck (inches)	14·5−15	15·5−16	16·5−17	17·5−18	18·5−19
Chest (inches)	Up to 37	38−40	41−43	44−46	47−49

   a Colin has a 16-inch neck. What size of shirt should he buy?

   b Ian has a 34-inch chest. What is the correct size for him?

   c What size of shirt should someone with a 45-inch chest buy?

2 The prices of tickets to an aquarium are given in the table.

	Door Price	Online Saving
Adult (13+)	£13.00	£2.50 per ticket
Child (3−12)	£9.00	£2.50 per ticket
Concession (OAP, etc.)	£11.00	£1.25 per ticket
Family (2 adults + 2 children)	£42.00	£8.00
Grandparents (2 concessions + 2 children)	£38.00	£5.50

(Note: children under 3 get in free.)

a Mr and Mrs Steel and their nine-year-old son buy tickets at the door.

  i What is the total cost?

  ii How much would they have saved by buying online?

b Mr and Mrs Zagni take their two grandchildren to the aquarium.
Both grandparents are OAPs and the children are aged five and two. They pay at the door.
What tickets should they buy to pay the least amount of money?

3

Pounds (£)	1	5	10	15	20	30	40	50	100	200	300	400	500
US dollars ($)	1.54	7.70	15.40	23.10	30.80	46.20	61.60	77.00	154	308	462	616	770

a Use the ready reckoner to find out how many US dollars ($) you would get for:

  i £40   ii £300   iii £25   iv £150   v £950.

b Estimate how many pounds are worth 100 US dollars.

4 The chart shows the distances, in kilometres, between five towns.

a How far is it from:

  i Darley to Ashfield   ii Barr to Eglinton?

b Gillian travels from Crosbie to Ashfield, then on to Eglinton
before returning directly to Crosbie.

Calculate the total distance she travelled.

Ashfield				
10	Barr			
14	15	Crosbie		
25	17	11	Darley	
19	9	6	8	Eglinton

5 Remember the table below is a **ready reckoner** that converts miles to kilometres.

Miles	1	2	3	4	5	6	7	8	9	10	20	30	40	50
Kilometres	1.6	3.2	4.8	6.4	8.0	9.7	11.3	12.9	14.5	16.1	32.2	48.3	64.4	80.5

a Write down the number of kilometres in:

  i 6 miles   ii 10 miles   iii 40 miles.

b Write down the number of km in:

  i 8 miles   ii 18 miles   iii 50 miles

c Estimate the number of miles in:

  i 10 km   ii 30 km   iii 100 km.

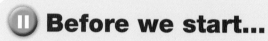

Before we start...

The parent/teacher committee wants to convince the council that a crossing near the school needs a 'lollipop man' to supervise the children.

Which graph might be most useful in highlighting their claim?

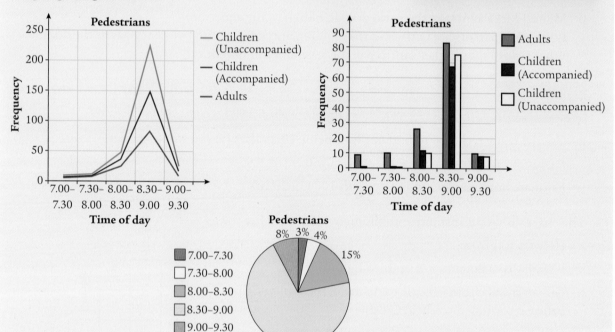

What you need to know

1 Glebe Street has several houses in it. Some of the houses have 2 rooms, while others have 3, 4 or 5 rooms.

The pictogram shows how many houses there are of each type.

Each picture represents 5 houses.

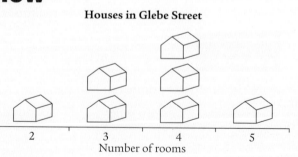

Houses in Glebe Street

a Which type of house occurs most often?

b How many houses are in Glebe Street?

c How many more houses had 3 rooms than 5?

2 James logged the types of birds that came to his bird table one morning.

This bar graph shows what he found.

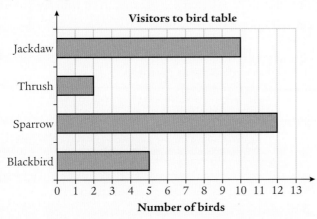

a Which type of bird had the highest count?

b How many more blackbirds than thrushes came to the table?

c How many birds did James count altogether?

3 Sandra records the amount of rain that falls in the first week of April.

The line graph shows the data that she recorded.

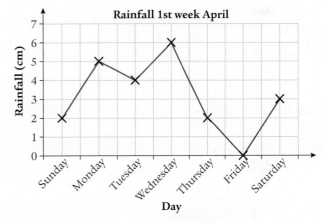

a Which day was the wettest?

b What was the rainfall on:
  i Monday   **ii** Friday?

c What was the total rainfall that week?

4 This pie chart shows how 360 students got to school.

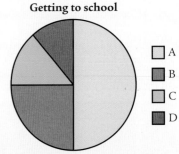

- 50 said they came by bus.
- 90 came by car.
- 180 walked.
- 40 used a bike.

a The key shows that A was the most popular method.

What does A stand for?

b Say what:
  i B
  ii C and
  iii D represent.

7.1 Bar graphs

In a bar graph the length of the bar gives us an idea of how often a score occurred (the **frequency**).

Example 1

As cars passed a checkpoint, the number of people in each car was counted.

The bar graph shows the findings.

Use the graph to help you complete the table.

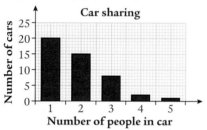

Number of people in car	Number of cars
1	
2	
3	
4	
5	

Number of people in car	Number of cars
1	20
2	15
3	8
4	2
5	1

Exercise 7.1A

1 Look at the 'car sharing' bar graph in Example 1.

   a How many cars had only 1 person in it?

   b How many cars had more than 2 people in it?

   c How many more cars had 2 people than 5?

   d Why would it be unlikely that there were no people in the car?

2 A car ferry company recorded the types of vehicles it carried.

   The results are shown in a **horizontal** bar graph.

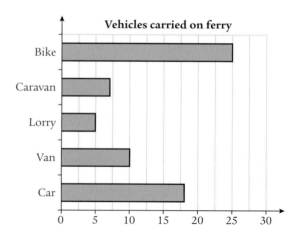

   a How many bikes were carried on the ferry?

   b Which vehicle type had a count of 10?

   c How many more vans than lorries were there?

3 After the bad weather, the council engineers went out to survey the potholes in the roads.

   a Which road was worst for potholes?

   b What was the difference between the number of holes in Arthur Street and Gwen's Way?

   c How many potholes were there in Camelot Crescent and Lancelot Lane put together?

   d If the total number of potholes goes over 100, then a special report will have to be written.

   Will the report have to be written?

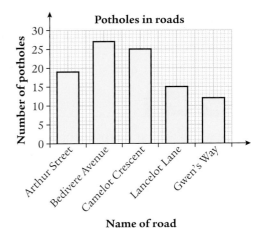

Exercise 7.1B

1 On midsummer's day each year the amount of seals basking on the rocks in the bay are counted.

   a What was the best year for spotting seals?

   b How many more seals were counted in 2011 than the previous year?

   c One year there was an flu epidemic in the spring among the seals. Which year was it?

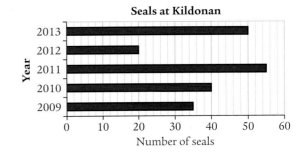

2 In Kenmore High, the number of students attending clubs was noted.

   a In which year group did equal numbers of boys and girls attend clubs?

   b What was the only year group where the girls outnumbered the boys?

   c What was the difference between boys and girls attending clubs in S1?

   d **i** In which year group was the difference between boys and girls the greatest?
   ii What was this difference?

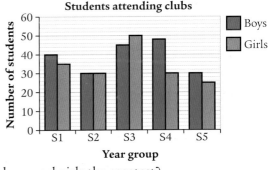

3 The daily count of people attending a cinema complex in the city is shown by a bar graph. Note that the people are being counted in hundreds.

   a On Monday, how many **i** children **ii** people **iii** adults attended?

   b How many children attended on Tuesday?

   c On which days were there more children than adults?

   d How many more adults attended on Wednesday than Tuesday?

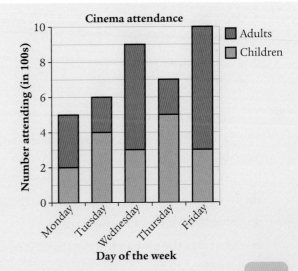

7.2 Line graphs

A line graph is useful to show changes happening over time.

Example 1

The graph shows an outbreak of measles in a school.

a How many cases of measles were there in week 3 of the outbreak?

b How many more people had the measles in week 4 than in week 2?

c Describe the trend of the outbreak.

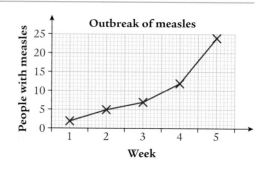

a In week 3, there were 7 cases of measles.

b In week 4, there were 12 cases. In week 2, there were 5 cases. There were 12 − 5 = 7 more cases in week 4 than in week 2.

c As the weeks pass, the number of cases of measles increases. This is called the **trend**.

Exercise 7.2A

1 A shop keeps a record of its sales of Easter eggs.

They record the number sold each week to the nearest five eggs.

a How many eggs were sold with 3 weeks to go till Easter?

b How many eggs were sold in the week containing Easter?

c How many fewer eggs were sold in the week after Easter than in the week before Easter?

d Describe the trend in egg sales:
   i before   ii after Easter.

2 The gas boiler in a house broke down on Friday.

The gas engineer couldn't come until the following Tuesday.

The graph shows the temperature at noon each day in the loft space.

a Describe the trend in the graph.

b What was the temperature on Saturday?

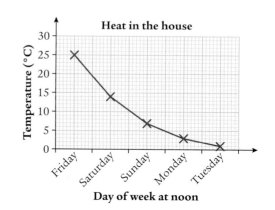

c What was the drop in temperature between noon on Sunday and noon on Monday?

3 This line graph shows the time of sunrise on the first of the month throughout the year.

The trend is **seasonal**, because every year it repeats itself.

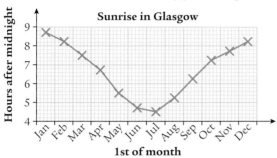

a **i** When is the earliest that the sun rises?
  ii In which month does this happen?

b When is the latest that the sun rises?

c In which months does the sun rise before 6 a.m.?

Example 2

Line graphs are often used as **ready reckoners**.

For example, when shopping abroad you can use a line graph to roughly change between euros and pounds quickly.

a How many euros do you get for:
  i £8 **ii** £80?

b How many pounds do you get for:
  i €7 **ii** €35?

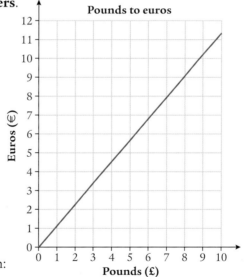

a **i** From the graph, £8 matches with €9.
  ii Using this, £80 will be 10 times as much: €9 × 10 = €90.

b **i** From the graph €7 matches with £6.
  ii Using this, €35 will be 5 times as much: £6 × 5 = £30.

Exercise 7.2B

1 Use the 'Pounds to euros converter' from Example 2 to change:

  a these amounts into euros:
    i £5 **ii** £50 **iii** £500.

  b these amounts into pounds:
    i €3 **ii** €30 **iii** €15.

2 This graph converts speed into 'thinking distance'.

'Thinking distance' is the distance your car travels as you think to brake.

a What is the thinking distance for:
   i 10 mph   **ii** 40 mph?

b How much further do you travel before you start to brake if you are going at 60 mph rather than 30 mph?

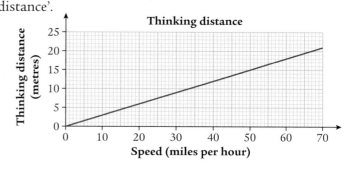

3 Sam is an electrician. When called out for a job, Sam charges a 'call-out' fee, plus a fixed amount per hour.

The chart helps him to estimate his charges.

a Sam's call-out fee can be found by finding the cost of a job that lasts no hours.
What is Sam's call-out fee?

b What is the charge for a job that takes:
   i 1 hour
   ii 2 hours?

c Sam's hourly rate can be calculated by subtracting the cost of a job that takes 1 hour from the cost of a job that takes 2 hours.
What is Sam's hourly rate?

d What would be the cost of a 10-hour job?

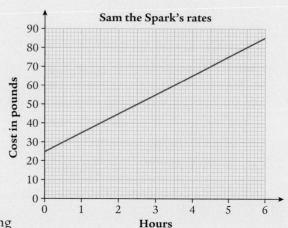

7.3 Pie charts

Pie charts are good for showing the **share** of the count that each object gets.

Things that happen more often will get a bigger share of the 'pie'.

In an election, the votes for the four main parties were put in a pie chart.

a What percentage voted Labour?

b List the parties in order, most popular first.

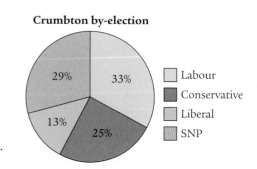

a The chart tells us that Labour got 33% of the vote.

b Labour(33%), SNP (29%), Conservatives (25%), Liberal (13%).

Exercise 7.3A

1 Sixty students visited the library during the English period. Each borrowed a book.

The pie chart shows what type of books were borrowed.

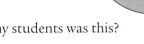

Books borrowed

a What was the most popular type of book?

b Which types were less popular than travel?

c Romance and travel accounted for half of the books borrowed.
How many students picked romance or travel?

d One-tenth of the students picked a science book.
What fraction didn't pick a science book?

e A quarter of the students picked history. How many students was this?

2 The pie chart shows the results of a survey into what students do for lunch.

a Half of the students asked take school dinners.
Which colour represents those who take school dinners?

b The green section represents those who go to the local shop
for a sandwich. What percentage of the students is this?

c For the survey, 90 students were asked.
The blue section represents the students who took a packed lunch.
How many took a packed lunch?

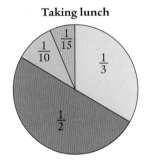

Taking lunch

Exercise 7.3B

1 Matthew kept a record of the time he spent on homework for different subjects.

This pie chart gives a picture of his record.

Over a term he recorded 60 hours of work.

a Which two subjects shared the top spot?

b What is: **i** 10% of 60   **ii** 5% of 60?

c How much time did Matthew spent on:
   i social studies   **ii** arts   **iii** technologies?

d How much more time did Matthew spend on science
than health?

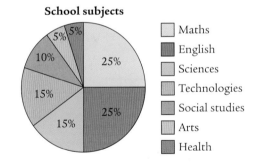

School subjects

Maths
English
Sciences
Technologies
Social studies
Arts
Health

2 This chart shows the estimated populations
of the countries of the UK in mid-2012.

The larger circle shows England
compared with Scotland, Northern
Ireland and Wales together.

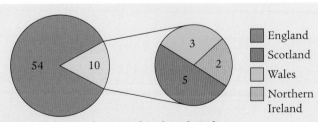

England
Scotland
Wales
Northern
Ireland

The smaller circle shows the relation between Scotland, Northern Ireland and Wales.

The figures show the populations in millions.

a What is the population of England?

b Which of the four countries has the fewest people?

c What is the difference between the population of Scotland and that of Northern Ireland?

Preparation for assessment

1 Sadiq spent an hour at the pier counting sea birds. He made a graph of his count.

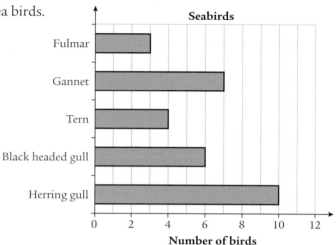

a Which bird did Sadiq see the most?

b How many more gannets did he see than terns?

c How many birds did he see altogether?

d What fraction of the birds were herring gulls?

2 A geologist collected pebbles from the beach and noted the type of rock each was made of.

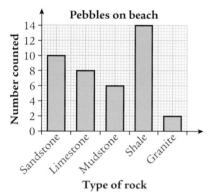

a What was the least common type of pebble collected?

b How many limestone pebbles were counted?

c How many more pebbles of shale were found than sandstone?

d How many pebbles were collected altogether?

3 The cars passing outside the school gates were counted one morning.

Two cars were counted at 8.10 a.m.

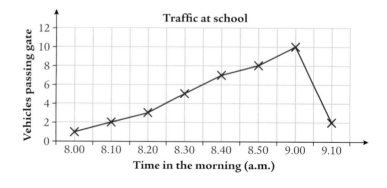

a How many cars were counted at 8.30 a.m.?

b At what time was the count highest?

c How many more cars passed at 8.50 a.m. than at 8.00 a.m.?

d What is the trend in the car count between 8 a.m. and 9 a.m.?

4 The type of vehicles that arrived outside the school gate just before 9 a.m. were noted.

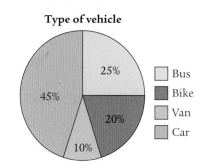

Type of vehicle

a What was the least common type of vehicle?

b What fraction of the vehicles were buses?

c If 40 vehicles were counted, how many of them were:
  i vans   ii bikes?

d Copy and complete the table:

Type	Count
Bus	10
Bike	
Van	
Car	

5 Remember the parent/teacher committee that wants to convince the council that a crossing near the school needs a 'lollipop man' to supervise the children.

Which graph might be most useful in highlighting their claim?

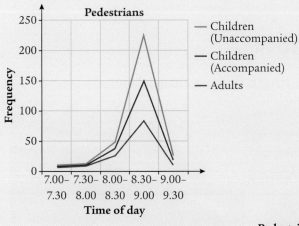

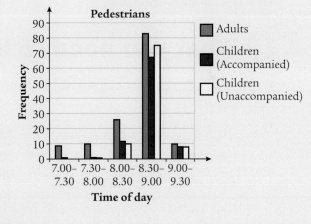

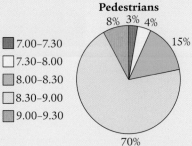

8 Length

Before we start...

North Gyles golf course is a nine-hole golf course.

The length of each hole in metres is shown in the table:

Hole	1	2	3	4	5	6	7	8	9
Length (m)	293	85	281	183	84	396	335	277	118

a What is the total length of the golf course:

  i in metres   **ii** in kilometres?

b The boundary of the golf course is shaped as shown.
  What is the perimeter of the course:

  i in metres   **ii** in kilometres?

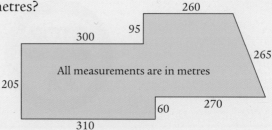

All measurements are in metres

260
95
300
265
205
60   270
310

▶ What you need to know

1 Choose from the list below the best unit of length for measuring these:

  a the length of your ruler

  b the height of the classroom

  c the width of an earthworm

  d the breadth of a tennis court

  e the distance between Paris and Edinburgh

  f the depth of water in the North Sea.

  centimetres (cm)
  metres (m)
  millimetres (mm)
  kilometres (km)

2 a Draw a rectangle 12 cm by 5 cm.

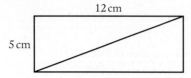

12 cm

5 cm

  b Draw in one diagonal.   **c** Measure the length of the diagonal in centimetres.

3 Write these lengths in metres and centimetres, and then in metres only.

Example: 318 cm = 3 m 18 cm = 3·18 m.

    a 124 cm   **b** 165 cm   **c** 537 cm   **d** 102 cm

4 Write these lengths in metres and centimetres, and then in centimetres only.

Example: 1·84 m = 1 m 84 cm = 184 cm.

    a 1·24 m   **b** 1·57 m   **c** 2·95 m   **d** 5·08 m

5 Are these possible? Copy and complete the table.

		Yes	No	Maybe
a	A tree 1 km high			
b	A rabbit 40 cm long			
c	A person running 30 km in a day			
d	A woman 2 metres tall			
e	A gull 8 mm long			
f	A person with hair 1 metre long			

8.1 Estimating length

You can estimate the length of objects by comparing them with lengths you already know.

- Your thumb will be about 2 cm wide.
- Your hand will be about 10 cm wide and 15 cm long.
- From your elbow to the tip of your middle finger is about 45 cm.
- Your foot is about 25 cm long.
- From your nose to the tip of your fingers is about a metre.

Check these out for yourself. They may come in handy.

Exercise 8.1A

1 The scissors in the picture are 4 cm.

    a Estimate the length of:

        i the paper clip

        ii the pen

        iii the puzzle

        iv the pencil sharpener

        v the postage stamp.

    b Now measure the length of each with a ruler to the nearest centimetre.

       Compare your estimates with your measurements.

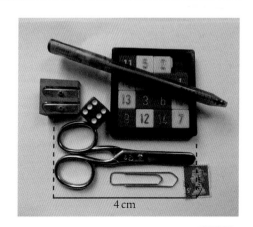

4 cm

2 a Use a ruler to measure: **i** the width of your thumb **ii** the width of your hand.

b Use this information to estimate: **i** the width of your textbook
ii the width of your desk
iii the height of your desk.

c Measure these distances accurately and compare them with your estimates.

3 Kirsty is 1·5 m tall. The standing stone is three times as tall.

a Estimate the height of the standing stone in metres.

b Use a similar idea to estimate the height of:
i your classroom **ii** your classroom door.

c If you have access to a digital camera, can you take a picture that would help you estimate the height of the school?

Exercise 8.1B

1 Estimate in metres or kilometres, the distance from the school:

a to your home **b** to the nearest supermarket **c** to the nearest railway station or bus station.

2 The sides of each small square on the road map are 1 cm long.

a Estimate the distance on the map from:
i Brent to Ashdown
ii Cairn to Brent.

b The distance of 1 cm on the map represents an actual distance of 2 km.

Estimate the actual distance from:
i Brent to Ashdown
ii Cairn to Brent.

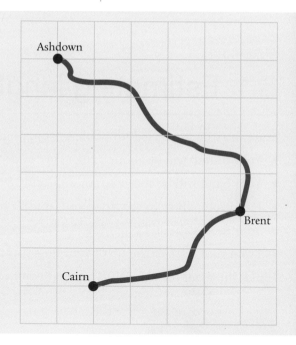

8.2 Using millimetres

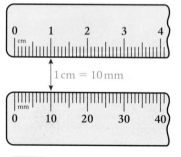

1 cm = 10 mm

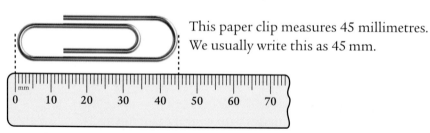

This paper clip measures 45 millimetres. We usually write this as 45 mm.

Exercise 8.2A

1 A picture of the PS *Waverley* is mounted into an album.

Measure the distances in millimetres between:

a A and B   **b** B and C   **c** A and C.

2 The length of the tennis court in the drawing is 120 mm.

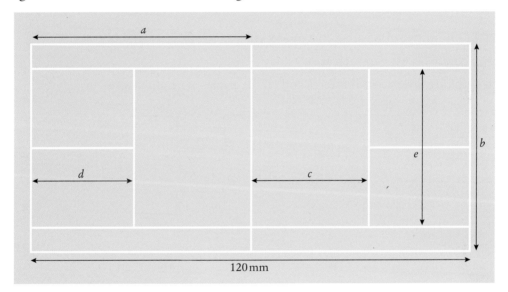

a Estimate the lengths *a*, *b*, *c*, *d* and *e* in millimetres.

b Measure each length with a ruler.

c Copy and complete the table.

	a	*b*	*c*	*d*	*e*
Estimate (mm)					
Measurement (mm)					

Exercise 8.2B

1 Make accurate drawings of each flag. All lengths are given in millimetres.

a
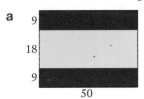

b
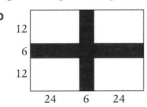

c
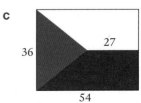

2 Four golf balls sit on the green.

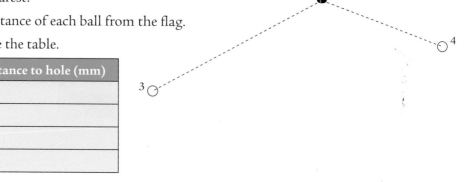

    a Which of the four golf balls looks furthest from the hole?

    b Which looks nearest?

    c Measure the distance of each ball from the flag.

Copy and complete the table.

Golf ball	Distance to hole (mm)
1	
2	
3	
4	

    d Which ball *is* furthest from the hole?

3 The sketches show two grass areas in a model village.

Make an accurate drawing of each area.

All the lengths are given in millimetres and all the angles are right angles.

a

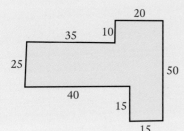

b

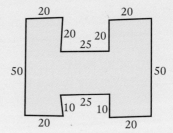

8.3 Changing to a smaller unit

Example 1

Over a day the redshank had paddled 4 km.

How far is this: **a** in metres **b** in centimetres **c** in millimetres?

a It walked **4 km** = 4 × 1000   = **4000 m.**

b   = 4000 × 100 = **400 000 cm.**

c   = 400 000 × 10 = **4 000 000 mm.**

    4 km = 4000 m = 400 000 cm = 4 000 000 mm

Exercise 8.3A

1 Change each length to millimetres by multiplying by 10:

    a 3 cm   **b** 8 cm   **c** 14 cm   **d** 75 cm.

2 Change each length to centimetres by multiplying by 100:

    a 6 m   **b** 12 m   **c** 25 m   **d** 40 m.

3 Change each length to metres by multiplying by 1000:

    a 2 km   **b** 7 km   **c** 13 km   **d** 42 km.

4 Shona's best friend lives 5 km away. How many metres is that?

5 The hedge round Ian's garden is 3 m high. When he cut it, he lowered its height by 80 cm.

    What is now the height of Ian's hedge, in centimetres?

6 A year ago Des was 1 m 98 cm tall. He has grown 5 cm since then.

    What height is he now:

    a in metres and centimetres   **b** in centimetres?

Example 2

Change:

a 7·9 cm to millimetres   **b** 6·5 m to centimetres

c 3·58 km to metres   **d** 8·27 m to millimetres.

65 mm

a 7·9 cm = 7·9 × 10 = 79 mm.

b 6·5 m = 6·5 × 100 = 650 cm.

c 3·58 km = 3·58 × 1000 = 3580 m.

d 8·27 m = 827 cm   (8·27 × 100)

    827 cm = 8270 mm   (827 × 10)

Exercise 8.3B

1 Change these lengths to millimetres:

    a 3·2 cm   **b** 14·7 cm   **c** 46·5 cm   **d** 2·46 m   **e** 5·3 m.

2 Express these measurements in centimetres:

    a 1·58 m   **b** 9·63 m   **c** 6·7 m   **d** 2·9 m.

3 Change these to metres:

    a 3·382 km   **b** 7·68 km   **c** 15·31 km   **d** 6·4 km.

4 A copper pipe is 3 metres long. A piece 84 cm is cut from it.

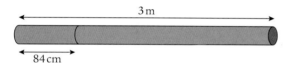

3 m

84 cm

What length of pipe remains? (Give your answer in centimetres.)

5 A length of cloth is 6 metres long. It is cut into eight equal lengths.

How long is each length in: **a** centimetres **b** millimetres?

6 The Forth Rail Bridge is 2·529 kilometres long.

a How many metres is this?

b The Forth Road Bridge is 2·517 kilometres long.
How many metres long is it?

c How many metres longer is the Rail Bridge?

d How many centimetres longer is the Rail Bridge?

8.4 Changing to a bigger unit

mm → ÷10 → cm → ÷100 → m → ÷1000 → km

Example 1

a The tallest man in the world was 272 cm.
How many metres high was he?

b A queen honey bee is about 24 mm long.
How many centimetres is this?

c The Clackmannanshire Bridge is 1190 metres long.
Give this length in kilometres.

a $272 \div 100 = 2.72$ m. The tallest man is 2·72 m tall.

b $24 \div 10 = 2.4$ cm. The queen bee is 2·4 cm long.

c $1190 \div 1000 = 1.190$ km. The Clackmannanshire Bridge is 1·19 km.

Exercise 8.4A

1 Change these lengths to centimetres by dividing by 10:

    a 20 mm   **b** 70 mm   **c** 160 mm   **d** 1300 mm.

2 Change these to metres by dividing by 1000:

    a 5000 mm   **b** 12 000 mm   **c** 38 000 mm   **d** 400 000 mm.

3 Change these measurements to metres:

    a 300 cm   **b** 900 cm   **c** 3400 cm   **d** 14 000 cm.

4 Change these measurements to kilometres:

    a 2000 m   **b** 8000 m   **c** 39 000 m   **d** 620 000 m.

5 Human hair grows at the rate of about 3 mm each week.
How much does it grow in a year? Give your answer in:

    a millimetres   **b** centimetres.

6 Carrie ran eight laps of an athletics track.
Each lap is 400 metres.

What distance did she run?
Give your answer in:

    a metres   **b** kilometres.

Example 2

Change:

a 59 mm to centimetres   **b** 2600 mm to metres

c 3680 cm to metres   **d** 5420 m to kilometres.

a 59 mm = 59 ÷ 10 = 5·9 cm.   **b** 2600 mm = 2600 ÷ 1000 = 2·600 m.

c 3680 cm = 3680 ÷ 100 = 36·80 m.   **d** 5420 m = 5420 ÷ 1000 = 5·420 km.

Exercise 8.4B

1 Change these lengths to centimetres:

    a 45 mm   **b** 81 mm   **c** 134 mm   **d** 408 mm.

2 Change these lengths to metres:

    a 3720 mm   **b** 7525 mm   **c** 148 cm   **d** 5238 cm   **e** 56 000 cm.

3 Change these lengths to kilometres:

    a 4700 m   **b** 35 400 m   **c** 19 750 m   **d** 500 m   **e** 645 m.

4 Gail and Greg went on a circular bike ride as shown.

The distances between the places are given in metres.

   a How many metres did they cycle altogether?

   b What is your answer to part **a**:

     i in kilometres and metres

     ii in kilometres?

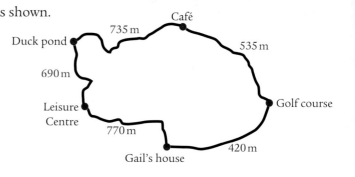

5 The table shows the rainfall each day during one week in Hayshill.

Day	Mon	Tues	Wed	Thu	Fri	Sat	Sun
Rainfall (mm)	7	0	36	28	19	14	5

   a How many millimetres of rain fell in Hayshill over the seven days?

   b What is your answer to part **a** in centimetres?

   c Which was the wettest day?

6 Kumar needs 5 m of edging to put at the side of his garden path.

He has six pieces of edging measuring 130 cm, 125 cm, 105 cm, 94 cm, 85 cm and 72 cm.

   a How much edging does Kumar have?

   b Does he have enough edging?

   c If your answer to part **b** is no, how much more edging does Kumar need?

     If your answer to part **b** is yes, how much extra does he have?

8.5 Perimeter

The **perimeter** of a shape is the total distance round the outside of the shape.

Example 1

Calculate the perimeter of:

a the red triangle

b the green rectangle.

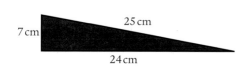

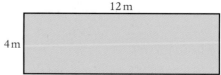

a 7 + 24 + 25 = 56. The perimeter of the red triangle is 56 cm.

b 12 + 4 + 12 + 4 = 32. The perimeter of the green rectangle is 32 m.

Exercise 8.5A

1 **i** Calculate the perimeter of each shape.

ii Write your answers to **d** and **e** in metres.

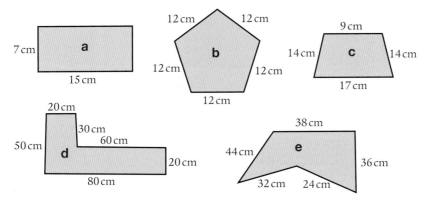

2 The pony is in an odd shaped field.

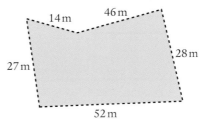

a Calculate the perimeter of the field.

b Fencing costs £10 a metre.
How much will it cost to put a fence round the field?

Exercise 8.5B

1 The blue shape is a rectangle of length 5 cm and breadth 3·6 cm.

The green shape has 2 long sides of length 26 mm and 10 small sides of length 12 mm.

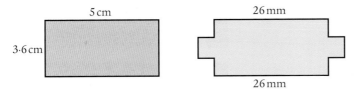

Which shape has the longer perimeter?

2 The green square has the same perimeter as the yellow rectangle.

What is the length of the rectangle?

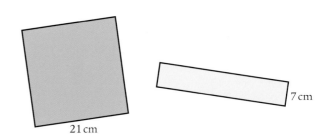

3 A strip of metal runs around the flat roof of a school building to act as a lightning conductor. The conductor is shown in red on the diagram.

All angles on the flat roof are right angles.

a What is the length of the conductor?

b The metal strip costs £5 a metre. What is the cost of the conductor?

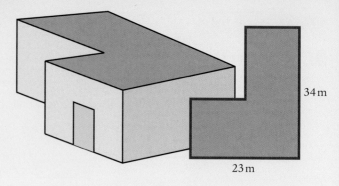

34 m

23 m

Preparation for assessment

1 The arrow below is 50 millimetres long.

Estimate in millimetres the length of each arrow:

a

b

c

d

2 A biologist photographed an insect beside a penny.

He knows the penny is 20 mm in diameter.

Estimate:

a the length of the insect

b the width of the insect.

3 Five friends are playing marbles.

The marble that stops closest to the 'steely' is the winner.

a Measure, in millimetres, the distance of each marble from the steely.

b Who wins?

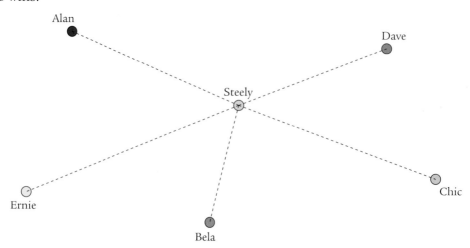

Alan

Dave

Steely

Ernie

Bela

Chic

4 The sketch shows a plan of the swimming pool at the Hotel Grande.

All the lengths are given in millimetres and all angles are right angles.

a Make an accurate drawing of the plan.

b What is the length of the unmarked side?

c Calculate the perimeter of the swimming pool on the plan:
  i in millimetres ii in centimetres.

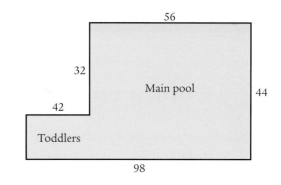

5 Change to centimetres: a 240 millimetres b 18 metres.

6 Express in metres: a 35 kilometres b 790 centimetres.

7 Remember the nine-hole golf course, North Gyles.

The length of each hole is shown in the table:

Hole	1	2	3	4	5	6	7	8	9
Length (m)	293	85	281	183	84	396	335	277	118

a What is the total length of the golf course:
  i in metres ii in kilometres?

b The boundary of the golf course is shaped as shown. What is the perimeter of the course:
  i in metres ii in kilometres?

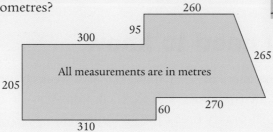

9 Managing time

⏸ Before we start...

Fraser works at the leisure centre.
He runs several keep fit classes.

The classes fall into three categories: low, medium, high intensity.

The length of time of each class is shown.

- Fraser works from 9 a.m. till 1 p.m. on a Monday.
- He is entitled to a 15-minute break during the shift.
- He does half an hour of paperwork during the shift.
- He can only do one high intensity class in a shift.

Make up a timetable for Fraser for a Monday morning.

Class	Intensity	Length of time
Easyline	Low	45 min
Zumba	Low	1 hour
Ultimate Abs	Low	35 min
Body Pump	Medium	50 min
Kettlebells	Medium	50 min
Jog Scotland	Medium	1 hour
Spinning	High	45 min
Metafit	High	30 min
Body Attack	High	55 min

▶ What you need to know

1 **a** How many days are there in: **i** 4 weeks   **ii** 6 weeks?

    b How many hours are there in: **i** 2 days   **ii** $\frac{1}{2}$ day?

    c Mandy went on a short city break for 72 hours. How many days was she away?

    d How many minutes are there in: **i** 3 hours   **ii** $\frac{1}{3}$ hour   **iii** $1\frac{1}{2}$ hours?

    e How many seconds are there in: **i** 3 minutes   **ii** $\frac{1}{2}$ minute?

    f Helena can swim a length of her local pool in 180 seconds.
    How many minutes is this?

2 **a** Hasim can drive from Nairn to Perth in 150 minutes. How many hours is this?

    b The summer holidays in one local authority lasted for 42 days. How many weeks is this?

    c A patient in hospital was told that the next 48 hours would be critical.
    How many days is this?

3 **a** Change these times to 24-hour times:
       i 6 a.m.   **ii** 10.25 a.m.   **iii** 7 p.m.   **iv** 9.16 p.m.

    b Change these times to 12-hour times:
       i 09 00   **ii** 13 50   **iii** 19 25   **iv** 02 10.

4 Sam drove to his granny's house in Edinburgh. It took him 2 hours and 45 minutes.
On his return journey there was an accident on the road and the traffic was diverted.
It took 3 hours and 5 minutes to get home.
How much longer did the return journey take?

5 a The 18th of July 2015 can be written as 18/07/15.
Write the 10th of November 2018 in the same way.

b King George V reigned between 1910 and 1936.
This stamp came off a letter which was dated 16/02/17.
Write 16/02/17 out in full.

9.1 The 12-hour and 24-hour clock

This is the timeline for one day.

It shows the 24-hour times on top and the matching 12-hour times on the bottom.

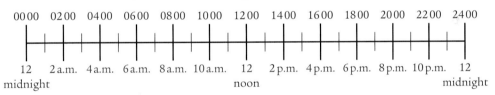

(In 24-hour time, 24 00 is usually written as 00 00.)

Example 1

Write 6.23 p.m. as a 24-hour time.

The letters 'p.m.' mean 'after noon' ...
so 6.23 p.m. = 6.23 + 12.00.
This gives us a 24-hour time of 18 23.   *Add 12 to the hours figure and drop the 'p.m.'*

Example 2

Change 08 32 to a.m./p.m. time.   *'a.m./p.m. time' is 12-hour time.*

08 is less than 12 which means it is 'before noon'.
This gives us an a.m./p.m. time of 8.32 a.m.   *Drop the zero at the front and add 'a.m.'*

Example 3

Change 22 15 to 12-hour time.

22 is more than 12 which means it is 'after noon'.

22 15 − 12 00 = 10 15.

This gives us a 12-hour time of 10.15 p.m.   *Subtract 12 from the hours and add 'p.m.'*

Notes:

- 12-hour times always need 'a.m.', 'p.m.', 'noon' or 'midnight'.
- 24-hour times never need 'a.m.', 'p.m.', 'noon' or 'midnight'.
- 12-hour times are written with a single dot to separate hours and minutes, e.g. 10.15 p.m.
- 24-hour times use a space (22 15), a colon (22:15), or no space (2215), but always use four digits.

Exercise 9.1A

1 Change these to 24-hour times:

a 4 a.m.	**b** 7 p.m.	**c** 2.50 a.m.	**d** 12 noon
e 3.45 p.m.	**f** 12.20 a.m.	**g** 8.15 p.m.	**h** 11.16 a.m.
i 12 midnight	**j** 11.40 p.m.	**k** 12.40 p.m.	**l** 5.36 a.m.

2 Change these times to a.m./p.m. times:

a 04:00	**b** 18:00	**c** 08 40	**d** 1352
e 23 20	**f** 02 40	**g** 11:49	**h** 1928
i 1200	**j** 0045	**k** 17:11	**l** 08 50.

3 For each clock, write:

   i the a.m./p.m. time   **ii** the 24-hour time.

a

Morning

b

Afternoon

c

Evening

d

Morning

e

Evening

f

Morning

4 Olivia has a busy day on Friday. All her appointments are scribbled on a piece of paper.

She wants to enter them on her phone. The phone only wants 24-hour times.

List the appointments she has, putting the earliest first, giving the times as 24-hour times.

- Hair 9am
- Dinner - Rhona 7.30 pm
- Visit grandad 5pm
- Dentist 2pm
- Coffee - Linda 3.30pm

5 Morag arrives at the bus stop at 7.17 p.m.

A part of the bus timetable is shown. It tells you when the buses arrive at that stop.

    1704   1724   1744   1804   1824   1844   1904   1924   1944   2004

   a When does the next bus arrive?

   b How long does Morag have to wait?

Exercise 9.1B

1 Copy and complete this cross-number puzzle by changing all the 12-hour times to 24-hour times.

Across	Down
1 11.02 a.m.	**1** 11.20 a.m.
5 10.42 a.m.	**2** 10.36 a.m.
6 11.15 p.m.	**3** 4.15 a.m.
7 6.52 a.m.	**4** 10.52 p.m.

1	2	3	4
5			
6			
7			

2 On a train timetable you might see **dep** and **arr**.

dep means 'departure time' and **arr** means 'arrival time'.

a What is the 12-hour time of this departure time?

dep
10 05

b Ahmed needs to be at a meeting at 2 p.m.
The venue is 5 minutes' walk from the train station.

Will this train get him there in time?

arr
13 45

c There are four trains arriving at the station from the following cities in the next hour.

London: 21 42   Perth: 9.22 p.m.

Edinburgh: 21 02   Inverness: 9.30 p.m.

Put them in order of arrival.

3 Here is part of a bus timetable.

A bus leaves Fairtown every 20 minutes. It arrives in Acetown 15 minutes later.

Copy and complete the timetable.

Fairtown	dep	08 05	08 25	08 45			
Acetown	arr	08 20	08 40	09 00			

4 Suzie had a business meeting in Glasgow at 2 p.m. The meeting lasted $2\frac{1}{2}$ hours.

Her pre-booked train back to Inverness leaves at 18 11.
How long will she have to wait for the train?

5 Nirmala has a dental appointment at 3.35 p.m.

The buses leave the stop outside her house at 10, 30 and 50 minutes past each hour. They arrive at the stop outside the dentist's 15 minutes later.

At what time should Nirmala catch the bus from her house to get to her dental appointment?

9.2 Units of time

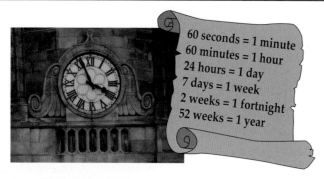

60 seconds = 1 minute
60 minutes = 1 hour
24 hours = 1 day
7 days = 1 week
2 weeks = 1 fortnight
52 weeks = 1 year

Thirty days hath September,
April, June, and November.
All the rest have thirty-one,
Except February alone,
Which has twenty-eight days clear,
And twenty-nine in each leap year.

- An ordinary year has 365 days.
- A leap year has 366 days.

Exercise 9.2A

1 Change:

   a 3 minutes to seconds   **b** 540 seconds to minutes

   c $\frac{1}{3}$ minute to seconds   **d** $1\frac{1}{4}$ minutes to seconds.

2 **a** Jonathan took 90 seconds to complete an online puzzle. How many minutes is this?

   b Sophia managed to do the puzzle in $1\frac{1}{5}$ minutes. How many seconds is this?

   c By how many seconds did Sophia beat Jonathan?

3 Change:

   a 5 hours to minutes   **b** $2\frac{1}{2}$ hours to minutes

   c 480 minutes to hours   **d** 210 minutes to hours.

4 Sandy was planning a new kitchen. He took $1\frac{1}{3}$ hours to make a scale drawing and plan where to position the new units. How many minutes was this?

5 Jessica planned a five-day city break in London. How many hours is this?

6 Joan is an ICT expert. Her company want to send her to New York to help set up a new branch. She is going for 84 days. How many weeks is that?

7 Stephen applied for a temporary job on a 24-month contract. How many years is this?

Exercise 9.2B

1 A planetary year is the length of time it takes that planet to go round the Sun.

The farther a planet is from the Sun, the longer its year.

   a A year on Mars is equivalent to 1 year and 322 days on Earth. How many Earth days is this?

   b A year on Mercury is equivalent to 88 days on Earth. How many hours is this?

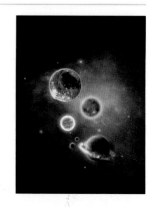

2 A planet's day is the length of time that it takes the planet to rotate on its axis.

  a A day on Venus is equivalent to 243 Earth days.
  How many weeks and days is this?

  b A day on the dwarf planet Pluto is equivalent to 6·4 Earth days.
  How many hours is this?

3 Copy and complete this cross-number puzzle.

Across

  1 7 days in hours
  3 15 weeks in days
  5 1 year + 100 days in days
  6 6 hours in minutes
  8 9 minutes in seconds
  10 4 years in weeks
  12 5 days in hours
  14 9 years in months
  15 1 leap year in days
  16 3 days in hours

Down

  1 $\frac{1}{2}$ leap year in days
  2 35 days in hours
  3 2 hours 35 minutes in minutes
  4 80 weeks in days
  7 50 years in months
  9 66 weeks in days
  10 29 weeks in days
  11 34 days in hours
  12 3 hours in minutes
  13 1 year in weeks

4 The Highland Cross is a duathlon event, coast to coast from Kintail, to Beauly.
It is 20 miles on foot followed by 30 miles cycling.

In 2013, the winning man took 3 hours 16 minutes 55 seconds.
The winning woman took 4 hours 1 minute 40 seconds. (*Source: The Highland Cross, 2013*)
What is the difference in these two times?

9.3 Duration

We can use a timeline to help us calculate the number of hours and minutes between clock times.

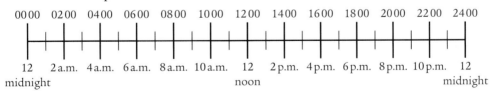

Example 1

Jin left Inverness at 2.45 p.m. He arrived in Glasgow at 6.15 p.m.

How long did Jin's journey take?

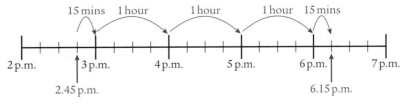

Jin's journey took 15 minutes + 3 hours + 15 minutes = 3 hours 30 minutes.

Example 2

A film starts at 10 35 and finishes at 13 20.

How long does it last?

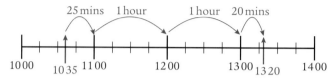

25 mins   1 hour   1 hour   20 mins

10 00   10 35 11 00   12 00   13 00 13 20   14 00

The length of the film is 25 minutes + 2 hours + 20 minutes = 2 hours 45 minutes.

Exercise 9.3A

1 Work out how long it is from:

    a 7 a.m. to 11 a.m.
    b 17 00 to 20 00
    c 2.40 p.m. to 3 p.m.

    d 08 25 to 09 00
    e 4.38 a.m. to 6.38 a.m.
    f 9.42 p.m. to 12 midnight

    g 13 20 to 14 40
    h 11 50 to 14 25
    i 05 18 to 07 10

    j 10 45 p.m. to 2.30 a.m. (next day).

2 A Benefits Advice 'Drop-in' Centre has the following opening times.

    a How long is the Tuesday morning session?

    b How long is the Thursday afternoon session?

    c Compare the two afternoon sessions. Which is longer and by how much?

Tuesday	10 a.m. to 11.45 a.m.
	2.50 p.m. to 4.45 p.m.
Thursday	9.40 a.m. to 11.30 a.m.
	2.20 p.m. to 3.50 p.m.

3 Look at Martina's timetable for Monday.

    a How long is period 1?

    b Work out the length of each period.

    c How long is it from the start of the school day to the end of the school day?

    d What is the total length of breaks (morning interval and lunch)?

    e How much time is spent in class, including registration?

Monday timetable		
Registration	09 00–09 10	
Period 1	09 10–10 05	French
Period 2	10 05–11 00	Maths
Interval	11 00–11 15	
Period 3	11 15–12 10	PE
Period 4	12 10–13 00	Technology
Lunch	13 00–13 55	
Period 5	13 55–14 50	English
Period 6	14 50–15 40	Chemistry

4 The times of two trains from Edinburgh to North Berwick are shown.

Edinburgh	**dep**	08 47	09 43
North Berwick	**arr**	09 19	10 16

    a How long does the 08 47 train take for the journey?

    b How long does the 09 43 train take?

Exercise 9.3B

1 Mayleen was admitted to hospital on Friday at 8 p.m. She was discharged on Sunday at 11 a.m. How many hours did Mayleen spend in hospital?

2 Look at the calendar for March 2017.

a Caitlin was 18 on 12th March 2013.
What age will she be on 12th March 2017?

b On what day of the week is 9th April 2017?

c On what day of the week is February 25th 2017?

d On what day is the last day in April?

March 2017						
Mon	Tues	Wed	Thur	Fri	Sat	Sun
		1	2	3	4	5
6	7	8	9	10	11	12
13	14	15	16	17	18	19
20	21	22	23	24	25	26
27	28	29	30	31		

3 Here is part of the calendar for March 2020.

What date is the Monday highlighted in yellow?

March 2020						
Mon	Tues	Wed	Thur	Fri	Sat	Sun
						1
2	3	4	5	6	7	8

4 There are 52 weeks and **one day** in an ordinary year.

That means if 10th June is a Tuesday one year, it will be on a Wednesday the next year, unless the next year is a leap year.

There are 52 weeks and **two days** in a **leap year**.

If 22nd November is on a Monday one year, it will be on a Wednesday the following year if the period includes the 29th February.

a 15th November 2013 is a Friday. On what day is 15th November 2014?

b 12th April 2015 is on a Sunday. On what day is 12th April 2016?

5 If 1st October 2014 is a Wednesday:

a what day is 1st October 2015

b what day is 3rd October 2016?

9.4 Planning ahead

Example 1

Florian has a few hours to pass in Glasgow before his train at 17 40.

He decides to go to the cinema. The film he wants to see starts at 2.55 p.m. It lasts for 135 minutes.

Does he have time to see the film?

135 minutes = 2 hours and 15 minutes.

17 40 is 5.40 p.m.

Note that you should either work in a.m./p.m. time or 24-hour time.

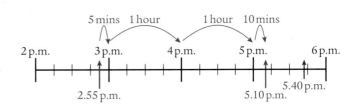

The film finishes at 5.10 p.m.

Florian does have time to see the film because his train leaves at 5.40 p.m.

Exercise 9.4A

1 The broadband service in Tain went off at 4.35 p.m. It was off for 4 hours and 20 minutes. When did it come back on?

2 June thinks it takes 3 hours and 45 minutes to drive to Carlisle from her house. What time should she leave her house to get to Carlisle for 11 30?

3 Jenny is opening a new café.

She decides to open at 7.45 a.m. on Monday to Saturday. On Sunday she will open at 9 a.m.

Jenny advertises that the café will be open for 10 hours on weekdays, 12 hours on Saturdays and $5\frac{1}{2}$ hours on Sundays.

Copy and complete the table:

	Opening time	Closing time
Monday		
Tuesday		
Wednesday		
Thursday		
Friday		
Saturday		
Sunday		

4 Leonora and Carlos are planning a holiday in Scotland.

They want to walk the Great Glen Way from Fort William to Inverness over five days.

They estimate the time they will be walking each day, including breaks.

		Estimated walking/resting time
Day 1	Fort William to Gairlochy	5 hours
Day 2	Gairlochy to Laggan	6 hours 15 minutes
Day 3	Laggan to Invermoriston	8 hours 30 minutes
Day 4	Invermoriston to Drumnadrochit	6 hours 30 minutes
Day 5	Drumnadrochit to Inverness	8 hours 15 minutes

Copy and complete the table to estimate their finishing time each day.

	Start	Finish
Day 1	10 a.m.	
Day 2	8.30 a.m.	
Day 3	8.15 a.m.	
Day 4	9.40 a.m.	
Day 5	7.45 a.m.	

Exercise 9.4B

1 George's watch is 25 minutes fast.

Write down the correct 24-hour times for each picture.

a

Afternoon

b

Evening

c

Morning

2 Maria's watch is 15 minutes slow.

Write down the correct 24-hour time for each picture.

a

Morning

b

Evening

c

Afternoon

3 Geoff and Samia applied for a mortgage on 27th June.
They have been told they will get a decision in 14 days.

On what day will they get a decision?

4 Copy and complete this cross-number puzzle.

Write all the answers in 24-hour time.

Across

1 2 hours after 1.32 p.m.

3 25 minutes after 3.56 p.m.

5 48 minutes before 10 p.m.

6 5 hours before 8.15 a.m.

8 1 hour 20 minutes
after 11 p.m.

10 6 hours 22 minutes
before 11.24 a.m.

12 $6\frac{1}{2}$ hours after 8.52 a.m.

14 $\frac{3}{4}$ hour before 4.30 a.m.

15 10 hours 30 minutes
before 7.40 a.m.

16 4 hours 50 minutes
after 9.30 p.m.

Down

1 3 hours 30 minutes
after 2.50 p.m.

2 3 hours 35 minutes
before midnight.

3 2 hours 40 minutes
before 2 p.m.

4 $4\frac{1}{2}$ hours after 5.30 a.m.

7 8 hours 25 minutes
after 3.25 a.m.

9 2 hours 35 minutes
before noon.

10 $2\frac{1}{4}$ hours after 6.37 a.m.

11 8 hours 20 minutes after noon.

12 7 hours 35 minutes after 7.45 a.m.

13 5 hours 30 minutes before 5.20 a.m.

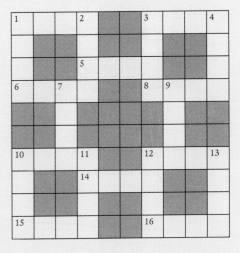

Preparation for assessment

1 Write the following times using the 24-hour clock:

  a 8.42 a.m.   b 12 noon   c 3.33 p.m.   d 11.20 p.m.

2 Each of these show different ways of writing a time as a 24-hour time.
  Write each using a.m./p.m.:

  a 05:25   b 1156   c 17 32   d 2005.

3 For each clock write: i the a.m./p.m. time   ii the 24-hour time.

a

Morning

b

Afternoon

c

Evening

4 Change:

  a 8 minutes to seconds   b 3 hours to minutes   c $1\frac{1}{2}$ minutes to seconds

  d 4 weeks to days   e 36 months to years   f 48 hours to days

  g 5 years to months   h 240 minutes to hours   i $1\frac{1}{4}$ days to hours.

5 Cheng's dinner party guests are arriving at 7 p.m. He plans to serve dinner at 7.30 p.m.

  The nut roast Cheng is making takes 40 minutes to prepare, 1 hour to cook and
  10 minutes to rest after cooking.

  At what time should he start preparing the dish?

6 Chris checks in for his flight at 16 50. The flight is 1 hour 30 minutes later.

  What time is the flight?

7 Gregory's plane is due to depart at 13 15.

  a Write 13 15 as a 12-hour time.

  b The latest check-in time for the flight is 1 hour 15 minutes
     before departure.

     It takes 45 minutes to drive from Gregory's house to the
     airport. He leaves his house at 10 55.

     Will Gregory be able to check in on time? Explain your answer.

8 Zarina lives in Fort Augustus. She is planning a trip to London by sleeper train from either
  Fort William or Inverness.

  There is a sleeper train leaving Fort William at 19 50 and one leaving Inverness at 20 44.

  The last bus she can get from Fort Augustus to Fort William leaves Fort Augustus at 17 48 and
  takes 57 minutes. The walk to the railway station takes about one minute.

  The last bus she can get to Inverness leaves Fort Augustus at 19 03 and takes 58 minutes.
  She then has a 5-minute walk to the station.

a What time would Zarina arrive at Fort William station?

b What time would she arrive at Inverness station?

c Which sleeper train would you advise Zarina to take?
   Explain your answer.

The trains join together before leaving Scotland and arrive
in London at 07 47.

d How long is the train journey from Fort William?

e How long is the train journey from Inverness?

9 The calendar shows November 2015.

   a What date is the first Wednesday in December?

   b What date is the last Sunday in October?

   c On what day of the week will Christmas day fall?

November 2015						
Mon	Tues	Wed	Thur	Fri	Sat	Sun
						1
2	3	4	5	6	7	8
9	10	11	12	13	14	15
16	17	18	19	20	21	22
23	24	25	26	27	28	29
30						

10 Remember Fraser, who works at the leisure centre. He runs several keep fit classes.

The classes fall into three categories low, medium, high intensity.

The length of time of each class is shown.

Class	Intensity	Length of time
Easyline	Low	45 min
Zumba	Low	1 hour
Ultimate Abs	Low	35 min
Body Pump	Medium	50 min
Kettlebells	Medium	50 min
Jog Scotland	Medium	1 hour
Spinning	High	45 min
Metafit	High	30 min
Body Attack	High	55 min

Fraser works from 9 a.m. till 1 p.m. on a Monday.

- He is entitled to a 15-minute break during the shift.
- He does half an hour of paperwork during the shift.
- He can only do one high intensity class in a shift.
- Make up a timetable for Fraser for a Monday morning.

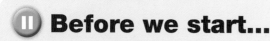

⏸ Before we start...

At the London 2012 Olympic Games, Usain Bolt won the 100 m final in 9·63 seconds.
Taoufik Makhloufi won the 1500 m in 3 minutes, 34·08 seconds.

a Write 3 minutes, 34·08 seconds in seconds.

b Find the speed of each runner in metres per second.

c Compare their speeds. Explain why there is a big difference.

▶ What you need to know

1 Each disc has to be placed in a box. For each disc, say which box.

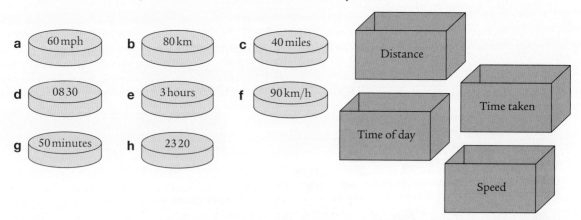

2 The diagram shows the distances between four locations.

a What is the distance from Glasgow to Carlisle?

b It is a further 120 miles from Carlisle to Manchester. How far is it from Lockerbie to Manchester?

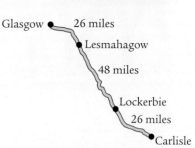

3 The table gives the times for a train and a bus journey from Inverness to Nairn.

	Train	Bus
Inverness	21 31	22 00
Nairn	21 45	22 54

a Copy the table but write each time as an a.m./p.m. time.

b How long does the train journey take?

c How long does the bus journey take?

4 a Write the speed shown on each speedometer:

i in km/h **ii** in mph.

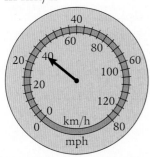

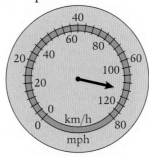

b Write 50 mph in km/h.

c Which speed is faster: 40 mph or 60 km/h?

5 Use the mileage chart to help you answer the questions.

What is the distance from:

a Glasgow to Dundee

b Edinburgh to Inverness

c Edinburgh to Glasgow?

Glasgow	Edinburgh	Aberdeen	Inverness	Dundee
46				
145	126			
169	156	104		
82	62	67	138	

Mileage chart

6 How long is it from:

a 08 12 to 11 42

b 6.45 p.m. to 9.15 p.m.

c 7.40 a.m. to noon

d 17 50 to 23 40?

10.1 Speed – how fast?

The speed limit for most cars on United Kingdom motorways is 70 mph.

70 mph means 70 miles in one hour.

Tracey likes walking.
She usually walks at 6 km/h.

This means she walks 6 kilometres in one hour.

Exercise 10.1A

1 25 m/s means 25 metres each second.

Write down what each of these speeds mean:

a 60 km/h

b 200 m/s

c 80 mph

d 20 miles/h

e 35 km/h

f 50 m/min.

2 Four women are training for a charity run.

Write down their speeds in order, with the fastest speed first.

Catriona 14 km/h   Jemima 12 km/h   Leanne 15 km/h   Saskia 9 km/h

3 Sean walked 10 km in 2 hours. What was his average speed in km/h?

Calculating average speed

To work out the average **speed**, you divide the **distance** travelled by the **time** taken.

$$\text{Speed} = \frac{\text{Distance}}{\text{Time}} = \text{Distance} \div \text{Time}$$

or

$$S = \frac{D}{T}$$

Example 1

Kevin cycled 90 km in 3 hours. Calculate his average speed.

Speed = Distance ÷ Time

= 90 ÷ 3

= 30 km/h   Make sure you use the units (km/h) in your answer.

Exercise 10.1B

1 Calculate the speed in each case. Remember to include the units in your answer.

a 75 miles in 3 hours

b 130 km in 2 hours

c 800 km in 5 hours

d 40 km in $\frac{1}{2}$ hour

2 Mervyn lives in Glasgow.

He can drive to his grandmother's house near Elgin in four hours. The distance is 212 miles.

Find Mervyn's average speed in mph.

3 Hayley does a run of 3 km some mornings.

a How many metres is this?

She takes 20 minutes to do the run.

b Calculate her speed in m/min

4 Luca can run 80 metres in 10 seconds.

a What is his speed in m/s?

He can run 800 metres in 200 seconds.

b What is his speed for this run?

c Why do you think he cannot run as fast on the longer run?

5 Here are some speed limit signs in the Republic of Ireland (ROI).

Copy and complete the table, matching each sign with a type of road.

Type of road (ROI)	Speed limit
Motorway/good dual carriageway	
National roads, which do not have motorway status	
Regional/local roads	
Built-up areas	

6 Here are some speed limit signs in the United Kingdom.

a What is the unit of speed on these signs?

b Copy and complete this table.

Type of road (UK)	Speed limit
Motorway/dual carriageway	
Single carriageway roads	
Built-up areas	

10.2 Distance – how far?

Example 1

Christopher's average speed on a car journey is 80 km/h.

He travelled for 4 hours.

How far did he drive?

The table shows the distances Christopher travelled over the 4 hours.

1 hour	2 hours	3 hours	4 hours
80 km	160 km	240 km	320 km

So in 4 hours he travelled 320 km.

Exercise 10.2A

1   Calculate the distance travelled in each case:

   a 3 hours at 75 km/h   **b** 4 hours at 35 mph   **c** 40 seconds at 4 m/s

   d $1\frac{1}{2}$ hours at 50 km/h   **e** $2\frac{1}{2}$ hours at 6 km/h   **f** $\frac{1}{4}$ hour at 60 mph.

2   Copy and complete this table for a jumbo jet with a cruising speed of 900 km/h.

1 hour	2 hours	3 hours	4 hours	5 hours
900 km				

3   Colin and Mary have rented a cottage on the Isle of Skye for a holiday.

   The journey from their home in Glasgow to the cottage took 5 hours. They drove at an average speed of 45 mph.

   What is the distance to the cottage?

4   Fraser and Jane went for a drive.

   They left home at 14 00. They drove around until 17 30, at an average speed of 50 mph.

   a How long did the journey last?   **b** How far did they travel?

Calculating distance travelled

To calculate the **distance** travelled, you multiply the average **speed** by the **time** taken.

> **Distance = Speed × Time**
>
> or
>
> $D = S \times T$

Example 2

Stefan went on a long cycle trip for 5 hours at 18 km/h.

How far did he travel?

Distance = Speed × Time
= 18 × 5
= 90 km

So Stefan travelled 90 km.

Exercise 10.2B

1 Find the distance between these places:

  a Inverness to Aberdeen: driving for 3 hours at an average speed of 55 km/h

  b Kirkcaldy to St. Andrews: cycling at 14 km/h for 3 hours

  c Milngavie to Drymen: walking for 4 hours at 3 mph

  d Edinburgh to Newcastle-upon-Tyne: driving for 3 hours at an average speed of 40 mph.

2 In the United Kingdom this sign means 'minimum speed of 30 mph'.

  a Why might there be a minimum speed on a road?

  b Corrine drove for 5 hours at this speed. How far did she travel?

3 In the United Kingdom, this sign means 'national speed limit applies'.

For most cars, this is 60 mph on single carriageways or 70 mph on motorways and dual carriageways.

Pujit is driving along the motorway at the national speed limit.

How far can he travel in half an hour?

4 Jessica and Dave had always wanted to walk the West Highland Way.

They plan to do it over nine days.

They walk at an average speed of 4 km/h.

Day	Stretch	Duration (hours)	Distance (km)
1	Milngavie to Drymen	4·8	
2	Drymen to Balmaha	3·2	
3	Balmaha to Rowardennan	2·8	
4	Rowardennan to Inverarnan	5·6	
5	Inverarnan to Tyndrum	4·8	
6	Tyndrum to Inveroran	4·0	
7	Inveroran to Kingshouse	4·8	
8	Kingshouse to Kinlochleven	3·6	
9	Kinlochleven to Fort William	5·6	

Fort William
Kinlochleven
Kingshouse
Inveroran
Tyndrum
Inverarnan
Rowardennan
Balmaha
Drymen
Milngavie

Calculate the distance travelled on each of the nine days.

5 Hamza's speedometer shows speeds in km/h.

He wants to know how fast he can drive on Scotland's motorways.

To change miles into kilometres, multiply the miles by 8 and then divide the result by 5.

What is the motorway speed limit in Scotland in km/h?

10.3 Time – how long?

Example 1

Jake can run at an average speed of 6 m/s.
How long will it take him to run 60 metres?

He can run 6 metres every second.

$60 \div 6 = 10$ seconds.

So it takes him 10 seconds to run 60 metres.

Exercise 10.3A

1 Work out the time taken for each of these journeys:

    a 120 kilometres at 60 km/h   **b** 24 metres at 6 m/s

    c 2000 kilometres at 500 km/h   **d** 45 miles at 15 mph.

2 Steve cycled from Durness to Tongue. The distance is 48 kilometres.

Steve can cycle at an average speed of 12 km/h.

How long did the journey take?

3 Use the mileage chart to help you calculate how long each journey takes.

    a Edinburgh to Inverness, at an average speed of 52 mph.

    b Edinburgh to Aberdeen, at an average speed of 42 mph.

    c Dundee to Inverness, at an average speed of 46 mph.

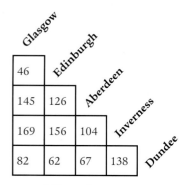

Mileage chart

4 (Use the mileage chart from Question **3** for this question.)

Eoin lives in Aberdeen. He plans to visit his grandmother near Forres.

He takes the road from Aberdeen to Inverness.

His grandmother lives 24 miles before Inverness.

    a How far is his grandmother's house from Aberdeen?

    b His average speed is 40 mph. How long will the journey take?

Calculating time taken

To work out the **time** taken, you divide the **distance** travelled by the average **speed**.

$$\text{Time} = \frac{\text{Distance}}{\text{Speed}} = \text{Distance} \div \text{Speed}$$

$$\text{or}$$

$$T = \frac{D}{S}$$

Example 2

Calculate the time taken on a flight from Glasgow to Barcelona.

The distance is 1600 kilometres. The average speed is 640 km/h.

Time = Distance ÷ Speed
    = 1600 ÷ 640
    = 2·5 hours

The time of 2·5 hours is the same as $2\frac{1}{2}$ hours = 2 hours 30 minutes.

The time taken on the flight is 2 hours 30 minutes.

Example 3

Celia travelled 105 miles at an average speed of 60 mph.

a How long did the journey take?

Celia started her journey at 3.30 p.m.

b When did she arrive at her destination?

a Time = Distance ÷ Speed
       = 105 ÷ 60
       = 1·75 hours

The time of 1·75 hours = $1\frac{3}{4}$ hours = 1 hour 45 minutes.

The journey took 1 hour 45 minutes.

b

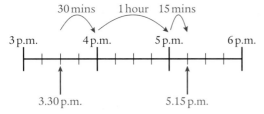

Celia arrived at her destination at 5.15 p.m.

Exercise 10.3B

1 Calculate the time taken for each of these journeys:

   a Robert travelled 150 km at 60 km/h

   b Lisa's plane travelled 400 km at 800 km/h

   c Jeanette cycled 10 miles at 8 mph

   d Tao swam 100 metres at 40 metres/minute

   e Zahra jogged 21 kilometres at 6 km/h

   f Douglas sails for 39 km at 12 km/h.

2 A train travels for 270 miles at 120 mph.

How long does the journey take?

3 I went for a walk. My speed was 5 km/h.

How long did it take me to walk 2·5 km?

4 The distance from Inverness to Glasgow is 169 miles.

Rajesh and Sunita drive from Inverness to Glasgow.

Sunita drives the first 75 miles at an average speed of 50 mph.

Rajesh drives the remaining distance at an average speed of 47 mph.

   a For how long did Sunita drive?

   b For how long did Rajesh drive?

   c If they left Inverness at 08 30, at what time did they arrive in Glasgow?

10.4 Timetables

Here is part of the train timetable for Inverness to Aberdeen.

Mondays to Saturdays						
Inverness	d	04 53	05 54	07 10	09 00	10 57
Nairn	d	05 08	06 09	07 26	09 16	11 14
Forres	d	05 19	06 20	07 37	09 27	11 25
Elgin	d	05 33	06 34	07 51	09 49	11 42
Keith	d	05 54	06 55	08 13	10 09	12 04
Huntly	d	06 09	07 11	08 38	10 23	12 18
Insch	d	06 25	07 27	08 56	10 48	12 35
Inverurie	d	06 37	07 43	09 08	11 00	12 47
Dyce	d	06 50	07 57	09 20	11 14	13 00
Aberdeen	a	07 03	08 09	09 32	11 25	13 12
Notes and codes						
a Arrival time						
d Departure time						

(Source: ScotRail, 2012)

Each **column** represents a different train making the journey from Inverness to Aberdeen.

Each **row** represents a different station on the journey.

A particular train is often referred to by its departure time from the first station.

The first train is 'the 04 53 from Inverness'.

Exercise 10.4A

1 Use the train timetable above to answer the following questions.

a When does the 04 53 train from Inverness arrive in Aberdeen?

b How long does the 04 53 take to travel from Inverness to Aberdeen?

c Helga lives in Forres. She is travelling to Aberdeen for a meeting at 10 a.m.
At what time should she catch the train in Forres?

d Gordon lives in Nairn and works in Elgin. He starts work at 8.15 a.m.
At what time should he take the train from Nairn?

2 This timetable shows the times of the Glasgow/London sleeper train.

Glasgow–London Euston

		Mon–Thurs	Fri	Sun (A)	Sun (B)
Cabins available from		22 00	22 00	22 00	21 00
Glasgow Central	d	23 40	23 40	23 15	21 40
Motherwell	d	2357	23 57	23 30	22 06
Carstairs	d	00 16	00 16	23 47	22 23
Carlisle	d	01 40	01 40	01 12	–
Watford Junction	a	06 22	06 22	06 22	–
London Euston	a	06 47	06 47	06 47	07 06
Vacate cabins by		08 00	08 00	08 00	08 00

London Euston–Glasgow

		Mon–Thurs	Fri	Sun (A)	Sun (B)
Cabins available from		23 00	23 00	22 45	21 00
London Euston	d	23 50	23 50	23 27	21 45
Watford Junction	d	00 10	00 10	23 47	–
Carlisle	a	05 10	05 10	05 10	–
Carstairs	a	06 19	06 19	06 19	07 00
Motherwell	a	06 53	06 53	06 53	07 27
Glasgow Central	a	07 18	07 18	07 18	07 59
Vacate cabins by		08 00	08 00	08 00	08 15

Notes: **a** Arrival time **d** Departure time
A January to March and July to September
B April to June

(Source: ScotRail, 2012)

a From which station in London does the sleeper train operate?

b How long does the train take to travel from Glasgow to London on a Monday?

c How long does the train take from London to Glasgow on a Monday?

d How long does the train take from Glasgow to London on a Sunday in June?

3 The timetable shows the times of the direct buses, each day, from Fort William to Portree on the Isle of Skye.

Fort William		10 15	14 15
Spean Bridge		10 30	14 30
Invergarry		10 53	14 53
Cluanie		11 24	15 24
Shiel Bridge		11 43	15 43
Dornie		11 53	15 53
Kyle of Lochalsh	arr	12 07	16 07
	dep	12 15	16 15
Kyleakin		12 20	16 20
Broadford		12 35	16 35
Sligachan		13 00	17 00
Portree		13 15	17 15

(Source: Scottish citylink, 2013)

a   How many buses are there from Fort William to Portree each day?

b   How long is it between buses?

c   How long does each bus wait in Kyle of Lochalsh?

d   How long does each bus take to travel from Fort William to Portree?

Exercise 10.4B

1   Here is part of a train timetable.

Mondays to Fridays										
Glasgow Central	d	08 34	08 38	08 48	09 00	09 04	09 18	09 34	09 38	09 48
Kilwinning	d	09 01	09 14	09 17	09 26	09 40	09 47	10 10	10 14	10 17
Ardrossan Harbour	a	09 20	▼	▼	▼	▼	10 02	▼	▼	▼
Largs	a	▼	▼	09 44	▼	▼	▼	▼	▼	10 44
Irvine	d	▼	09 18	▼	09 30	▼	▼	10 14	▼	▼
Prestwick Airport	d	▼	09 29	▼	09 42	▼	▼	10 25	▼	▼
Prestwick Town	d	▼	09 31	▼	09 43	▼	▼	10 27	▼	▼
Ayr	a	▼	09 40	▼	09 51	▼	▼	10 34	10 37	▼
Stranrear	a	▼	▼	▼	▼	▼	▼	▼	12 00	▼

(Source: ScotRail, 2012)

a   What do you think ▼ means?

b   How long does the 09 18 from Irvine take to travel to Ayr?

c   Craig boards a train at Kilwinning. He arrives in Ayr at 10 34.
    How long did his train journey take? Explain your answer.

d   How long does the train journey from Glasgow Central to Stranrear take?

2   Here is an extract from the Glasgow Queen Street to Edinburgh Waverley train timetable.

Mondays to Fridays									
Glasgow Queen Street	d	08 45	09 00	09 15	09 30	09 45	10 00	10 15	10 30
Croy	d	▼	09 12	▼	09 42	▼	10 12	▼	10 42
Falkirk High	d	09 03	09 22	09 33	09 52	10 03	10 22	10 33	10 52
Palmont	d	09 08	▼	09 38	▼	10 08	▼	10 38	▼
Linlithgow	d	09 14	▼	09 44	▼	10 14	▼	10 44	▼
Edinburgh Haymarket	a	09 32	09 46	10 01	10 12	10 32	10 46	11 01	11 12
Edinburgh Waverley	a	09 37	09 51	10 10	10 19	10 37	10 51	11 10	11 19

(Source: ScotRail, 2012)

a   How often is there a train from Glasgow Queen Street to Edinburgh on this route?

b   How long does the 09 15 from Glasgow Queen Street take to get to Edinburgh Waverley?

c   How long does the 09 45 from Glasgow take to get to Waverley?

d   Which trains from Glasgow Queen Street stop at Polmont?

e   Which trains from Glasgow Queen Street stop at Croy?

Preparation for assessment

1 a Brendon can type 120 words in four minutes.
   What is his average speed in words per minute?

   b Helen walks 8 km in 2 hours.
   What is her average speed in km/h?

   c Kenny cycles 42 km in three hours.
   What is his average speed in km/h?

2 Joan and Ian are travelling from Newcastle-upon-Tyne to Glasgow.
   The distance is 150 miles. Their average speed for the journey is 50 mph.
   How long will the journey last?

3 Ruairidh strolled round York sightseeing.
   He covered 4·2 km and walked at an average speed of 2·1 km/h.
   How many hours did he take?

4 Frédérique decided to visit three shops
   she owns in one morning.

   She drives at an average speed of 40 mph.
   The map shows how long it takes to travel
   between the shops.

   Work out the distances between the shops.

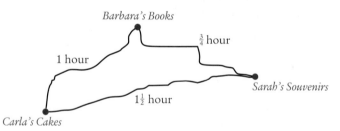

Barbara's Books

$\frac{3}{4}$ hour

1 hour

Sarah's Souvenirs

$1\frac{1}{2}$ hour

Carla's Cakes

5 The tables show part of the summer ferry
   timetable between Stornoway and Ullapool.

   a How long does the ferry take from
      Ullapool to Stornoway?

   b To which days of the week does this
      part of the timetable refer?

   c One Friday, Jordan took the first ferry
      from Ullapool to Stornoway and the
      last ferry back.
      How long did he spend in Stornoway?

Wed/Fri – Extra sailings

Stornoway depart	Ullapool arrive	Ullapool depart	Stornoway arrive
06 00	08 45	09 30	12 15
13 00	15 45	16 30	19 15
19 45	22 30	23 00 A	01 45 A

Code
A Arrives following morning   *(Source: Caledonian MacBrayne, 2013)*

6 Remember at the London 2012 Olympic Games, Usain Bolt won
   the 100 m final in 9·63 seconds.
   Taoufik Makhloufi won the 1500 m in 3 minutes, 34·08 seconds.

   a Write 3 minutes, 34·08 seconds in seconds.

   b Find the speed of each runner in metres per second.

   c Compare their speeds. Explain why there is a big difference.

Before we start...

Hannah is planning a new wet room for her house.

She is going to put in a corner shower.

She wants to tile the two walls that form that corner.

The dimensions of the two walls to be tiled are shown. They have different widths but the same height.

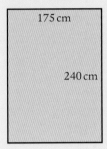
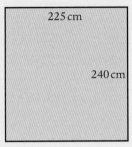
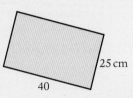

Each tile is 25 cm by 40 cm.

Hannah hasn't decided whether to put them like this: or like this:

Tiles are £3·45 each. They have to be bought in boxes of 10.

Work out how many tiles are needed to tile the two walls for each way.

Calculate the cost in each case.

 What you need to know

1 a Make a full size copy of this rectangle.

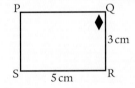

b Mark in the lengths of all four sides.

c ∠PQR is marked with a ◆. Mark ∠PSR with a ●.

d What is the size of each angle in the rectangle?

e How many lines of symmetry has a rectangle?

f Use a coloured pencil or dotted line to show the lines of symmetry.

119

2 a Make a full size copy of this square.

b Mark in the lengths of the other three sides.

c Mark a ✖ in ∠LKN.

d What is the size of each angle in the square.

e How many lines of symmetry has the square?

f Use a coloured pencil or dotted line to show the lines of symmetry.

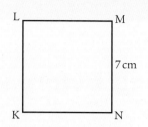

3 Work out the size of each missing angle.

a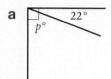

b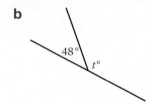

c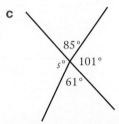

4 Copy and complete this table by naming each labelled part of the circles.

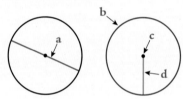

	Part of circle
a	
b	
c	
d	

11.1 Triangles

Angles in a triangle

Draw a triangle and cut it out.

Mark each angle in some way.

Tear off each angle.

Fit the three angles together on a ruler as shown.

They should fit snuggly to form a straight line.

This always works because ...

the angles in a triangle add up to 180°.

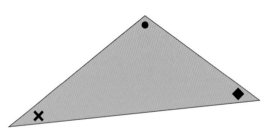

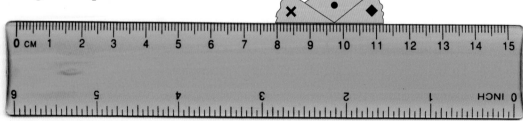

Example 1

Find the size of ∠ACB.

$102° + 36° = 138°$

$180° - 138° = 42°$ The three angles add up to $180°$.

So $∠ACB = 42°$.

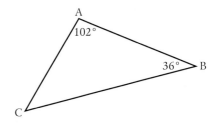

Exercise 11.1A

1 Work out the size of each angle named.

a

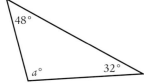

48°

a°

32°

b

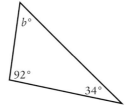

b°

92°

34°

c

56°

c°

2 Find the value of: **a** $p°$ **b** $q°$ **c** $r°$.

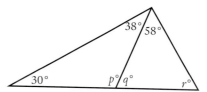

38° 58°

30°

p° q°

r°

3 The sails on Ronan's model boat are shown in the diagram.

    a Calculate the size of angle $x°$.

    b Calculate the size of angle $y°$.

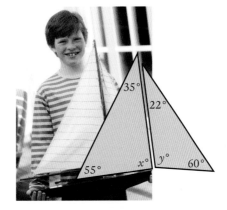

35°

22°

55°

x° y°

60°

4 An American company is opening a branch in Canada.

The managing director wanted a picture showing the flags of both countries.

She considered the shape shown in the diagram. The angles marked $s°$ are the same size.

Work out the size of $s°$.

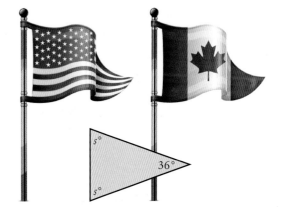

s°

36°

s°

5 The picture shows a new development of eco-friendly houses.

The **pitch** of each roof is the angle, $x°$, the roof makes with the horizontal.

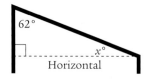

What is the angle of the pitch of each roof?

Special triangles

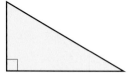

The yellow triangle has a right angle.

It is called a **right-angled triangle**.

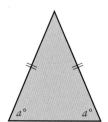

The blue triangle has two equal sides ... and two equal angles.

It is called an **isosceles triangle**.

It has **one line of symmetry**.

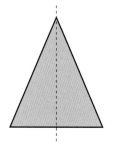

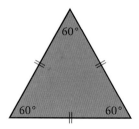

The red triangle has three equal sides ... and three equal angles.

$180 ÷ 3 = 60$ ... so each angle is $60°$.

It is called an **equilateral triangle**.

It has **three lines of symmetry**.

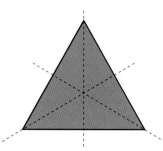

Exercise 11.1B

1 The side of the ramp for a wheelchair user is a right-angled triangle.

What is the size of the angle marked $a°$?

2   Bunting at a summer fete is made up from identical isosceles triangles.

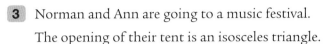

   a   What size is the angle marked $p°$?

   b   What size is the angle marked $q°$?

3   Norman and Ann are going to a music festival.

   The opening of their tent is an isosceles triangle.

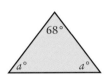

   Calculate the size of $a°$.

4   The legs of a table form two **equilateral** triangles.

   Copy the diagram and fill in the sizes of all the angles.

11.2 Quadrilaterals

Quadrilaterals are four-sided shapes.

- A rectangle has two lines (axes) of symmetry.
- All its angles are right angles.
- Opposite sides are equal.
- The diagonals are **equal** and cut each other in **half**. They cut the rectangle into isosceles triangles. Because of the symmetry of the rectangle, the isosceles triangles of the same colour are identical ... we say they are **congruent**.

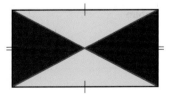

Example 1

Find the size of all the angles in this rectangle.

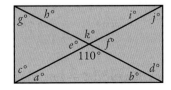

Step 1: Draw an axis of symmetry

... 110° becomes two angles of 55°

... right angles are formed

... angle $a° = 180° - 55° - 90° = 35°$

... angle $b°$ **is the same as angle** $a° = 35°$.

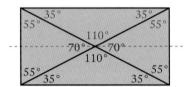

Step 2: The corners of the rectangle are all right angles

... so both $c°$ **and** $d° = 90° - 35° = 55°$.

The diagonals make straight lines

... so both $e°$ **and** $f° = 180° - 110° = 70°$.

Step 3: Draw the other axis of symmetry

... you can now fill in the rest of the missing angles.

Exercise 11.2A

1 Copy this rectangle.

  a Find the size of each angle.

  b Find the length of each side.

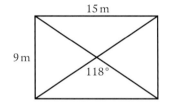

2 Copy this rectangle.

What other lengths can you find?

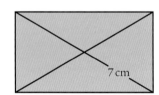

3 Copy these diagrams and fill in as many lengths and angles as you can.

  a 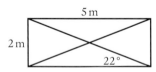   **b** 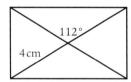   **c**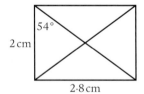

4 John is building a small greenhouse from a kit.

He makes a cement base for it.

He measures the diagonals of the base.
One diagonal is 3·5 m and the other is 3·6 m.

Is the base a perfect rectangle?
Give a reason for your answer.

5 The size of a television is given as the length of the diagonal.

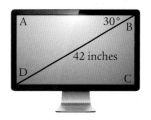

a If BD is 42 inches, what is the length of AC?

b What is the size of ∠DBC?

c What is the size of ∠BDC?

6 Chas and Sara bought a new rug for their living room.

It is made from a patchwork of rectangles.

Work out the sizes of all the marked angles.

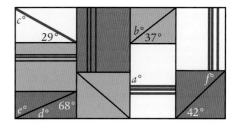

A very special rectangle – the square

- A square has four axes of symmetry.
- It has four right angles.
- It has four equal sides.
- The diagonals cut each other in **half** and at **right angles**.
  A diagonal makes an angle of
  45° with a side.

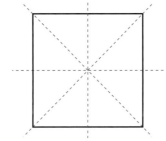
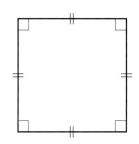
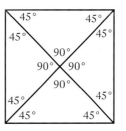

Exercise 11.2B

1 Draw a square of side 6 cm accurately. Label all the sides.

a Mark in its diagonals.

b Fill in the sizes of all the angles.

c Check that both diagonals are about 8·5 cm long.

2 The picture shows a square antique table top.

The inside section is a pattern of 25 small squares.

a Find the size of angle $a°$.

b Find the length of side p.

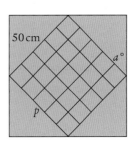

3 Gerry is tiling his kitchen floor.

He is using square tiles each of side 50 cm.

Here is a plan of the floor.

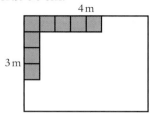

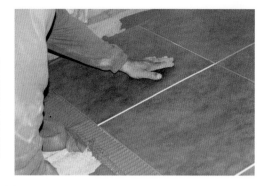

a How many tiles will fit along the 4 m wall?

b How many rows of tiles will be needed?

c How many tiles are needed altogether?

d Tiles come in boxes of 10. How many boxes of tiles will be needed?

4 A **rhombus** is a quadrilateral which can be made from two identical **(congruent)** isosceles triangles placed base to base.

A lot of people call it a diamond.

How many axes of symmetry does a rhombus have?

5 ABCD is a rhombus. Copy this rhombus.

a Fill in the lengths of all the sides.

b Fill in the sizes of all the angles.

c What is the size of ∠ABC?

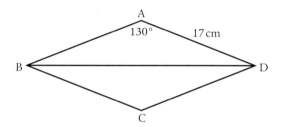

6 A **kite** is a quadrilateral. It can be made from any two isosceles triangles whose bases are equal in length.

PQRS is a kite.

a How many axes of symmetry does a kite have?

b Sketch the kite and fill in the sizes of all its sides and angles.

c What is the size of ∠PSR?

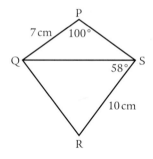

7 Copy this diagram of a tiling of kites onto squared paper.

Continue the pattern for at least six more tiles.

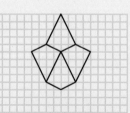

8 Here is a tiling of parallelograms.

A **parallelogram** is a quadrilateral whose opposite sides are **equal** and **parallel**.

Copy the tiling and add at least six more tiles.

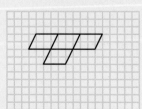

11.3 Working with circles

The **circumference** is the distance around the circle.

A **diameter** is a line which joins two points on the circumference and passes through the centre.

A **radius** is a line which joins the centre to a point on the circumference.

Diameter = 2 × radius   Radius = diameter ÷ 2

Exercise 11.3A

1 Find the diameter of each circle.

a
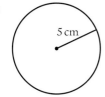
5 cm

b

16 mm

c
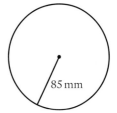
85 mm

2 Work out the radius of each circle.

a

36 mm

b
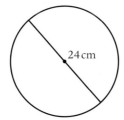
24 cm

c
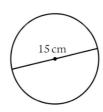
15 cm

d
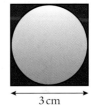
3 cm

3 The radius of the centre circle of a football pitch is 9·15 metres.

What is its diameter?

Exercise 11.3B

1 This basket holds two footballs exactly.

The diameter of the football is 22 cm.

a What is the width, w cm, of the basket?

b What is the height, h cm, of the basket?

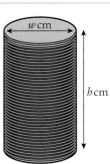
w cm

h cm

2 This circular window and frame is 200 cm wide.

The width of the window frame is 35 cm.

a What is the diameter of the glass window?

b What is the radius of the glass window?

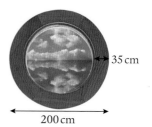

35 cm

200 cm

3 Jeff wanted to have a stone picnic table with two stools built for his garden.

Here is the top view of the table and stools.

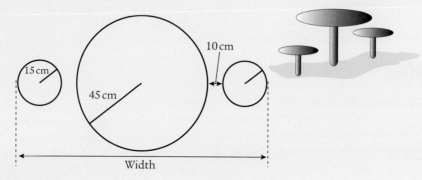

15 cm

45 cm

10 cm

Width

The radius of the table is 45 cm. The radius of each stool is 15 cm.
There is a 10 cm space between the table and a stool.

Find the width of the whole set-up, as shown in the diagram.

4 Cans of soup are to be packed in cardboard trays.

This can ...   packed like this ...   in one of these trays ...

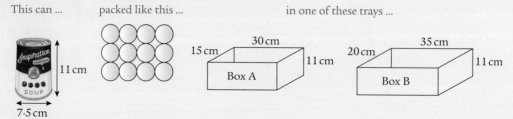

11 cm

7·5 cm

15 cm   30 cm
11 cm
Box A

20 cm   35 cm
11 cm
Box B

Which tray would be better? Explain your answer.

Preparation for assessment

1 This sign is in the shape of an equilateral triangle.

a What is the size of the angle marked $a°$?

b What is the length of AB?

2 What is the size of the angle marked $b°$?

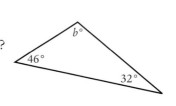

$b°$

46°

32°

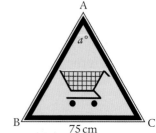

A

$a°$

B   C
75 cm

3 PQR is an isosceles triangle.

   a What is the size of each angle marked ✖?

   b Name another side of the triangle that is 8 cm long.

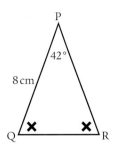

4 a Copy this rectangle and fill in the sizes of all the sides and angles.

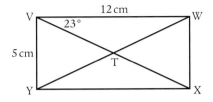

   b WT = 6·5 cm. What is the length of VT?

5 Doris is putting a little fence along the edge of a flower bed.

It is made with semicircular sections joined by straight-line sections.

Each semicircle has a radius of 40 cm.

The straight-line sections joining them are also 40 cm long.

Find the total length of this part of the fence.

6 Remember Hannah's new wet room.

She is going to put in a corner shower.
She wants to tile the two walls that form that corner.

The dimensions of the two walls to be tiled are shown.
They have different widths but the same height.

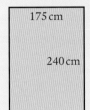

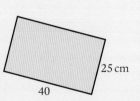

Each tile is 25 cm by 40 cm.

Hannah hasn't decided whether to put them like this: or like this:

Tiles are £3·45 each. They have to be bought in boxes of 10.

Work out how many tiles are needed to tile the two walls for each way.

Calculate the cost in each case.

12 Handling data

⏸ Before we start...

Lisa wanted to buy a small flat in Glasgow. She had two areas in mind.

a What things should she consider when choosing an area to live?

The cheapest suitable flats she found had the following prices:

Glasgow City Centre
£77 500, £79 000, £70 000,
£73 500, £75 000, £75 000

Glasgow West End
£73 000, £79 000, £90 000,
£85 000, £85 000, £86 000.

b Which area do you think she should concentrate on?

Explain your answer.

▶ What you need to know

1 What do the following tallies represent?

   a ||| **b** ⏜⏜   **c** ⏜ ⏜ ⏜ ||

2 Ayesha did a survey of door colours in her street.

The results are in this graph.

a Copy and complete the bar graph to show that:

    six houses had brown doors,

    four houses had black doors,

    two houses had red doors

b How many houses were in the street altogether?

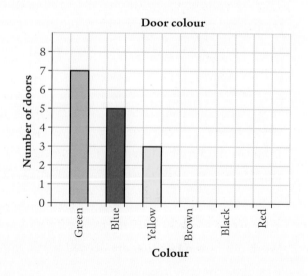

3 Here are the results in a competition with four rounds.

a Who got the highest score in Round 1?

b Who won the game?

Round	1	2	3	4
Saleem	7	5	3	6
Lauren	6	4	4	3
Nicole	8	5	5	2
Michael	3	8	5	4

4 The pictograph shows the number of people attending a gym one week:

Monday	☺ ☺ ☺ ☺ ☺
Tuesday	☺ ☺ ☺ ☺ ☺
Wednesday	☺ ☺ ☺ ☺
Thursday	☺ ☺ ☺ ☺
Friday	☺ ☺ ☺
Saturday	☺ ☺ ☺
Sunday	☺ ☺ ☺ ☺ = 5 people

a How many people attended the gym on Tuesday?

b What seems to be happening to gym attendance as the week goes on?

c What was the total attendance at the gym that week?

12.1 Frequency tables

Example 1

Colin is buying a new mobile phone.

To help him decide what phone to get, Colin asks his friends what phone they have.

These are the results of his survey.

Samsung	MobPhone	no phone	MobPhone
MobPhone	Nokia	Nokia	BlackBerry
MobPhone	MobPhone	HTC	Samsung
Samsung	no phone	Samsung	HTC
BlackBerry	MobPhone	no phone	BlackBerry
Nokia	BlackBerry	Samsung	HTC
Nokia	MobPhone	BlackBerry	Samsung

a What is the most popular type of phone?

b How many of Colin's friends have no phone?

c How many friends did he ask altogether?

You can sort the data into a table using tally marks.

Enter the data one row at a time. Cross out each item as you record the tally.

This makes sure you don't miss any out and that you don't count any twice.

Samsung	MobPhone	no phone	MobPhone
MobPhone	Nokia	Nokia	BlackBerry
MobPhone	MobPhone	HTC	Samsung
Samsung	no phone	Samsung	HTC
BlackBerry	MobPhone	no phone	BlackBerry
Nokia	BlackBerry	Samsung	HTC
Nokia	MobPhone	BlackBerry	Samsung

Phone	Tally	Frequency
BlackBerry		
Samsung		
Nokia	||	
MobPhone	|||	
No phone		
HTC		

When the tallies are complete, you can count them up and enter the **frequencies**.

This gives you a **frequency table**.

With the data are sorted, you can answer the questions.

Phone	Tally	Frequency
BlackBerry	|||||	5
Samsung	|||||		6
Nokia	||||	4
MobPhone	||||| ||	7
No phone	|||	3
HTC	|||	3

a The MobPhone is most popular.

b Three people have no phone.

c $5 + 6 + 4 + 7 + 3 + 3 = 28$ friends were asked.

Exercise 12.1A

1 Members of a drama group were asked for their favourite type of live theatre.

The results of the survey are shown below.

Musicals	Opera	Dance	Musicals	Plays
Musicals	Dance	Musicals	Dance	Comedy
Comedy	Dance	Musicals	Opera	Comedy
Plays	Musicals	Comedy	Opera	Opera
Musicals	Dance	Musicals	Plays	Opera
Opera	Plays	Dance	Dance	Plays

Type	Tally	Frequency
Musicals		
Opera		
Dance		
Plays		
Comedy		

a Sort the data into a frequency table.

b What is the most popular type of theatre?

c How many members were in the survey?

2 Katryna is considering buying a car.

She checked the local paper for secondhand cars on sale in her price range.

Here are the makes of cars she finds in the adverts.

Toyota	Ford	Mini	VW	Mazda
Ford	Mini	Toyota	Mazda	Ford
Toyota	VW	Mini	Ford	Mazda
Ford	Ford	VW	Ford	Mazda
VW	Mazda	Ford	Ford	Mini

Model	Tally	Frequency
Toyota		
Ford		
VW		
Mazda		
Mini		

a Copy and complete the frequency table.

b Which make gives her the most choice?

c Which make gives her the least choice?

3 A group of people were asked to name their most memorable team GB gold medal winners in the London 2012 Olympics.

The top ten winners are shown in the frequency table.

Gold medal winners	Frequency
Mo Farah	7
Chris Hoy	10
Andy Murray	8
Ben Ainslie	7
Jessica Ennis	10
Katherine Grainger and Anna Watkins	7
Bradley Wiggins	8
Laura Trott	4
Victoria Pendleton	4
Katherine Copeland and Sophie Hosking	5

a How many people's choices are recorded in the table?

b Who were the most popular choices for this group of people?

4 All the voters in a street were asked which party they would vote for.

Party	Frequency
SNP	25
Labour	30
Conservative	10
Liberal Democrat	10
Undecided	8
Won't vote	7

a How many of the voters in the street have made up their minds about voting?

b How many voters were asked?

c Copy and complete this bar chart for the information given in the table.

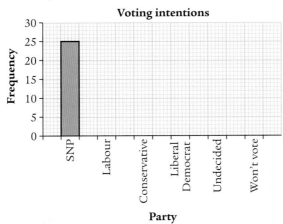

Code breaker

Example 2

What are the five most commonly used letters in the rhyme for remembering how many days are in each month?

Set up a frequency table and count the use of every letter in the rhyme.

Thirty days hath September,
April, June, and November.
All the rest have thirty-one,
Except February alone,
Which has twenty-eight days clear,
And twenty-nine in each leap year.

Letter	A	B	C	D	E	F	G	H	I	J	K	L	M
Frequency	15	3	4	4	22	1	1	11	7	1	0	6	2
Letter	N	O	P	Q	R	S	T	U	V	W	X	Y	Z
Frequency	11	3	4	0	10	5	14	2	2	3	1	8	0

By inspection we can see that the five most commonly used letters are E(22), A(15), T(14), H(11) and N(11).

Exercise 12.1B

1 Use the data sorted in Example 2 above to help you answer the following.

  a Which is the most frequent letter in the rhyme?

  b Which letters do not appear in the rhyme?

  c If you were looking at a message in a secret code and found that three letters occurred a lot more than any others, what would you guess the three letters stood for?

2 **Morse code** is a way of transmitting messages using a series of dots and dashes.

It is often transmitted using a telegraph key like in the picture, but sometimes using light signals.
- A dot takes one unit of time to send.
- A dash takes three units of time.
- The space between letters is one unit of time.

Here are the codes for each letter.

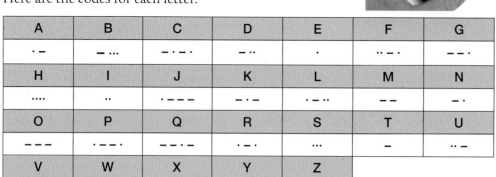

A	B	C	D	E	F	G
· —	— · · ·	— · — ·	— · ·	·	· · — ·	— — ·
H	**I**	**J**	**K**	**L**	**M**	**N**
· · · ·	· ·	· — — —	— · —	· — · ·	— —	— ·
O	**P**	**Q**	**R**	**S**	**T**	**U**
— — —	· — — ·	— — · —	· — ·	· · ·	—	· · —
V	**W**	**X**	**Y**	**Z**		
· · · —	· — —	— · · —	— · — —	— — · ·		

  a How many units of time does it take to send: **i** C **ii** J **iii** E?

  b What is the symbol for E?

c Why do you think this is the symbol for E?

d The international distress signal is SOS (save our souls).
  i Write this in Morse code. Leave a space between each letter.
  ii How many units of time does it take to send?

e **i** The most commonly used letters are E, T, I and A. How many units of time does it take to send each?
  ii The least used letters are J, Q and Y. Comment about how much time it takes to send these.

3 Pick a passage of your own.

Investigate whether the frequency of use of letters is the same as in Example 2 above.

4 A large firm gives each member of staff a unique code.

They have offices in Glasgow, Aberdeen, Inverness, Manchester and Birmingham.

The code is based on various pieces of information about the member of staff.

The code has 10 characters.

For example, this is the code for Helen Stock, whose birthday is on 12th June and works in the Glasgow office.

S	T	1	2	G	L	0	6	H	E

Every character in the code means something.

a Write down the code for Carol Proctor. Her birthday is 5th November.
She works in the Manchester office.

b Get the code for Jamie Collins. He works in the Inverness office. His birthday is New Year's Day.

c This is the code for Fiona Gordon.

G	O	2	9	A	B	0	2	F	I

  i She works in the office of a Scottish city. What city might she work in?
  ii What is unusual about Fiona's birthday?

d Twins Gemma and George Ferguson both work in the Birmingham office.

Why might there be a problem with the firm's codes?

12.2 Averages

When we talk about 'average' we are interested in what is a **typical** score for a set of data.

There are different ways of thinking about average.

The mean

When most people talk about 'average' they are thinking about the **mean**.

Mean score = **total of the scores** divided by **number of scores**.

Example 1

Omar took a note of his supermarket bill each week for six weeks.

He spent:

£54·82, £46·38, £37·75, £54·53, £42·58, £38·74.

Calculate the mean bill.

54·82 + 46·38 + 37·75 + 54·53 + 42·58 + 38·74 = 274·80

274·80 ÷ 6 = 45·80

So his mean weekly bill is £45·80.

Notice that a calculator will give the answer 45·8. We must make sure that when we write the answer, we write it as £45·80.

Example 2

Jacqui had a dinner party. She put a bowl of crisps out for herself and her six guests.

The total amount of crisps eaten was 250 grams.

Find the mean weight of crisps eaten per person.

250 ÷ 7 = 35·714 ...

So the mean weight is 35·7 grams (to 1 d.p.).

Exercise 12.2A

1 Find the mean of each set of data:

   a morning walks: 20 min, 26 min, 25 min, 22 min, 30 min, 32 min, 27 min

   b weights of babies: 3·35 kg, 3·77 kg, 2·32 kg, 3·22 kg, 3·54 kg

   c heights: 156 cm, 151 cm, 162 cm, 153 cm, 149 cm, 148 cm, 159 cm, 162 cm

   d cost of mobile phone batteries: £4·99, £4·49, £3·99, £3·49.

2 The total amount of sunshine in Wales in June was 200·3 hours.

   a How many days are there in June?

   b Find the mean hours of sunshine per day. (Give your answer correct to 1 d.p.)

   c The total amount of sunshine in Scotland in June was 161·4 hours.

      Find the mean hours of sunshine per day in Scotland. (Give your answer to 1 d.p.)

   d Compare the hours of sunshine in Wales and Scotland.

3 Mei supports Inverness Caledonian Thistle FC.

They joined the Scottish Premier League (SPL) in season 2004–2005.

Here are the points they scored over the period 2004 to 2013.

Season	2004/2005	2005/2006	2006/2007	2007/2008	2008/2009	2010/2011	2011/2012	2012/2013
Points	44	58	46	43	37	53	39	54

  a Find the mean number of points per season.

  b What was their lowest points score?

  c In which season did they not play in the SPL?

  d Looking at their points scores, why do you think they didn't play in the SPL that season?

4 Karen wanted to go to Barcelona before the winter.

She checked November's air fares on the internet. She found the following fares on offer:

  £73   £88   £99   £171   £184   £225

  a Calculate the mean flight cost.

She also checked the first week in December. She found the following prices:

  £88   £117   £179   £189   £212   £229

  b What is the mean price for the first week in December?

  c Can you think of a reason for the difference in mean price?

5 Jacob prided himself in his school attendance record.

He looked back over his secondary school reports and recorded his absences.

Year	1st	2nd	3rd	4th	5th	6th
Absences	2	0	20	2	1	5

  a Find the mean number of absences per year.

  b During which year do you think he had a knee operation?

  c What would the mean have been if we don't include that year?

  d What effect does an unusually high result have on the mean?

6 Six friends compare how many hours they studied over the weekend.

  a Find the mean number of hours spent on study per person.

  b Which friends did more than the average hours of study?

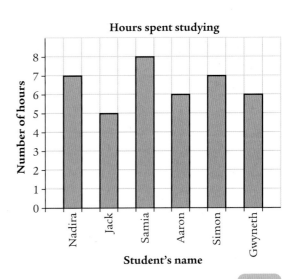

Hours spent studying

The mode and the median

The **mode** is another measure of average. It is the result or score with the **highest frequency**.

Example 3

The frequency table shows the number of orders for the 'specials' one evening at a restaurant.

Dish	Frequency
Chicken with haggis	12
Sea bass	15
Steak with pepper sauce	20
Mediterranean vegetable moussaka	11
Pork, apple and Stornoway black pudding tower	12

What is the **mode** or **modal** order?

The most commonly requested dish was steak.

So we would say that steak with pepper sauce was the mode.

Example 4

Kai tossed a dice several times.
He recorded the results in a table.

a How many times did he toss the dice?

b What was the modal score?

a $4 + 6 + 5 + 6 + 5 + 4 = 30$.

He tossed the dice 30 times.

b The scores 2 and 4 both have the same frequency.
There is not one single modal score.

There are two modes, 2 and 4.

The **median** is a third kind of average. It is the **middle result** when the **data are arranged in order**.

Score on dice	Frequency
1	4
2	6
3	5
4	6
5	5
6	4

Example 5

Jenny's cousins visited for her birthday.

Her cousins are: Peter aged 12, Anne aged 15, Thomas aged 7, Helen was 10 and Mark 8.

What is the median age of Jenny's cousins?

Putting the ages in order we get: 7, 8, 10, 12, 15.

We can see that 10 is the age in the middle of the list.

So we say that 10 years old is the median age of Jenny's cousins.

Exercise 12.2B

1 A group of students were asked about the number of people in their family.

Family size	3	4	5	6	7
Frequency	5	9	4	1	1

The results of the survey are shown.

What size of family is the mode?

2 The lengths of Ameena's mobile calls, in minutes, for the last month are listed:

5	1	1	1	5	1
1	1	1	6	1	4
0	1	1	1	24	

  a What is the modal length of a phone call?

  b Would you say Ameena is a heavy user of her mobile phone?

3 Shelley did a survey of motor vehicles that passed her house one morning.

Vehicle	Frequency
Car	20
Motorbike	12
Small van	5
Large van	2
Lorry	3
Bus	7

  a What is the modal type of vehicle?

  b How far was the lorry below the mode?

  c How does the bus compare with the mode?

  d Which vehicle was only a quarter as common as the mode?

4 Five friends compared their hourly rate of pay.

   £9·50   £9·75   £8·30   £10·50   £8·90

  a Arrange the amounts in order with the smallest rate first.

  b What is the median rate of pay?

5 A group of employees in a small firm were asked how long it took them to travel to work each day.

20 min	1 hour	35 min	40 min	10 min	1 hour 10 min	50 min	45 min	15 min

  a Arrange the times in order with the smallest first.

  b What is the median length of time taken to travel to work?

12.3 What's the chance?

We can use our past experience to judge the **likelihood** of an event occurring.

We know for sure that if today is Sunday then tomorrow will be Monday ... certain.

We know that if we throw a normal dice that we won't get a 7 ... impossible.

For everything else the chances of it happening must fall somewhere between these two.

Example 1

Draw a likelihood line with '**Impossible**' at one end and '**Certain**' at the other.

Place the following events on the line, to show which is more likely when you throw a dice.

A: getting an even number.

B: getting a 6.

C: getting a number that can be divided by 3.

D: throwing a dice and not getting a 6.

When you throw a dice there are 6 things that can happen ... 1, 2, 3, 4, 5, or 6.

D has the most **favourable** outcomes ... 1, 2, 3, 4 or 5 ... 5 chances in 6 ... $\frac{5}{6}$.

A is next. There are three favourable outcomes, 2, 4, 6 ... 3 chances in 6 ... $\frac{3}{6}$.

C is next. There are two favourable outcomes, 3, 6 ... 2 chances in 6 ... $\frac{2}{6}$.

B is the least likely. There is only one favourable outcome ... 1 chance in 6 ... $\frac{1}{6}$.

Exercise 12.3A

1 From each pair of events, say which one is more likely.

    a **i** Getting a head when tossing a coin.   **ii** Getting a 4 when throwing a dice.

    b **i** Picking a day at random and it starts with 'M'.

       ii Picking a month at random and it starts with 'M'.

    c **i** Picking a card from a pack and getting a red card.

       ii Picking a card from a pack and getting a diamond.

2 Draw a likelihood line and place on it the following events.

    a Tossing a coin and getting a tail.

    b Getting a number that divides into 12 exactly when you throw a dice.

    c When your dad gets a puncture in his car, it will be the tyre on the front right-hand side of the car.

    d A surprise visit to the school by a councillor will be on a Thursday.

3 In Meg's purse there are two 1p, three 2p, four 5p, two 10p, one 20p and three 50p coins.

    a How many coins are there all together?

    b A coin falls out. What is the likelihood of the coin being:

       i a copper coin   **ii** a 50p coin?

    c For the coin that falls out, which is more likely?

       i It is worth more than 10p.   **ii** It is worth less than 5p.

    d Meg loses a coin. What is the probability that she'll have £2·17 left?

       (Hint: 'probability' is another word for 'likelihood' here.)

4 For a history project, the students were asked to bring in any old pre-decimal coins they had in their house.

The table shows that 100 coins were brought in.

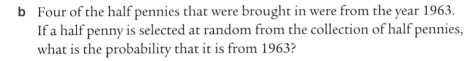

Half crown	2 shillings	Threepence	Half penny	Penny
10	15	25	20	30

a The teacher picks up one coin to talk about it.

What is the probability that it is:

i a half crown   ii a threepence   iii a silver coin?

(Hint: the half crown and 2 shilling coins were silver)

b Four of the half pennies that were brought in were from the year 1963. If a half penny is selected at random from the collection of half pennies, what is the probability that it is from 1963?

5 The diagram shows the result of a survey on who takes school dinners.

a How many are: i boys ii girls?

b What is the probability that a student picked at random will be:

i a boy who takes school dinners

ii a girl who takes a packed lunch.

	School dinner	Packed lunch
Boy	8	2
Girl	14	4

c What is the likelihood that a boy picked at random will take school dinners?

d A student who has a packed lunch is called out. Are they more likely to be a boy or a girl?

Estimates of chance

If we don't have all the information, we can still estimate chance by taking a sample and assuming that the sample is typical of what usually happens.

Example 2

John was offered a holiday in the first week of May.

Using the internet, he gathered information about how often it had rained in that week over the past 20 years.

The table shows that there were 6 years when there was no rain, 4 years when there was 1 day of rain, etc.

Days of rain	0	1	2	3	4	5	6	7
Frequency	6	4	3	2	1	3	1	0

a What is the probability that it will not rain during John's holiday?

b What is the likelihood that there will be rain on fewer than 4 days?

We can't predict the future, but assuming that the past 20 years are typical of the weather for that week ...

a There were 6 years out of 20 that there was no rain that week ... a probability of $\frac{6}{20}$ ... which we can simplify to $\frac{3}{10}$ or 0·3.

b Altogether there were $6 + 4 + 3 + 2 = 15$ years when it rained on fewer than 4 days ... a probability of $\frac{15}{20}$ ... which we can simplify to $\frac{3}{4}$ or 0·75.

Exercise 12.3B

1 The teacher studied how many days students took off to recover from the common cold.

She looked at the last 24 cases. (Note that 5 people took 3 days off, 7 took 4 days off, etc.)

Days off	3	4	5	6	7
Frequency	5	7	8	3	1

a Use the results to estimate the probability that a student will take:
  i 5 days off   **ii** 6 days off.

b Mary catches the cold. She has an exam in 5 days' time. Unfortunately she has to take some sick leave. What is the likelihood that she will miss the exam? (i.e. what is the likelihood that she will be off for 5 or more days?)

2 Pedro was worried about the length of time his light bulbs were lasting in the kitchen.

He kept a record.

Lifetime (weeks)	5	6	7	8	9
Frequency	2	4	5	10	9

a How many bulbs lasted seven weeks?

b Use the record to estimate the probability that a new bulb will last:
  i 8 weeks
  ii more than 6 weeks
  iii 6 weeks or less.

3 A bus driver said, 'There are 100 excuses for leaving late, none for leaving early.'

The inspector noted how many minutes late the buses left the station.

Minutes late	0	1	2	3	4	5
Frequency	10	9	5	3	2	1

a How many buses did the inspector log?

b Estimate the chance that the bus you are on will be:
  i 2 minutes late
  ii more than 3 minutes late.

c What is the likelihood that the bus will not leave the station on time?

d I arrive at the station a minute late for my bus. I will catch my bus as long as it's running at least 2 minutes late.

What are the chances that I will catch my bus?

Preparation for assessment

1 A hospital recorded the number of missed appointments each day over a four-week period.

5	5	3	5	2	6	5	1	3	9
4	6	2	1	7	3	5	2	6	3

Missed appointments	Tally	Frequency
1		
2		
3		
4		
5		
6		
7		
8		

a Copy and complete the frequency table.

b What is the modal number of missed appointments?

2 Here is the month FEBRUARY in code.

Letter	F	E	B	R	U	A	R	Y
Code letter	H	G	D	T	W	C	T	A

The code for FEBRUARY is HGDTWCTA.

Write the word BEAR using the same code.

3 The bar chart shows the number of students in each third year class in a school.

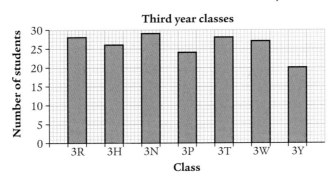

a What is the modal class size?

b Write down the numbers of students in all seven classes.

c Calculate the mean class size.

d What is the median class size?

4   What is the probability that:

   a   when a day of the week is picked at random, it will start with a T

   b   when a month is chosen at random, it will start with a T

   c   when a month is chosen at random, it will start with a vowel?

5   A random selection of students was asked if they belonged to a school club.
The table shows the responses.

	Club	No club
S1–S3	5	12
S4–S6	25	8

If one of these students is picked at random, what is the probability that:

   a   they will be an S1–S3 club member

   b   they will be in S4–S6 but not belong to a club

   c   they will belong to a club?

6   Remember Lisa who wanted to buy a small flat in Glasgow. She had two areas in mind.

   a   What things should she consider in choosing an area to live?

The cheapest suitable flats she found had the following prices:

Glasgow City Centre
£77 500, £79 000, £70 000, £73 500,
£75 000, £75 000

Glasgow West End
£73 000, £79 000, £90 000, £85 000,
£85 000, £86 000.

   b   Which area do you think she should concentrate on?
Explain your answer.

13 Earnings

⏸ **Before we start...**

This is Pete's pay slip for June.

Pete knows that during June he will spend £1300 on things like rent, food, electricity, and so on.

Payslip for June			
Name: P. Simpson	NI Number: AB 12 34 56 C		Employee No: 00382
Earnings		**Deductions**	
Description	**Amount**	**Description**	**Amount**
Basic Pay	£2,015.30	Income Tax	£289.13
Overtime	£69.47	National Insurance	£182.47
Bonus	£35.66	Pension	£125.23
Others		Others	
Gross Pay:		**Total Deductions:**	

Net Pay:

Can he afford a £250 holiday from his June pay?

Work out the missing values from his pay slip to help you decide.

▶ What you need to know

1 In one year, say how many there are of each of these:
   a months **b** weeks.

2 How long is it from:
   a 09 30 to 12 00   **b** 13 30 to 17 00   **c** 8.45 a.m. to 12.30 p.m.?

3 Write these in hours:
   a 1 hour 30 min
   b 2 hours 45 min
   c 3 hours 15 min.

   > 15 min is 0·25 hour
   > 30 min is 0·5 hour
   > 45 min is 0·75 hour

4 Round: **a** 12·5p to the nearest whole penny   **b** £13·59 to the nearest £1.

5 Calculate:

   a 10% of £40·00   **b** 1% of £147·00   **c** 5% of £8   **d** 2% of £200.

6 Calculate:

   a £9 + 5p   **b** £32 − 14p

   c £196·72 + £37·14 − £5·03   **d** £8·30 × 12

   e £2796·96 ÷ 12   **f** £28 340 ÷ 52.

7 Iain earned £340 in the first week of October.

In each of the next three weeks he earned £420.

Calculate his total earnings for these four weeks of October.

13.1 Wages and salaries

Remember these facts:

Salary is used for what you earn in a month or a year.
A salary is usually paid once a month.

Wage is used for what you earn in a day or a week.
A wage is usually paid once a week.

Example 1

Amir works as a nurse.

Each month he earns a **salary** of £2217.

How much does he earn in a year?

           Monthly salary = £2217

Total earned in one year = £2217 × 12

                 = £26 604

Amir earns £26 604 in one year.

Example 2

Eric drives a forklift truck.

He earns £19 344 in one year.

Each week he earns the same wage.

Calculate his weekly wage.

Total earned in one year = £19 344

         Weekly wage = £19 344 ÷ 52

               = £372

Eric's weekly wage is £372.

Exercise 13.1A

1 Noah earns £6·35 per hour in a bakery.

How much is he paid for 6 hours' work?

2 Sophie worked at a Theme Park for 8 weeks in the summer. She earned a total of £1856.

How much was she paid each week?

3 Emily applied for this job and was successful.

   a What is her annual salary?

   b What is her monthly salary?

> **PRINT ENGINEER**
> Salary £30K
> Apply Now

4 Quarry workers earn £550 per week.

Nick is a quarry worker. How much does he earn in one year?

5 Clare packs shelves part-time at her local supermarket. Last year her total pay was £4836.

Calculate her average weekly pay last year.

6 If Richard got this job how much would he earn in a year?

> **Professional Photographer Required**
> *£1943 per month*

Exercise 13.1B

1 Jiao earns £15·50 an hour as an aerobics instructor.

   a What is she paid for taking a 3-hour class?

   b Each week she takes four 3-hour classes.
How much does she earn in a week?

2 Mirek works 6 hours each day from Monday to Friday at his local supermarket. His hourly rate is £6·48.

   a How much does he earn each day?

   b Calculate his total earnings for the week.

3 Rachel works at a Call Centre. She earns £7·62 for each hour she works.

   a Copy and complete this table:

Number of hours	1	2	3	4	5	6	7	8
Amount earned (£)	7·62	15·24						

Rachel's mobile phone bill is £43·66.

   b How many complete hours of work cover her phone bill?

4 Mrs Morgan is a freelance games developer.

She is paid £15·26 per hour.

Her workday is 9 a.m. to 4 p.m. with a one-hour lunch break.

She works on Monday, Thursday and Friday each week.

a How many hours a week does she work?

b How much does she earn working for five weeks?

5 Here is a list of jobs:

Office Worker   Electrician   Shop Assistant   Plumber

Dental Nurse   Waiter/Waitress   Joiner

Do some research using the internet to find out what you can earn for doing these jobs.

Try to put the jobs in order – highest paid to lowest paid.

Write a short report on what you found and any difficulties you had.

You may add your own choice of jobs to the list.

13.2 Hourly rates

Timesheets

A **timesheet** records when you started working and when you stopped.

You can calculate the number of hours you worked from a timesheet.

Example 1

Look at Jacob's timesheet for Friday. Explain how the figure 8·5 was calculated.

TIMESHEET	Time In	Time Out	Time In	Time Out	Hours Worked
Monday	09 00	13 00	14 00	17 00	7
Tuesday	09 00	13 00	14 00	17 30	7·5
Wednesday	08 30	12 30	13 30	17 00	7·5
Thursday	09 00	12 30	13 30	17 00	7
Friday	08 00	12 30	14 00	18 00	8·5
				Total Hours =	37·5

Name: Jacob Greene   Week No. 15

Hours worked in morning:

$$\begin{array}{r} 12\,30 \\ -\ 08\,00 \\ \hline 4\,30 \end{array}$$

Hours worked in afternoon:

$$\begin{array}{r} 18\,00 \\ -\ 14\,00 \\ \hline 4\,00 \end{array}$$

This is 4 hours 30 minutes.   This is 4 hours.

This gives a total of 8 hours 30 minutes or 8·5 hours that he worked on Friday.

Overtime

Any extra hours you work over your normal hours are called **overtime**.

Often a higher rate per hour is paid for overtime.

For example, if your overtime is paid at **double time** then your normal basic rate per hour is doubled.

Example 2

Steve is a painter and decorator. His basic rate of pay is £11·30 per hour.

On Sunday he is paid double time.

a Steve normally works 35 hours a week.
How much is he paid for a week's work?

b He works 4 hours' overtime on a Sunday.
How much is he paid for this overtime?

a 35 hours at basic rate = £11·30 × 35 = £395·50.

b Overtime rate (double time) = £11·30 × 2 = £22·60.
4 hour's overtime = £22·60 × 4 = £90·40.

Exercise 13.2A

1 **a** On Monday Imari started work at 8.30 a.m. He finished for lunch at 1.00 p.m.
How many hours did Imari work in the morning?

b He starts work again at 2.30 p.m. and finishes work at 5.00 p.m.
How many hours does he work after lunch?

c Calculate the total hours he worked on Monday.

2 Yvonne started work at 9.30 a.m. She had one-and-a-half hours for lunch.
In total she worked 6 hours.
What time did Yvonne finish work?

3 Calculate the overtime rate at 'double time' for these basic rates:

   a £7·30   **b** £8·90

   c £11·50   **d** £9·48.

4 Jennifer works as a shop assistant. Her basic rate of pay is £7·50 per hour.
She is paid 'double time' for any overtime she works.

   a How much is she paid for one hour's overtime?

   b On Tuesday she worked overtime from 18 00 to 21 00.
How much did she earn for this overtime?

5 Kevin works as a shop assistant.

This is his timesheet for one week in September. It has not been completed.

TIMESHEET		Name: Kevin Smith			Week No. 27
	Time In	Time Out	Time In	Time Out	Hours Worked
Monday	08 00	12 00	13 00	17 00	
Tuesday	08 00	13 00	14 00	17 30	
Wednesday	08 30	12 30	13 30	16 30	
Thursday	08 00	12 30	14 30	18 00	
Friday	08 30	13 30	14 00	16 30	
				Total Hours =	

a Work out how many hours Kevin worked each day.

b How many hours did he work in total this week?

c Kevin's normal hours are 35 hours each week.
How many hours overtime did he do?

d Kevin's basic rate of pay is £7·50 per hour.
How much did he earn **at the basic rate** for this week?

e He is paid 'double time' for overtime.
How much did he earn doing overtime?

Exercise 13.2B

1 Tyrone's basic rate of pay is £8·80 an hour. Overtime is paid at 'double time'.

On Friday he works 6 hours at basic rate and does 2 hours' overtime.

Calculate his Friday pay.

2 a i Who earns the most for the week shown, Stephanie or Trevor?

ii By how much?

b Swap their hours of overtime.
Now answer the same questions!

Stephanie
Basic rate: £7·35
Normal hours: 36
Overtime: 3 hours
(at 'double time')

Trevor
Basic rate: £8·16
Normal hours: 30
Overtime: 5 hours
(at 'double time')

13.3 Piecework

Apple pickers are paid by how many crates of apples they pick.

This is called piecework payment.

Piecework is when you are paid for completing a task.

You are not paid for the time you take.

Example 1

Jamelia is picking apples.

She is paid £18 for each crate (400 kg) of fruit she picks.

On Monday she fills 3 crates. On Tuesday she fills 5 crates.

How much did Jamelia earn:

a on Monday   **b** on Tuesday   **c** for the two days?

a Monday: 3 × £18 = £54.

b Tuesday: 5 × £18 = £90.

c Total = Monday's total + Tuesday's total = £54 + £90 = £144.

Exercise 13.3A

1 Nathan works as a 'room attendant' at a hostel.
He is paid £12·50 for each room he cleans.
How much is he paid for cleaning seven rooms?

2 Sisters Melanie and Abigail do hair braiding at festivals.
They charge £1·50 for one braid.
One Saturday they did 26 braids.

    a How much did they make?

    b If they split their income equally, how much did each make?

3 Robert is a 3-D printer operator.
His pay is worked out from the number of objects he prints.
For small objects he is paid £2·45. For large objects he is paid £5·25.

    a How much is he paid for printing four small objects?

    b How much is he paid for printing nine large objects?

    c On Wednesday, Robert prints six small objects. He also prints 14 large objects.
How much is he paid on Wednesday?

4 Felicity goes berry picking to earn some extra money.
She is paid £6 for each tray she picks.

    a How much does she get for picking seven trays?

    b Felicity finds she can pick two trays per hour.
At this rate what is she paid per hour?

    c On Thursday she works at this rate for five hours.
How much did she earn on Thursday?

5 Simba delivers leaflets. He gets paid £1·50 for every 20 leaflets he delivers.
He wants to earn £15.

    a How many leaflets does he need to deliver?

    b Simba's pay is increased to £2 for every 20 leaflets delivered.
To earn £15 how many leaflets does he now need to deliver?

Exercise 13.3B

1 Brian works for a Craft Company making bookmarks.

He hand-paints three different types of bookmark.

The table shows how much he is paid for each type.
It also shows how long he takes to make each type.

Use the information given in the table to answer the questions.

Type of bookmark	Oriental	American	Australian
Payment for 1	£2·41	£4·48	£3·75
Hours to make	2	3·5	2·5

a In the first week, Brian makes six of each type of bookmark.

   i How much does he earn?

   ii How many hours does he work?

   iii Calculate how much he earned per hour.

b In his second week, he makes these bookmarks:
Oriental – 7, American – 11, Australian – 3.

   i Did he earn more or less than in his first week?

   ii Was his pay per hour better or worse than his first week?

13.4 Commission

Mrs Hughes works for a computer company.
She sells tablet computers.
Her pay depends on how many she sells.
This type of pay is called **commission**.

Example 1

Mrs Hughes is paid commission of £17 for each tablet she sells.
If she sells 30 tablets, how much commission does she earn?
Commission = 30 × £17 = £510.

Example 2

Mrs Hughes is offered a new way of calculating her commission.
She will get 5% of the total value of her sales.
Each tablet is sold for £360.
Will she be better off accepting this new offer?

1% of £360 = £3·60.   Divide by 100 to find 1%

5% of £360 is £3·60 × 5 = £18·00.

So Mrs Hughes will be £1 better off on the new offer for each tablet she sells.

She would therefore be £30 better off if she sells 30 tablets.

Exercise 13.4A

1 Amelia sells e-book readers.

She is paid £12 commission for each one she sells.

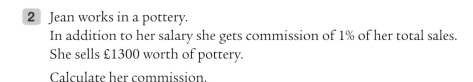

a On Monday she sells nine e-book readers.
How much is her commission?

b On Tuesday she earns £120 commission.
How many e-book readers did she sell?

2 Jean works in a pottery.
In addition to her salary she gets commission of 1% of her total sales.
She sells £1300 worth of pottery.

Calculate her commission.

3 Balkar sells broadband packages.

His commission is £35 for each package sold.

Day	Mon	Tue	Wed	Thur	Fri
No. of packages	4	3	6	2	7
Commission (£s)					

a Copy and complete the table to show Balkar's commission for each day.

b How much commission did he earn that week?

4 Tracey works in a computer shop.

She gets a basic wage and is paid a commission of 2% of her sales.

How much commission does she get for selling computers worth £3400?

5 At 'The Four Wheels' secondhand car sales company the staff are
paid 5% of the value of their sales.
Adam sells a car to a customer for £1800.
How much commission does he earn?

Exercise 13.4B

1 Mr MacDonald sells tropical fish. His commission is 6% of the value of his sales.

How much commission will he receive for selling:

a fish with a value of £160

b 200 fish, each worth £2·50?

2 Sahib works for Bright Stage Agency.

She is paid 85p commission for each adult ticket she sells.
Her commission for a child's ticket is 35p.

a On Thursday she sells 25 adult tickets. What is her commission?

b On Friday she sold tickets to Mr and Mrs Vaughan and their two children. How much was her commission for this sale?

3 Paul sells cactus plants.

His commission for selling a 'Mexican Grass Tree' is £2·60.
His commission for selling a 'Pony Tail' is £3·15.

In each case, find his commission.

a He sells five 'Mexican Grass Trees'.

b He sells ten 'Pony Tails'.

c He completes an order for eight 'Mexican Grass Trees' and seven 'Pony Tails'.

4 Mr Drazek runs a factory that produces hand-made rugs.

His workers earn a basic weekly wage.

They also get commission for each rug they make.

Can you decide what the smallest commission for each rug should be?

You may find it easier to work in groups to solve this problem.

Try to explain your solution to another group.

> It takes 3 hours to make 1 rug.
> Each worker works a 30-hour week.
> Legally each worker has to earn at least £8·40 per hour.
> Each worker has a basic weekly wage of £150.

13.5 Take-home pay

When you work you will get a **pay slip**. This shows you how much you have earned.

It will tell you what has been taken off your pay.

These amounts that are taken off are called **deductions**.

The main deductions are income tax and national insurance.

You may also pay into a pension fund.

Find out what **gross pay** and **net pay** are.

Example 1

Wendy has a new job. She gets her first pay slip.

She finds three deductions have been made from her weekly pay:

Income tax	£29·36
National insurance	£11·20
Pension	£35·79

Calculate the total amount deducted.

Total deductions = £29·36 + £11·20 + £35·79

= £76·35.

Example 2

This is Zara's pay slip.

Calculate her:

a gross pay

b total deductions

c net pay or take-home pay.

Payslip for Week 27				
Name: Z. Docherty		NI Number: AB 12 34 56 D		Employee No: 24/B
Earnings			**Deductions**	
Description	Amount		Description	Amount
Basic Pay	£772.56		Income Tax	£131.05
Overtime	£45.47		National Insurance	£55.18
Bonus			Pension	£63.47
Others			Others	
Gross Pay:			**Total Deductions:**	
			Net Pay:	

a Gross pay = basic pay + overtime

= £772·56 + £45·47

= £818·03

b Total deductions

= income tax + national insurance + pension

= £131·05 + £55·18 + £63·47

= £249·70

c Take-home pay = gross pay − total deductions = £818·03 − £249·70

= £568·33

Exercise 13.5A

1 Leo is a laboratory assistant.

In the boxes you can see his deductions for two weeks' work.

Week 1
Income tax £34·70
National Insurance £18·63
Pension £13·80

Week 2
Income tax £37·25
National Insurance £19·04
Pension £13·80

Find the total deductions from his pay for:

a week 1

b week 2

c week 1 and week 2 combined.

2 This is part of Kasey's pay slip. It shows one week's deductions.

    a Calculate her total deductions for the week.

    b Kasey's pension deduction was missing. It was £15·80.
Calculate her correct total deductions.

Deductions	
Description	**Amount**
Income Tax	£84.30
National Insurance	£23.55
Pension	
Others	£23.00
Total Deductions:	

3 Harrison is a kennel attendant.

His gross pay for one week is £248.

His total deductions for that week are £46·10.

What is his take-home pay?

4 Kirsten works as a sound engineer.

Look at this part of her week's pay slip.

    a Calculate Kirsten's gross pay for this week.

    b Her deductions for this week were £142·35.
Calculate her take-home pay for the week.

Earnings	
Description	**Amount**
Basic Pay	£354.00
Overtime	£86.46
Bonus	£30.00
Others	
Gross pay:	

Exercise 13.5B

1 Work out the missing values in these two pay slips to find the net (take-home) pay.

a

Payslip for August

Name: D. Bell   NI Number: GH 23 45 67 J   Employee No: 023

Earnings		Deductions	
Description	**Amount**	**Description**	**Amount**
Basic Pay	£1,340.00	Income Tax	£222.37
Overtime	£235.00	National Insurance	£87.60
Bonus	- - - - - - -	Pension	£144.05
Others	£144.70	Others	£23.00
Gross Pay:		**Total Deductions:**	

Net Pay: [ ]

b

Payslip for Week 12

Name: Ahmed Bell   NI Number: KL 98 76 54 M   Employee No: AT/07

Earnings		Deductions	
Description	**Amount**	**Description**	**Amount**
Basic Pay	£435.17	Income Tax	£97.16
Overtime	£121.78	National Insurance	£28.76
Bonus	- - - - - - -	Pension	- - - - - - -
Others	- - - - - - -	Others	£14.17
Gross Pay:		**Total Deductions:**	

Net Pay: [ ]

Calculate the missing entries for this pay slip.

 You might want to work in pairs or in a group to discuss the solution to this question.

Try to explain to another group how you got your solution.

Payslip for Week 12

Name: Danielle Robertson   NI Number: EF 87 65 43 A   Employee No: Z-02

Earnings		Deductions	
Description	**Amount**	**Description**	**Amount**
Basic Pay	£392.38	Income Tax	?
Overtime	?	National Insurance	£23.14
Bonus	£43.00	Pension	£14.76
Others	£25.00	Others	£12.00
Gross Pay:	**£529.46**	**Total Deductions:**	?

Net Pay: £404.26

13.6 Benefits and the Universal Credit

Universal Credit

The UK government runs a benefit system for people who cannot do full-time work.

Universal Credit is the main benefit for people of working age.

It is paid monthly but not everyone is entitled to it.

Universal Credit can help pay for your housing or for looking after your children.

If you are disabled or caring for someone, it can help pay some of your costs.

Example 1

Ailsa is a single unemployed parent over 25. She has one child aged 6.
Her Universal Credit entitlement is £210 per week.
She also receives weekly child benefit of £20·30.

What is her weekly income?

Total household income: Universal Credit	£210·00
Child Benefit	£20·30
Total	£230·30

Example 2

Ailsa manages to get a part-time job which pays £112·48 per week.

Her mum is very happy to do the child minding.

Ailsa's Universal Credit goes down by £47·11.
Her child benefit does not change.

a How much Universal Credit does Ailsa get now?

b How does this affect her total household income?

a
Original Universal Credit	£210·00
Deduction	£47·11
Revised Universal Credit	£162·89

b
Universal Credit	£162·89
Earnings	£112·48
Child Benefit	£20·30
Total household income	£295·67

Ailsa is better off by £295·67 − £230·30 = £65·37 each week.

Exercise 13.6A

1 Zygmunt and Zofia have one child aged three.

Zygmund earns £184 per week. Zofia does not work and looks after their child.

Their Universal Credit entitlement is £106·45. They also receive child benefit of £20·30.

What is their total household income?

2 Yvonne and Zak have an elderly aunt staying with them.

They have two children.

Zak works and Yvonne stays at home to care for her aunt and look after their child.

Their Universal Credit entitlement per week is £76·83.
They receive child benefit of £33·70 each week.

Zak earns £185 per week.

They also receive a carer's allowance of £55·55 per week for looking after their aunt.

Calculate their total household income per week.

3 This table shows the various earnings and entitlements that Paul and Sonia get each week:

Universal Credit	Earnings (Paul)	Earnings (Sonia)	Child benefit	Council Tax support
£218·37	£41·50	£78·20	£20·30	£56·30

a Calculate their total weekly household income.

b If Paul's earnings are increased by £100, their Universal Credit entitlement is reduced by £65.

What effect will this have on their total income each week?

Exercise 13.6B

1 Universal Credit is paid monthly. It useful to know your average weekly Universal Credit.

Alison is a single parent with one child. She receives £1053 Universal Credit monthly.

Calculate her average weekly credit.

> 52 weeks = 1 year
> 12 months = 1 year
> Not all months have the same number of days or weeks

2 Maz and Tom have no children but Maz is pregnant.

Tom earns £283·50 per week. Maz receives £136·78 maternity allowance. Their Universal Credit is £15·80 per week.

After their baby is born their Universal Credit will be increased to £68·40. Maz will still be paid her maternity allowance. They will also get £20·30 child benefit. Tom's earnings are set to go down to £249·70 per week.

Will they be better or worse off after the baby is born?

Preparation for assessment

1 Irene works as a 3-D printer operator and earns £447·25 a week.

  a How much does she earn in four weeks?

  b What is her yearly income?

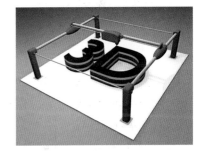

2 This is Richard's time sheet.

TIMESHEET	Name: Richard Manning			Week No. 18
	Time In	Time Out	Time In	Time Out	Hours Worked
Monday	08 30	12 30	13 30	17 30	
Tuesday	08 00	12 30	14 00	17 30	
Wednesday	09 00	13 30			
Thursday	08 00	12 00	14 30	18 30	
Friday	07 30	12 30	14 00	16 30	
				Total Hours =	

  a Work out how many hours Richard worked each day.

  b How many hours did he work in total this week?

3 Austin works for a picture framing company.

He is paid piecework.

His rates are: small frames £5·20, large frames £7·75.

How much is he paid for making:

  a 3 small frames

  b 18 large frames

  c 6 frames of each type?

4 Bryan sells software packages to large companies.

He is offered two different commission payment schemes.

> **Scheme 1**
> £47·50 for each package sold

> **Scheme 2**
> 3% of total sales

One week he sold nine packages with a total sales value of £15 000.

a Work out what Bryan's week's pay would be for each scheme.

b Which scheme should he choose? Give a reason.

5 Elena normally works a 37-hour week. Her rate of pay is £9·22 per hour.

a Calculate her basic weekly wage.

b One Saturday she worked five hours overtime at double pay.

How much was she paid for this overtime?

6 Ameena has a part-time job paying £112·48 per week.

She has Universal Credit entitlement of £164·79. She also receives child benefit of £33·70 for her two children.

a What is Ameena's total weekly income?

b If her pay is increased by £50, then her Universal Credit goes down by £32·50.

What would her new weekly income be?

7 Remember Pete's wage slip for June.

Pete knows that during June he will spend £1300 on things like rent, food, electricity, and so on.

Payslip for June			
Name: P. Simpson	NI Number: AB 12 34 56 C		Employee No: 00382
Earnings		**Deductions**	
Description	**Amount**	**Description**	**Amount**
Basic Pay	£2,015.30	Income Tax	£289.13
Overtime	£69.47	National Insurance	£182.47
Bonus	£35.66	Pension	£125.23
Others		Others	
Gross Pay:		**Total Deductions:**	

Net Pay: [   ]

Can he afford a £250 holiday from his June pay?

Work out the missing values from his pay slip to help you decide.

160

14 Proportion

⏸ Before we start...

Packets of tea bags are on sale in the supermarket.

Super-brew comes in three sizes as shown.

Which of the packets is the 'best buy'?

Super-brew
180 tea bags
£3·42

Super-brew
100 tea bags
£2·10

Super-brew
250 tea bags
£5·00

▶ What you need to know

1 a There are 100 pence in £1. How many pence are there in £5?

   b There are 12 months in a year. How many months are there in three years?

2 a 1 cm = 10 mm. Change 4 cm to mm.

   b 1 kg = 2·2 pounds. Change 6 kg to pounds.

3 a Three car tyres cost £291. How much does one tyre cost?

   b A book of 10 postage stamps costs £5·10. How much does one stamp cost?

   c Sending 40 texts costs £3·20. How much does it cost to send one text?

4 A model ship is 65 cm long.

   Each centimetre stands for 2 metres.

   How long is the actual ship?

5 In two minutes Joss can type 90 words.

   How many words would you expect her to type in:

   a one minute   **b** five minutes?

14.1 Rates

The word '**per**' means 'for each'.

A phrase that contains the word 'per' is called **a rate**.

Example 1

Tessa cycles at 18 km **per** hour (km/h). (This means that if Tessa cycled at this speed
Travelling at this speed, how far would she cycle in: for one hour she would travel 18 km.)

a   three hours   **b**   half an hour?

a   In 1 hour Tessa cycles 18 km.

   In 3 hours she would cycle $18 \times 3 = 54$ km.

b   In half an hour she would cycle $18 \times \frac{1}{2} = 9$ km.

Example 2

A bamboo plant grew 24 cm in 6 hours.

Calculate its **rate** of growth per hour.

In 6 hours it grows 24 cm.

In 1 hour it grows $24 \div 6 = 4$ cm.

So the rate of growth is 4 cm per hour.

Example 3

The express train travels 270 miles in 3 hours.

a   Calculate its rate of travel in miles per hour.
   (How far does the train travel in 1 hour?)

b   How many miles will it travel in 4 hours?

a   Rate of travel = $270 \div 3 = 90$ miles per hour.

b   In 4 hours it will travel $90 \times 4 = 360$ miles.

Exercise 14.1A

1   To have a swim at the leisure centre costs £2 **per** person.
   How much does it cost for five people to have a swim?

2   Entry to the rock concert is £25 **per** ticket.
   What is the cost of four tickets?

3 The bus fare from Bo'ness to Linlithgow is £2·50 **per** person.

How much does it cost six people to make the journey by bus?

4 One ticket to the cinema costs £6.

What is the cost of five tickets?

5 One orange costs 65p. What is the cost of eight oranges?

6 Ahmad earns £42 for six hours work. What is his rate of pay per hour?

7 Five school lunches cost £7. What is the cost of one school lunch?

8 Ten litres of petrol cost £15. What is the cost of petrol per litre?

9 Terry and June are moving house.

They hire a van for three days at a cost of £105.

What is the daily rate for the hire of the van?

10 A Boeing 737 aircraft flew 4800 kilometres in six hours.

  a Calculate its rate of travel in kilometres per hour (km/h).

  b Travelling at the same rate, how far can the aircraft fly in five hours?

11 Three cans of fruit juice cost £1·50.

  a What is the cost of one can?

  b What is the cost of five cans?

12 Susie hires a carpet shampooer for three days.

It costs her £120.

  a Calculate the daily rate for hiring the shampooer.

  b How much would it cost her to hire it for four days?

Example 4

Nine chocolate yoghurts cost £5·40.

How much would six of them cost?

9 yoghurts cost £5·40.

$\Rightarrow$ 1 yoghurt costs £5·40 ÷ 9 = £0·60.

$\Rightarrow$ 6 yoghurts cost £0·60 × 6 = £3·60.

Exercise 14.1B

1   Sam pays £165 per month Council Tax.

How much Council Tax does he pay in total for the year?

2   A 20 pence coin weighs 5 grams.

What is the weight of £10 worth of 20 pence coins?

3   A tennis match lasted 3 hours and 30 minutes.

The score was 6-4, 6-3, 3-6, 5-7, 6-4.

a   Check that there were 50 games in total in the match.

b   Calculate the rate of play in minutes per game.

4   Marina drives her lorry 595 km in seven hours on Monday.

a   Calculate her speed in kilometres per hour.

She drives 440 km in five hours on Tuesday.

b   Calculate her speed on Tuesday in kilometres per hour.

c   On which day was her speed greater?

5   **a**   Rose received 75 US dollars in exchange for £50.

i   Calculate the rate of exchange in US dollars per £.

ii   How many US dollars would she get for £125?

b   Harry received 120 euro in exchange for £100.

i   Calculate the rate of exchange in euro per £.

ii   How many euro would he get for £240?

6   Five kerbstones of equal length laid end-to-end cover 6 metres.

How far would nine of the kerbstones cover?

7   Tony's electric fire uses 36 units of electricity if it is on for 4 hours.

How many units of electricity will it use if it is burning for 7 hours?

14.2 Best buys

Example 1

Which is the better buy?

The cost **per can** for the first offer is
£1·80 ÷ 3 = 180p ÷ 3 = 60p per can.

The cost **per can** for the second offer =
£2·80 ÷ 5 = 280p ÷ 5 = 56p per can.

So the 5-can offer is the better buy.

Note: You will often find it is better to change pounds to pence before calculating the cost of one item.

> **3 cans of
> SPRING FRUIT
> for £1·80**

> *Spring*
> *Fruit*

> **5 cans of
> SPRING FRUIT
> for £2·80**

Exercise 14.2A

1 **a** Calculate the cost of one battery with each offer.

   b Which is the better buy?

> **Ready Power
> AA Batteries
> *3 for £1·08***

> **Ready Power
> AA Batteries
> *8 for £2·64***

2 Pusti was looking for wood stain. She saw two offers:
- 6 litres for £84
- 4 litres for £60.

   a Calculate the cost of one litre with each offer.   **b** Which is the better buy?

3 **a** Calculate the cost of one egg
with each offer.

   b Which is the better buy?

> **Half Dozen**
> Free range eggs
> 6 for £1·80

> **Dozen**
> Free range eggs
> 12 for £3·24

4 **a** Calculate the cost per litre with each offer.

   b Which is the better buy?

SUPAPAINT EMULSION IN 2 HANDY SIZES	
4-litre tin	*6-litre tin*
£10	**£13·80**

Exercise 14.2B

1 Two electricity companies advertise their costs.

   a Calculate the cost per unit for each electricity company.

   b Which company offers the better deal?

> *POWERPLUS*
> *150 units £24*

> *MEGAPOWER*
> *250 units £41·25*

2 Sometimes it is cheaper buying in bulk.

   a Calculate the cost per sheet of plasterboard for each offer.

   b Which is the better deal?

> ***ACE Plasterboard***
> **30 sheets £225**
> **50 sheets £360**

3 The cake shop buys lots of boxes of small candles

    a Calculate the cost per candle for each size of box.

    b Which box is the better deal?

MINI-CANDLES
Box of 5 £1·40
Box of 9 £2·25

4 **a** Calculate the cost per gram of strawberries for each pack.

    b Which pack of strawberries is the better deal?

Strawberries
250-gram pack £3·00
400-gram pack £4·40

5 This sign was seen at the garden centre.

    Which offer is the better deal?

ROSE BUSHES
5 for £37·50
6 for £43·50

6 At the DIY store different packs of sandpaper are on sale.

    Which pack offers the best deal?

Sandpaper
10 sheets £6·40
15 sheets £9·30
25 sheets £15·75

14.3 Proportion

Example 1

Shona mixes blackcurrant cordial with lemonade to make 'blackcurrant fizz'.

She uses 1 part cordial with 5 parts lemonade.

How many glasses of lemonade should she mix with:

a 1 glass of cordial   **b** 4 glasses of cordial?

a 1 **part** cordial needs 5 **parts** lemonade,

   so, 1 **glass** of cordial needs 5 **glasses** of lemonade.

b 4 glasses of cordial need 5 × 4 = 20 glasses of lemonade.

Example 2

Charlie makes tomato soup.

He uses this recipe. It makes enough soup for 6 people.

How much of each ingredient would he need to make soup for:

a 3 people   **b** 9 people?

Tomato Soup   **Serves 6**
30 g butter
2 onions
800 g tomatoes
4 tablespoons pesto

a **3 is half of 6,** ... so for 3 portions, divide the 6-portion amounts by 2, giving:

15 g butter, 1 onion, 400 g tomatoes, 2 tbsp pesto.

b **9 is 3 times 3,** ... so for 9 portions, multiply the 3-portion amounts by 3, giving:

45 g butter, 3 onions, 1200 g tomatoes, 6 tbsp pesto.

Exercise 14.3A

1 Joe mixes sand and cement to make the base of a garage.

He mixes 1 part sand with 3 parts cement.

How many bags of cement should he use with:

a 1 bag of sand

b 6 bags of sand?

2 Sid makes dough by mixing 1 part butter with 2 parts plain flour.

How many grams of flour does he use with:

a 100 g of butter   **b** 200 g of butter   **c** 250 g of butter?

3 Ann mixes 1 part red paint with 5 parts yellow paint to make orange paint.

a The amount of red paint she uses is 2 litres.

How many litres of yellow paint does she need?

b How much yellow paint does she need if she uses 5 litres of red paint?

4 The recipe gives ingredients for an omelette for two people.

List the ingredients needed to make an omelette for:

a 1 person

b 3 people.

> *Mexican omelette*   **(Serves 2)**
> 6 eggs   2 tbsp olive oil
> 30 g butter   2 ripe tomatoes
> 150 g button mushrooms

5 **a** How many people does this recipe serve?

b List the ingredients needed to make the pudding for:

    i 2 people

    ii 8 people.

> *Bread and butter pudding*   **Serves 6 people**
> 12 thin slices of bread
> 120 g butter
> 180 g mixed dried fruit
> 150 g demerara sugar
> 600 ml milk
> 3 eggs

Exercise 14.3B

1 Georgie makes wallpaper paste by mixing 1 packet of powdered paste with 4 litres of water.

a How much water is needed for 3 packets?

b How many packets of powdered paste are needed for 8 litres of water?

2 Sunnyside Nursery has these rules for trips outside the nursery:

Sunnyside Nursery	
Age	**Teachers needed**
Under 3 years	1 teacher to 4 children
3 years and over	1 teacher to 6 children

  a Twelve children under 3 are going on a picnic. How many teachers are needed?

  b Thirty 3- and 4-year olds are going to the zoo. How many teachers are needed to take them?

  c Sixteen 2-year-olds and sixteen 3-year-olds are going to the pantomime. How many teachers are needed?

3 Here is what we need to make a plum crumble.

Plum Crumble	Serves 6
240 g plain flour	
150 g muscovado sugar	
90 g butter	
1 kg plums	

  a How many does it cater for?

  b If we make it for two people, how much sugar is needed?

  c We want to make it for eight people. How much butter is needed?

  d How much flour is needed for a 10-person crumble?

4 Making Mississippi mud pie ...

Mississippi Mud Pie	Serves 8
200 g plain chocolate	
120 g butter	
3 eggs	
140 ml single cream	
180 g sugar	
140 ml whipping cream	

  a How many people is the recipe for?

  b How much: **i** single cream

               ii butter is needed for a two-person pie?

  c How many eggs would you suggest are needed for the two-person pie?

  d How much: **i** chocolate

               ii sugar is needed for a six-person pie?

14.4 Scales, models and maps

Example 1

A model castle is built to a scale of 1 to 6.

(The real castle is six times bigger than the model castle.)

The model castle is 15 metres long.

What is the length of the real castle?

Length of real castle = 6 × 15 = 90 m.

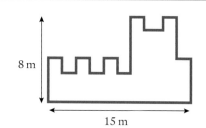

8 m

15 m

Example 2

The engine on a miniature railway is 5 metres long.

It is modelled on a real engine 20 metres long.

What scale was used to make the model engine?

5 metres represents 20 metres.

So 1 metre represents 20 ÷ 5 = 4 metres.

So the scale used is 1 m to 4 m or 1 to 4.

Exercise 14.4A

1 The height of the **model** castle in Example 1 above is 8 metres.
What is the height of the real castle?

2 Stephen makes a wheelbarrow for his young son. It is 80 cm long.
It is modelled on his own wheelbarrow which is 240 cm long.
What scale did Stephen use to make his son's wheelbarrow?
(Write your answer in the form '1 to ?'.)

3 Jean has a model yacht that is 60 cm long.
It is a model of an actual yacht that is 1800 cm long.
What scale was used to make the model yacht?

4 A map is drawn using a scale of 1 cm to 5 km.
The distances between the three places on
the map are shown.
What is the **actual** distance between:
  a the bridge and Barnton
  b Barnton and Bonsyde
  c Bonsyde and the bridge?

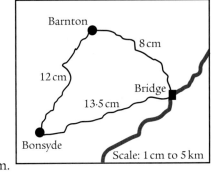

5 On a map, the distance between Dumfries and Dornoch is 15 cm.
The actual distance between the two towns is 270 miles.
How many miles does 1 cm on the map stand for?

6 A doll's pram is made using a scale of 1 to 3.
(The full-sized pram is three times bigger than the doll's pram.)
  a The length of the doll's pram is 45 cm.
    What is the length of the full-sized pram?
  b The doll's pram is 20 cm wide.
    How wide is the full-sized pram?
  c The height of the full-sized pram is 120 cm.
    What is the height of the doll's pram?

Exercise 14.4B

1 Class 3 are making a plan of their maths classroom.
On the plan the room is 50 cm long.
The actual classroom is 900 cm long.
  a What is the scale used on the plan?
  b On the plan the room is 45 cm wide.
    How wide is the actual room?

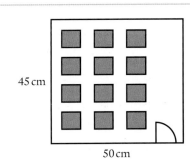

45 cm

50 cm

2 A toy manufacturer makes model vehicles.

The real vehicles are 50 times larger than the models.
(The scale is **1 to 50**.)

The table gives some of the models' dimensions in millimetres.

Draw a new table like the one below but giving the actual dimensions of the four vehicles in centimetres.

Model	Length (mm)	Width (mm)	Height (mm)
Sports car	90	40	25
Ford Focus	87	36	30
Ambulance	130	49	56
Double-decker bus	226	50	84

3 A toy fire engine is made using a scale of 1 to 7.

The toy is 100 cm long, 36 cm wide and 47 cm high.

Give your answers to **a**–**c** in: **i** centimetres **ii** metres.

  a How long is a real fire engine?

  b How wide is a real fire engine?

  c What is the height of a real fire engine?

4 The pitch for a table football game is modelled on Hampden Park.

The scale used is 1 to 50.

  a The length of the pitch for the table game is 220 cm.

    How long is the pitch at Hampden Park in metres?

  b The breadth of the game's pitch is 140 cm.

    How broad is the pitch at Hampden Park in metres?

Preparation for assessment

1 Sally fishes on Coylton Loch.

The cost of hiring a rowing boat is £7·50 per hour.

How much does it cost her to hire the boat for five hours?

2 Gary went on a diet.

He lost 21 pounds in 14 weeks.

At what rate did Gary lose weight in **pounds per week**?

3 Twenty maths books cost £300.

   a How much does one of the maths books cost?

   b How much do fifty of them cost?

4 Theresa sold 3 ounces of gold for £2400.

How much should she get for 10 ounces of gold?

5 A supermarket sells tins of Beanie coffee in three sizes as shown.

   a Calculate the number of grams you get for £1 for each size of tin.

   b Which tin is the best value for money?

   c Which tin is the worst buy?

Beanie Coffee

240 g	£3
300 g	£4
500 g	£5

6 A machine produces 18 000 metal washers in 5 hours.

Operating at the same speed, how many washers should it produce in 8 hours?

7 The Scott Monument in Edinburgh is approximately 60 metres high.

Cheryl makes models of the monument that are 30 cm tall.

What is the scale of the models?

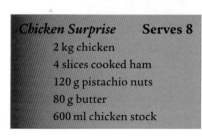

8 We have a recipe for chicken surprise.

   a For how many does this recipe cater?

   b How much chicken would you need if you were only making the dish for two people?

   c Write out the recipe you would need to serve six.

Chicken Surprise   Serves 8

2 kg chicken

4 slices cooked ham

120 g pistachio nuts

80 g butter

600 ml chicken stock

9 Remember packets of tea bags are on sale in the supermarket.

Super-brew comes in three sizes as shown.

Which of the packets is the 'best buy'?

Super-brew
180 tea bags
£3·42

Super-brew
100 tea bags
£2·10

Super-brew
250 tea bags
£5·00

15 Perimeter and area

⏸ Before we start...

Mike and Sara are getting their old carpet restored.
It will be cleaned and edged.
Cleaning costs £1·32 per m².
Edging costs 87p per metre.
The carpet measures 5 metres long by 6 metres wide.
How much will it cost to restore the carpet?

▶ What you need to know

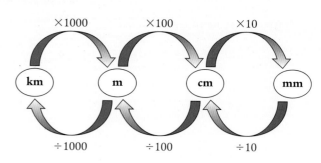

1 Change to metres: **a** 2 km   **b** 1300 cm   **c** 6000 mm.

2 Change to centimetres: **a** 450 mm   **b** 6 m.

3  A length of optic fibre is cut into three pieces.
These are 47 cm, 316 cm and 231 cm long.
What is the total length of the three pieces:
   a in centimetres
   b in metres?

4 This large square shape is made from four square metre tiles.
  a What is the shape's area?
    Write your answer like this: Area = ... m².
  b What is the shape's perimeter?
    Write your answer like this: Perimeter = ... m.

15.1 Perimeter

The pentominoes

Solomon Golomb is a mathematician who invented puzzles.

He used five 1 cm squares to make shapes called **pentominoes**.

He made 12 different shapes.

Each of these shapes has an area of 5 cm².

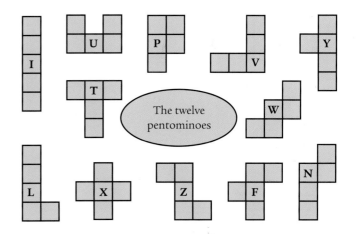

The twelve pentominoes

Example 1

Find the **perimeter** of the V pentomino.

Perimeter = 2 + 2 + 1 + 3 + 3 + 1 = 12 cm.

This is the total length of the red edges.

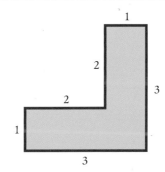

Exercise 15.1A

1 Here are shapes made from pairs of pentominoes.

Find the perimeter of each shape.

a P and V

b P and T

c N and U

d L and I

e I and L

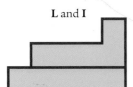

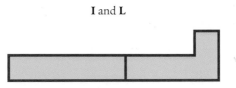

2 **Measure** the perimeters of the shapes in these diagrams.

Give your answer in a whole number of millimetres as accurately as you can.

Remember the perimeter is the total length of just the **outside** edge of the shape.

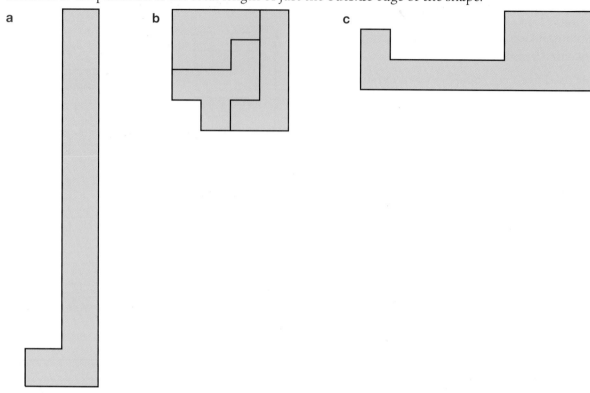

a b c

3 Write each perimeter from Question **2** in centimetres.

Exercise 15.1B

1 Barry is an archaeologist. He uses a magnetometer to trace the outlines of ancient buildings under the soil.

The diagrams below show some of these outlines.

Find the lengths labelled with question marks.

(All angles are right angles.)

a

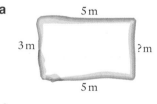

5 m

3 m

? m

5 m

b

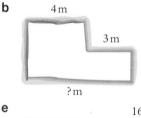

4 m

3 m

? m

c

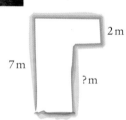

2 m

7 m

? m

d

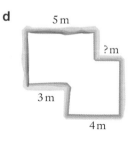

5 m

? m

3 m

4 m

e

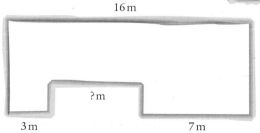

16 m

? m

3 m

7 m

2 Barry has to mark the outlines of the following houses on the surface using special tape. For each outline, calculate the total length of tape needed (i.e. calculate the perimeter).

a

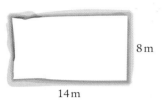

8 m
14 m

b

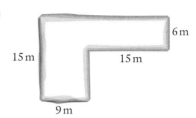

6 m
15 m   15 m
9 m

c

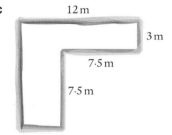

12 m
3 m
7·5 m
7·5 m

d

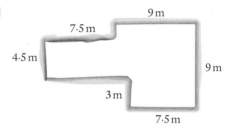

9 m
7·5 m
4·5 m
9 m
3 m
7·5 m

3 You may want to work in pairs or groups for this question.

Make a set of pentominoes using centimetre squares.

a For shapes using two pentominoes (like the shapes in Exercise 15.1A, Question **1**), how many different perimeters can you find?
What is the greatest?
What is the least?

b Investigate shapes made from three different pentominoes. What's the greatest and least perimeter you can find?

c Make up a poster showing what you found.

Keep your set of pentominoes for later in this chapter.

> **Joining rules**
> - No overlapping
> - No corner-to-corner
> - Square-to-square only

15.2 Estimating an area

How do you measure area?

Choose a square. It can be a square centimetre (cm²), a square metre (m²) or a square kilometre (km²).

Choose another shape to measure.

How many times does your chosen square fit into the shape you are measuring?

This answer tells you the area of the shape.

Always add cm² or m² or km² to the area to show the size of the square you used.

> How many squares fit?

Example 1

Here is a saw blade.

The grid shows square centimetres.

Estimate the area of the blade.

Estimate the area of the blade by counting squares.

Some squares are more than half full.

You should count these as 1 square.

Some squares are less than half full.

You should not count these squares.

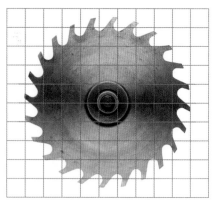

The area is roughly 44 cm².   Remember to add cm² after your estimate

 Why is it unlikely that everyone will give the same estimate?

Exercise 15.2A

1 Estimate the area of each of these.

a A cucumber slice
(the grid shows cm squares).

b A wasp's wing
(the grid shows mm squares).

c The lake inside this crater
(the grid shows km squares).

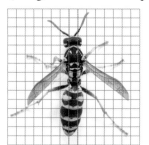
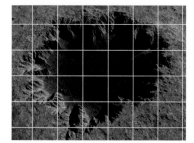

2 This is part of an indoor archery target.

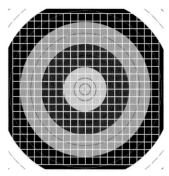

Keith and Sue are arguing about the size of the rings.

Keith says the red and gold rings together have a larger area than the blue ring.

Sue thinks the area of the blue ring is larger than the total area of the red and gold rings.

Use the grid of cm squares to find out who is right.

Record your results.

Exercise 15.2B

1 **a** Estimate the area of the small red X using the grid of mm squares.

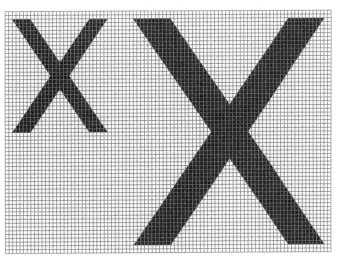

b Each edge on the large X is twice the length of the corresponding edge on the small X.

Will it have twice the area?

Use the grid of mm squares to find out.

2 Take any six pentominoes.

Arrange them so they enclose an empty space in the middle.

Akram's attempt is shown on the right.

Check that the area enclosed by Akram's shape is 21 cm^2.

Akram says this is the biggest empty space possible using these six pentominoes.

Show that he is wrong.

See if you can make a class record using **any** six pentominoes for enclosing the largest space in the middle.

Work in pairs or groups to make class records for seven pentominoes, eight pentominoes, and so on.

Make a wall chart showing the winning records and the names of the record holders.

Joining rules
• No overlapping
• No corner-to-corner
• Square-to-square only

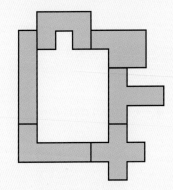

15.3 Area of rectangles

A formula for counting squares

The length of a football pitch is 100 m.

The breadth of the pitch is 75 m.

If it were marked off in metre squares we would get 100 rows with 75 squares.

$100 \times 75 = 7500 \text{ m}^2$

> **Area = Length × Breadth**

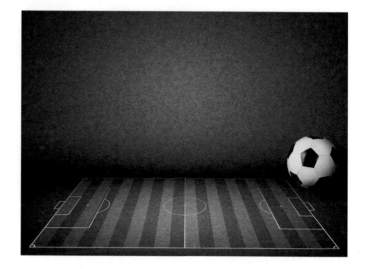

Example 1

a Find the area of the screen of this touch phone.

6·5 cm

10 cm

b Find the area of this square QR code.

2·5 cm

a Area = length × breadth
    = 10 × 6·5
    = 65 cm²

b Area = length × breadth
    = 2·5 × 2·5   For a square, length = breadth
    = 6·25 cm²

Exercise 15.3A

1 Find the area of ...   Remember to add the units: mm², cm², m² or km²

a A British passport.   **b** This garage door.   **c** The screen of this e-book reader.

9 cm

12 cm

4·5 m

3 m

7·6 cm

10 cm

d This warning sign.

e The area represented by one square on the grid of this map.

f This square computer chip.

1·2 m

0·3 m

25 km

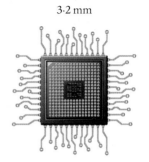

3·2 mm

2 Touch phone screens come in a variety of sizes.

	Length (cm)	Breadth (cm)
Type 1	9.5	5.4
Type 2	8.9	4.9
Type 3	8.2	5.5
Type 4	8.8	6.6

a Calculate the area of the screen of each type.

b List the screens in order of area, smallest to largest.

Exercise 15.3B

This is the ground floor plan of Richard and Audrey's new house.

1 Find the area of the:

a living room

b kitchen

c garage

d square vestibule

e hall (you will need to find the width)

f stairwell

g bathroom.

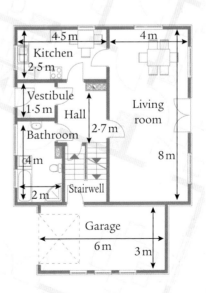

4·5 m   4 m

Kitchen

2·5 m

Vestibule

1·5 m   Hall

Living room

Bathroom   2·7 m

4 m

8 m

2 m   Stairwell

Garage

6 m   3 m

2 Put the seven areas on this ground floor plan in order, smallest first.

3 Carpet for the living room costs £13·50 per m².
How much will the carpet cost them?

4 The square tiles Richard and Audrey want for the kitchen floor have sides measuring 0·5 m.

    a How many tiles will they need?   **b** How much will they cost at £9 per tile?

5 Calculate the total area covered by the house and garage.

6 As a project, try to construct a plan of your own house.

Show all the room dimensions to the nearest 0·1 metre (to 1 d.p.).

You should ignore the thickness of the walls.

Make a poster showing your plan.

You might like to find the cost of reflooring some of the rooms. Do research on the internet to find out what it would cost.

15.4 Area and perimeter problems

Example 1

A 12-foot snooker table requires a 6·7 m by 4·9 m playing space.

How many snooker tables can fit into a 14 m by 13 m room?

Four tables will fit. The sketch shows how.

You need to show your calculations and reasons:

6·7 + 6·7 = 13·4 m, which is less than 14 m.

4·9 + 4·9 = 9·8 m, which is less than 13 m.

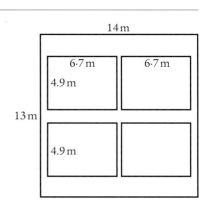

Exercise 15.4A

Here is the plan of a sports centre.

A youth club is planning to use the centre for some of their activities.

They need to know various measurements to plan ahead.

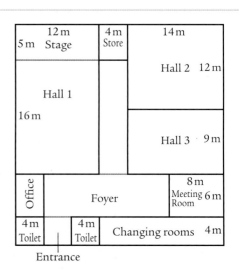

1 Calculate the area and perimeter of:

    a Hall 1   **b** Hall 2   **c** Hall 3.

2 Place the halls in increasing order of:

    a area   **b** perimeter.

3 A badminton court is 13·4 m by 6·1 m.

It needs 2 m of space at each end.

Is it possible to set up one of the halls for badminton?
Explain your answer.

4 Junior Judo requires an area of side 6 m for a square mat.

It also needs a 2 m safety border on all sides.

Which halls can be set up for Junior Judo?

5 Karate requires an 8 m square mat.

It needs the same size safety border around the mat as Judo.

Which halls are suitable for karate?

6 Each chair needs a 50 cm wide space.

a How many chairs fit around the walls of each of the halls?
Make sure you have thought about the corners.

b Explain how you can use the perimeter measurements from
Question **1** to work out the answer to part **a**.

Exercise 15.4B

Here is a table showing information about the minimum playing area required for various sizes of
snooker table.

Table size	8-foot	9-foot	10-foot	12-foot
Playing area	5·5 m × 4·3 m	5·8 m × 4·4 m	6·1 m × 4·6 m	6·7 m × 4·9 m

Use the plan of the sports centre from Exercise 15.4A to answer the following questions.

1 **a** What is the largest size of table that can be set up in the meeting room?
Give reasons for your answer.

b Is it possible to use the stage area for one or more of the tables?
Give reasons for your answer.

c Is the foyer large enough to set up some of the tables?
Explain your answer.

d Is it possible to set up a table in the corridor from the foyer to the store cupboard?
Explain your answer.

2 **a** How many 10-foot tables can be set up in Hall 1?
You should sketch a diagram and show your calculations.

b A 1-metre wide border is needed around the sides of the hall for chairs for the audience.
Does this alter the number of tables that can fit in the hall?

c How many more tables can be set up if they are 9-foot tables?
You will still need the audience area.

3 Most of the members of the Youth Club want to play volleyball.

 A volleyball court measures 18 m by 9 m (minimum).

In pairs or groups discuss possible structural alterations to the sports centre that would allow volley ball to be played.

Write a short report on your plans.

4 A snooker club buys the sports centre.

They need to set up exactly 15 tables.

They need at least two tables of each of the four sizes.

They are using Hall 1, Hall 2, Hall 3, the meeting room and the stage area for their tables.

Draw up a plan showing how they could set up their tables.

You might like to work with a partner or in a group.

Make a poster showing your plan.

Preparation for assessment

1 a This shape is made from 1 cm squares.

Find its perimeter and area.

b This shape is made from 5 cm squares.

Find its perimeter and area.

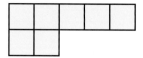

2 a Measure the length and breadth of this rectangle.

b Use your measurements to find: **i** the area **ii** the perimeter.

3 This lawn needs edging.

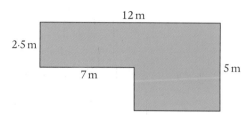

a What is the total length of edging needed?

b Edging costs £1·75 per metre.
How much will the edging cost?

4  Estimate the area of the surface of the coffee in the cup.
The grid shows centimetre squares.

5 Write down the formula for finding the area of a rectangle.

6 Find the area of ...

    a The solar panels on this roof.

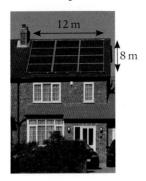

    b This ink stamp.

7 Remember Mike and Sara are getting their old carpet restored.

It will be cleaned and edged.

Cleaning costs £1·32 per m².

Edging costs 87p per metre.

The carpet measures 5 metres long by 6 metres wide.

How much will it cost to restore the carpet?

16 Volume and weight

⏸ Before we start...

Adam wants a private swimming pool in his garden.

Running costs depend on the volume of water.

He can get a pool that is 4 m wide by 7 m long by 1·5 m deep ... or one that is 3·5 m wide by 7 m long by 2 m deep.

a Which pool has the lower running costs?

b How many tonnes of water are needed to fill this pool?

▶ What you need to know

1 These two puzzles are made from small cubes.

   a How many small cubes are in the larger puzzle?

   b How many more cubes are there in the larger puzzle than in the smaller puzzle?

   c State the dimensions of:
     i the smaller puzzle   **ii** the larger puzzle.

2 This cube has a side of 1 cm. It is called a cubic centimetre (1 cm³).
How many cubic centimetres make up each of these shapes?

a 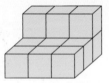   **b** 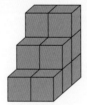   **c**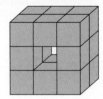

3 Put the three tins, red, blue and green, in order, heaviest first.

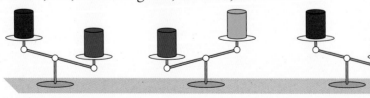

16.1 Volumes of cuboids

The **volume** of an object is a measure of how much space it occupies.

For a cuboid, we count how many cubes of a fixed size it would take to 'fill' it.

We would count **cubic millimetres (mm³)** if we want the volume of a small cuboid such as a sweet.

We would count **cubic centimetres (cm³)** if we want the volume of something like a shoe box.

We would count **cubic metres (m³)** if we want the volume of a room or a house.

Example 1

This cuboid is made of cubic centimetre cubes.

What is the volume of the cuboid?

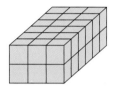

One layer of the cuboid is made of 6 rows of 3 cubes ... 6 × 3 = 18 cubes.

There are 2 layers ... 2 × 18 = 36 cubes.

The volume of the cuboid is 36 cubic centimetres.

Example 2

Find the volume of this shoe box.

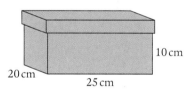

Imagine the bottom layer is
20 rows of 25 cubes of edge 1 cm ... 20 × 25 = 500 cubes.

There would be 10 such layers to fill the box ... 10 × 500 = 5000 cubes.

The volume of the shoe box is 5000 cm³.

Exercise 16.1A

1 These cuboids are made from cubic centimetre cubes.

For each cuboid, find:

  i the number of cubes in one layer   **ii** the number of layers   **iii** the volume.

  a 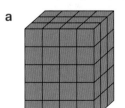   **b** 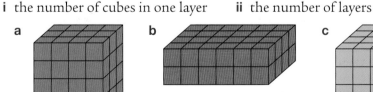   **c** 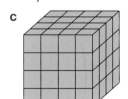   **d**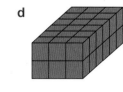

2 Fab Gems sells earrings in a small cuboid box.

Imagine the box is filled with cubes of edge 1 centimetre.

  a How many cubes will form a layer in the bottom of the box?

  b How many layers of cubes will fit in the box?

  c What is the volume of the box?

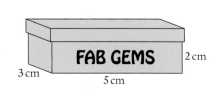

3 Calculate the volume of each box.

a

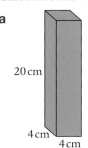

20 cm

4 cm
4 cm

b

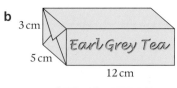

3 cm

5 cm

Earl Grey Tea

12 cm

c

2 cm

12 cm

Ginger Biscuits

20 cm

Exercise 16.1B

1 A juice manufacturer has the choice of two cartons in which to sell his juice.

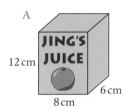

A

JING'S JUICE

12 cm

8 cm

6 cm

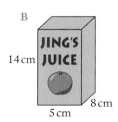

B

JING'S JUICE

14 cm

5 cm

8 cm

a Work out the volume of each carton.

b Which one should Jing pick if he wants to get as much juice in the carton as possible?

c Jing is going to charge a fixed price whichever carton he picks.
Which one should he pick to make the most profit?

2 Sugar **cubes** have an edge of 1 centimetre.
They are sold in the supermarket in boxes of two sizes.
Both boxes are cubes. One has a side of 10 cm. The other a side of 12 cm.

a How many sugar cubes does each box hold?

b The smaller box is to be sold for £2.
How many suger cubes do you get per £1?

c The larger box is to be sold at £3.
Which of the two boxes is the better deal?

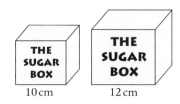

THE SUGAR BOX

10 cm

THE SUGAR BOX

12 cm

3 A company sold flour in cuboid boxes of length 6 cm, breadth 10 cm and height 15 cm.

a Calculate the volume of one box.

b James was asked to design a box that would hold double the amount.
He doubled the length, breadth and height of the box.
  i Calculate the volume of the new box.   **ii** Does the box meet the requirements?

c James then tried doubling only the length and the breadth.
He kept the height as it was.
Does the box meet the requirements?

d Can you find a box with suitable dimensions?

4 In a factory, boxes are filled to the top with cereal.

By the time the boxes arrive at the shops, the contents have settled.

When you open a new packet of cereal, there is always an empty space.

a What is the volume of the cereal box?

b What is the volume of the empty space?

c What fraction of the box is empty space?

16.2 A formula and units ⊞

Counting cubes can be difficult when the edges of an object are not whole numbers.

Instead of counting cubes, a formula is a helpful way to calculate volume.

> **Volume of a cuboid = Length × Breadth × Height**
>
> or
>
> $V = L \times B \times H$

Example 1

Find the volume of a box with length 12·5 mm, breadth 35·2 mm and height 30 mm.

$$\text{Volume} = \text{length} \times \text{breadth} \times \text{height}$$
$$= 12\cdot5 \times 35\cdot2 \times 30$$
$$= 13\,200 \text{ mm}^3$$

When numbers are big like in this volume, it can be helpful to swap between units.

Example 2

a How many cubic millimetres make one cubic centimetre?

b Express 13 200 mm³ in cubic centimetres.

a One centimetre = 10 mm.

So a cubic centimetre can be drawn as:

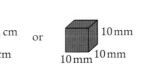

$$\text{Volume} = 1 \text{ cm} \times 1 \text{ cm} \times 1 \text{ cm}$$
$$= 10 \text{ mm} \times 10 \text{ mm} \times 10 \text{ mm}$$
$$= 1000 \text{ mm}^3.$$

So $1 \text{ cm}^3 = 1000 \text{ mm}^3$.

b So 13 200 mm³ = 13 200 ÷ 1000 = 13·2 cm³ ... roughly 13 cm³.

Exercise 16.2A

1 Use the formula to calculate the volume of each box.

a
5·0 mm
2·4 mm
6·5 mm

b
10·5 mm
10·0 mm
17·8 mm

c
7·5 mm
1·6 mm
1·4 mm

2 A private swimming pool is 400 cm wide, 700 cm long and 150 cm deep.

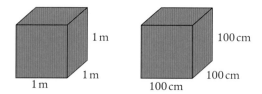

1 m
1 m
1 m

100 cm
100 cm
100 cm

  a Calculate its volume in cubic centimetres.

  b A cubic metre has an edge of length 1 metre.
  (1 metre = 100 cm.)

  Calculate how many cubic centimetres make one cubic metre.

  c How many cubic metres of water will fill the pool?

3 **a** How many millimetres are in a metre?

  b How many cubic millimetres are in a cubic metre?

4 The cost of heating a room depends on its volume.

  a Calculate the volume of each of these rooms.

Room	Length (m)	Breadth (m)	Height (m)
Living room	10·5	8·5	4·0
Dining room	8·6	7·5	4·0
Kitchen	6·6	5·5	3·0
Bedroom 1	6·5	5·0	2·8
Bedroom 2	6·0	4·5	2·8

  b What is the difference in volume between the living room and bedroom 1?

  c Which will cost more to heat, bedroom 1 or bedroom 2?

Exercise 16.2B

1 A publisher sells a trilogy (3 books) in a box.

The three books fit snuggly in the box.

Each book is 1·5 cm thick, 16 cm tall and 12 cm wide.

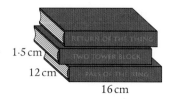
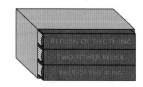

1·5 cm
12 cm
16 cm

  a What is the volume of one book?

  b What is the volume of the box?

2 Belinda wants a storage box.

She has the choice of three.

The 'Room Tidy': 35 cm tall by 45 cm wide and 60 cm long.

The 'Packem Up': 40 cm tall by 45 cm wide and 55 cm long.

The 'Litter Tray': 40 cm tall by 35 cm wide and 70 cm long.

   a Which box should Belinda buy if:

      i she wants it to take up the least space   **ii** she wants it to hold the most?

   b How much more can the 'Packem Up' hold than the 'Litter Tray'?

3 The supermarket sells loose tea in boxes which are 7·5 cm by 15 cm by 12 cm.

Each box costs £2.

   a What is the volume of one box?

   b If the whole box is filled with tea, how many cubic centimetres do you get for:

      i £1   **ii** 1p?

4 A shop sells coffee refills in two sizes.

The Jumbo Pack costs £8·50. It is 17 cm by 25 cm by 11 cm.

The Economy Pack costs £1·50. It is 9 cm by 12·5 cm by 6 cm.

   a For each pack, work out:

      i the volume   **ii** how much coffee you get for a penny.

   b Which is the better buy?

16.3 Capacity and litres

The volume that a container can hold is called its **capacity**.

Rather than working with big numbers we usually work in **litres** where:

     1 litre = 1000 cubic centimetres.

A cubic centimetre is also called a millilitre ... one thousandth of a litre.

Example 1

The inside of a fridge has a compartment that is 30 cm by 55 cm by 120 cm.

a What is the capacity of the fridge?

b How many litres is this?

a Capacity of fridge $= L \times B \times H$

                     $= 30 \times 55 \times 120$

                     $= 198\,000 \text{ cm}^3$.

b $198\,000 \text{ cm}^3 = 198\,000 \text{ ml}$

                    $= 198\,000 \div 1000$

                    $= 198 \text{ litres}$.

Exercise 16.3A

1 Calculate the capacity of each of these containers.

Give your answer in:
 i cm^3 **ii** ml **iii** litres.

	Container	Length (cm)	Breadth (cm)	Height (cm)
a	Water tank	180	90	25
b	Trough	120	60	20
c	Cupboard	20	55	110
d	Plastic container	20	25	10
e	Juice carton	8	8	6

2 An old unit of volume is the gallon.

A container holding 15 cm by 15 cm by 20 cm will hold about a gallon.

a Roughly how many cm^3 make a gallon?

b How many litres is this?

3 **a** How many cubic centimetres are in a cubic metre?

b How many litres are in a cubic metre?

c Copy and complete this number machine.

4 A drinks maker sells his juice in cartons.

The label says that there is 1 litre of juice.

The carton is a cuboid with dimensions 7 cm by 8 cm by 18 cm.

a What is the capacity of the container?

b How much empty space will there be in the carton when it contains a litre of juice?

Tangy

1 litre

Exercise 16.3B

1 A room is 10 m by 3 m by 15 m.

a Write these dimensions in centimetres.

b Find the volume of the room in:
 i cm^3 **ii** litres **iii** m^3.

2 A pack of cards forms a cuboid, which is 60 mm by 80 mm by 15 mm.

a What is the volume of the cuboid in cubic millimetres?

b The pack contains 55 cards.

What is the volume of one card?

3 Mandy feeds her pigs from a cuboid trough.

The dimensions of the trough are 60 cm by 70 cm by 14 cm.

  a What is the capacity of the trough in litres?

  b Mandy fills the trough from a cuboid bowl of kitchen scraps.

    It is 16 cm by 18 cm by 20 cm.

    What is the bowl's capacity in litres?

4 After flooding, Neil's basement had to have the water pumped out.

The basement is a cuboid. Its floor is 1200 cm by 2000 cm.

The water filled it to a depth of 150 cm.

  a What volume of water was in the basement?
    Give your answer in litres.

  b The water pump took out 2 litres every second.
    How long did it take to empty the basement?

16.4 Volume and weight connection

If you work with water, the connection between weight and volume is easy.

The scientists who invented the metric system decided:

1 cubic millimetre of water ... weighs ... 1 milligram (mg).

1 cubic centimetre of water ... weighs ... 1 gram (g).

1 litre of water ... weighs ... 1 kilogram (kg).

1 cubic metre of water ... weighs ... 1000 kg = 1 tonne (t).

Example 1

A tank has dimensions 120 cm by 60 cm by 80 cm.

It is filled with water.

What weight of water is in the tank?

$$\text{Volume} = 120 \times 60 \times 80$$
$$= 576\,000 \text{ cm}^3$$
$$= 576 \text{ litres.}$$

Weight of water in the tank is 576 kg.

Exercise 16.4A

1 How many grams are in:

    a 4000 milligrams

    b 2 kilograms

    c 3 tonnes?

2 A chef has a 1 kg bag of flour.

    He used 720 g to make a cake.

    What weight of flour is left?

3 Five calves were getting loaded on to a truck for market.

    Their weights were 252 kg, 300 kg, 285 kg, 310 kg and 285 kg.

    What is the total weight in tonnes and kilograms?

4 State the weight of water with a volume of:

    a 500 ml

    b 50 ml

    c 2 litres.

5 A bottle contains 250 ml of water.

    Mabel pours 100 ml into a glass.

    a What volume of water remains in the bottle?

    b What weight of water remains in the bottle?

6 A plastic bottle weighs 15 grams.

    It has 250 ml of water poured into it.

    What does the bottle of water weigh?

7 A tank is 60 cm by 50 cm by 100 cm.

    It weighs 2 kg when empty.

    What is its weight when it is filled to capacity with water?

Exercise 16.4B

1 **a** Write 29 450 g in kilograms.

    b Write 30 kg 5 g in grams only.

    c What is the difference between 29 450 g and 30 kg 5 g?

2 A load of 2·5 tonnes of sand is split into five equal piles.

    a How much does each pile weigh in tonnes?

    b How much does each pile weigh in kilograms?

3 At the garden centre Mac is putting six sacks on a lorry.

He wants them arranged so that the load is placed evenly.

Arrange the six sacks into two sets of equal weight.

4 Jahida and her four friends are packing their rucksacks in the car for a hiking holiday.

The weight of each rucksack is:

Adam	18 kg 240 g
Bahira	15·5 kg
Cathy	17 540 g
Latif	15 kg 15 g
Jahida	16·7 kg

a Who had the lightest rucksack?

b What was the difference in weight between the rucksacks of :
   i Bahira and Jahida
   ii Adam and Latif
   iii Cathy and Latif?

c What is the total weight of the rucksacks?

Preparation for assessment

1 Calculate the volume of butter in the pack.

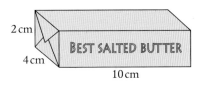

2 How many cubic centimetres make a millilitre?

3 Chloe bought a piece of vanilla cake and a piece of chocolate cake in the shape of cuboids.

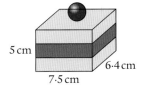

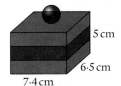

a Which cake has the bigger volume?   b How much bigger is it?

4 A car was described as having a 1200 cc engine. This means 1200 cubic centimetres.
   How many litres is this?

5 The space inside a fridge is a cuboid with dimensions 55 cm by 90 cm by 35 cm.
   a Calculate the capacity of the fridge in cubic centimetres.
   b What is this in litres?

6 A container is 30·0 cm by 15·5 cm by 20·4 cm.
   a Calculate its capacity.
   b What weight of water can it hold?

7 Helen has six glasses of water.
   The volumes in the glasses are 25 ml, 22 ml, 19 ml, 24 ml, 32 ml, and 20 ml.
   She wants to pour three glasses into one jug and the other three into another jug.
   She wants the two jugs to hold the same amount.
   a What volume of water should be in each jug?
   b Show how the split can occur.
   c What weight of water will be in each jug?

8 Remember Adam who wants a private swimming pool in his garden.

   Running costs depend on the volume of water.

   He can get a pool that is 4 m wide by 7 m long by 1·5 m deep ... or one that is 3·5 m wide by 7 m long by 2 m deep.

   a Which pool has the lower running costs?
   b How many tonnes of water are needed to fill this pool?

⏸ Before we start...

The number of visitors to Edinburgh Castle in 2009 was 1 190 000.

In 2010, the percentage increase in the number of visitors was 11%.

a How many visitors to the castle were there in 2010?

b Round your answer to the nearest 1000.

▶ What you need to know

1 Calculate:

  a 4827 + 146   **b** 6524 − 286   **c** 236 × 5   **d** 3854 × 8

  e 732 ÷ 3   **f** 4722 ÷ 6   **g** 57 ÷ 2   **h** 411 ÷ 5.

2 Calculate:

  a 47 × 10   **b** 268 × 100   **c** 67·2 × 10   **d** 3·74 × 100

  e 0·73 × 10   **f** 430 ÷ 10   **g** 81 ÷ 10   **h** 325 ÷ 100

  i 7·6 ÷ 10   **j** 3 ÷ 100   **k** 13 ÷ 100   **l** 0·16 ÷ 100.

3 David bought a shirt for £24·99.
   His friend Neil bought a shirt for £6·50 less.
   How much did Neil pay for his shirt?

4 The school gardening club bought six hand forks at £3·50 each.
   It bought two garden spades at £17·25 each.
   How much did the club spend in total?

5 Last year Sabeena ran 1500 metres in 5 minutes 14 seconds.
   This year she ran the distance 23 seconds quicker.
   What is Sabeena's time this year?

17.1 Fraction values

We often need to find fractions of quantities.

First we will look at fractions that have a numerator (top number) of 1, for example, $\frac{1}{2}, \frac{1}{3}, \frac{1}{10}$.

Example 1

Calculate $\frac{1}{4} \times 56$.

$\frac{1}{4} \times 56 = 56 \div 4 = 14$.

Example 2

Calculate $\frac{1}{5}$ of 100.

'of' means '×'

$\frac{1}{5}$ of $100 = 100 \times \frac{1}{5}$

$= 100 \div 5 = 20$.

 You can use your calculator to find fractions.

Example 3

Calculate $\frac{1}{12}$ of 672.

On your calculator, enter: 6 7 2 ÷ 1 2 =

The calculator reads 56.

So $\frac{1}{12}$ of $672 = 56$.

Exercise 17.1A

You should not use a calculator for questions 1–6.

1 Find:

   a $\frac{1}{2}$ of 20   **b** $\frac{1}{3}$ of 84   **c** $\frac{1}{4}$ of 92   **d** $\frac{1}{5}$ of 160

   e $\frac{1}{4}$ of 156   **f** $\frac{1}{10}$ of 70   **g** $\frac{1}{3}$ of 555   **h** $\frac{1}{10}$ of 800.

2 Calculate:

   a $\frac{1}{2} \times 3170$ **b** $\frac{1}{3} \times 4521$ **c** $\frac{1}{4} \times 3360$ **d** $\frac{1}{10} \times 2770$.

3 Work out:

   a $\frac{1}{3} \times 1.8$ **b** $\frac{1}{5} \times 2.5$ **c** $\frac{1}{2} \times 17.6$ **d** $\frac{1}{10} \times 8.4$

   e $\frac{1}{4} \times 18.24$ **f** $\frac{1}{3} \times 26.16$ **g** $\frac{1}{10} \times 45$ **h** $\frac{1}{5} \times 37.95$.

4 Last season Van Persil scored 27 goals.

This season he has scored one-third of last year's total.

How many goals has he scored this season?

5 One-tenth of the 190 students in Third Year are left-handed.

How many students in Third Year are left-handed?

6 Sally made 35 jars of redcurrant jam.

She gave away one-fifth of them to relatives and friends.

a How many jars did she give away?

b How many jars of the jam did she keep?

 You may use a calculator for questions 7 − 9.

7 Calculate:

a $\frac{1}{12}$ of 828   **b** $\frac{1}{15}$ of 555   **c** $\frac{1}{18}$ of 522   **d** $\frac{1}{25}$ of 1200

e $\frac{1}{26}$ × 1456   **f** $\frac{1}{52}$ × 8632   **g** $\frac{1}{40}$ × 6960   **h** $\frac{1}{24}$ × 2256.

8 Find:

a $\frac{1}{12}$ of £46·08   **b** $\frac{1}{15}$ of £56·10   **c** $\frac{1}{24}$ of £191·52   **d** $\frac{1}{11}$ of £389·51.

9 Tommy works part-time in the local garage.

Last year he earned £7488.

a How much did he earn per month?

b How much did he earn per week?

 Example 4

Find $\frac{1}{25}$ of £972·48. Round your answer to the nearest penny.

Using a calculator, $\frac{1}{25}$ of £972·48 = 972·48 ÷ 25 = £38·8992.

So, to the nearest penny, $\frac{1}{25}$ of £972·48 = £38·90.

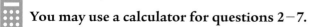 **Exercise 17.1B**

1 Calculate:

a $\frac{1}{6}$ of 564   **b** $\frac{1}{8}$ of 376   **c** $\frac{1}{7}$ of 329   **d** $\frac{1}{9}$ of 756.

 You may use a calculator for questions 2−7.

2 Find:

a $\frac{1}{7}$ of £3584   **b** $\frac{1}{8}$ of £17·60   **c** $\frac{1}{9}$ of £26·01   **d** $\frac{1}{6}$ of £40·74.

3 Work out:

a $\frac{1}{15}$ of 435

b $\frac{1}{11}$ of 957

c $\frac{1}{12}$ of 444

d $\frac{1}{25}$ of 170

e $\frac{1}{52}$ of 1222

f $\frac{1}{80}$ of 6112

g $\frac{1}{13}$ of 625·3

h $\frac{1}{24}$ of 66.

4 Work out each fraction. Round your answers to the nearest penny.

a $\frac{1}{12}$ of £38·45

b $\frac{1}{15}$ of £54·40

c $\frac{1}{18}$ of £76·34

d $\frac{1}{36}$ of £94·58

5 Council workers planted 1425 new trees.

A severe storm destroyed $\frac{1}{15}$ of them.

a How many trees were destroyed?

b How many trees survived the storm?

6 Last month at the Hilltop Health Centre, 3872 patients made an appointment to see their doctor.

$\frac{1}{11}$ of these patients failed to keep their appointment.

a How many appointments were not kept?

b How many appointments were kept?

c Over the same month 1014 appointments were made to see one of the nurses.

$\frac{1}{13}$ of these appointments were not kept.

How many patients failed to keep their appointment with the nurse?

7 Edinburgh Airport had 8280 passengers flying out one day.

$\frac{1}{18}$ of them flew to the Canary Islands.

$\frac{1}{24}$ flew to the Channel Islands.

a Did more passengers fly to the Canary Islands or the Channel Islands?

b How many more flew there?

17.2 Percentages

A common way of writing a fraction is as a percentage.

Per cent means **out of a hundred**.

The sign **%** is often used for **per cent**.

So 6% means 6 out of a 100. This is written as $\frac{6}{100}$.

12% means 12 out of a 100 ... the same as $\frac{12}{100}$.

Percentages can be written as decimal fractions or common fractions.

$$1\% = \frac{1}{100} = 1 \div 100 = 0{\cdot}01.$$

To find 1%, divide by 100.

Example 1

Find 1% of £92.

$$92 \div 100 = 0{\cdot}92.$$
So   1% of £92 = £0·92.

Example 2

Find 6% of £74.

$$1\% \text{ of } 74 = 74 \div 100 = 0{\cdot}74.$$
So 6% of £74 $= 0{\cdot}74 \times 6 = £4{\cdot}44.$

Some percentages are easier to calculate if you treat them as common fractions.

It is worthwhile learning the ones in this list:

50 is half of 100	...	$50\% = \frac{1}{2}$
$33\frac{1}{3}$ is a third of 100	...	$33\frac{1}{2}\% = \frac{1}{3}$
25 is a quarter of 100	...	$25\% = \frac{1}{4}$
20 is a fifth of a 100	...	$20\% = \frac{1}{5}$
10 is a tenth of a 100	...	$10\% = \frac{1}{10}$
1 is a hundredth of 100	...	$1\% = \frac{1}{100}$

Example 3

Find: **a** 10% of £120   **b** $33\frac{1}{3}\%$ of £162   **c** 25% of £92.

a   10% of 120 $= \frac{1}{10}$ of 120
$= 120 \div 10$
$= 12.$
So 10% of £120 = £12.

b $33\frac{1}{3}\%$ of 162 $= \frac{1}{3}$ of 162
$= 162 \div 3$
$= 54.$
So $33\frac{1}{3}\%$ of £162 = £54.

c   25% of 92 $= \frac{1}{4}$ of 92
$= 92 \div 4$
$= 23.$
So 25% of £92 = £23.

Example 4

Last year Martina earned £9420.

This year she has been given a 3% increase in her salary.

a Calculate the increase in her salary.

b What is her new salary?

a 1% of £9420 = £94·20.   Remember: To find 1% divide by 100.

So 3% of £9420 = 94·20 × 3 = £282·60.

The increase is £282·60

b Martina's new salary is £9420 + £282·60 = £9702·60.

Using a calculator to find percentages

Example 5

Find 35% of 842.

35% of 842 = 842 ÷ 100 × 35

On your calculator, key in:

... to find that 35% of 842 = 294·7.

Exercise 17.2A

You should not use a calculator for questions 1–14.

1 Write each percentage as a fraction out of 100:

  a 50%   **b** 20%   **c** 9%   **d** 37%.

2 Write each fraction as a percentage:

  a $\frac{36}{100}$ **b** $\frac{73}{100}$ **c** $\frac{9}{100}$ **d** $\frac{13}{100}$.

3 Write each percentage as a fraction in its simplest form:

  a 50%   **b** 20%   **c** 60%   **d** 1%.

4 Write each percentage as a decimal. For example, 40% = 40 ÷ 100 = 0·4.

  a 30%   **b** 45%   **c** 60%   **d** 5%

5 Write each decimal as a percentage. For example, 0·8 = 0·8 × 100% = 80%.

  a 0·1   **b** 0·4   **c** 0·6   **d** 0·35

6 Find 1% of:

a 23   b 7   c 475

d 851   e 4·6   f 2·8.

7 Calculate these by finding 1% first:

a 2% of 60   b 4% of 78   c 5% of 120   d 3% of 360.

8 Calculate:

a 10% of 54   b 10% of 98   c 50% of 90   d 50% of 360

e $33\frac{1}{3}$% of £15   f $33\frac{1}{3}$% of £75   g 25% of £144   h 25% of £1008

i 20% of 30 m   j 20% of 875 m   k 10% of 170 m   l 10% of 68 m.

9 Last year Ethan paid £85 to be a member of the local sports club.

This year the price has gone up by 10%.

How much will Ethan have to pay this year?

10 Jon's car insurance was £465.

It is increased by 25%. What is it now?

11 The flight from Glasgow to Tenerife took five hours.

The return flight took 20% longer.

a How much longer did the return flight take?

b How long, in hours, was the return flight?

12 Gary bought a painting at an auction for £225.

He sold it six months later and made a $33\frac{1}{3}$% profit.

How much did he sell it for?

13 Last year Gianni drove 9500 miles.

This year the miles he has driven increased by 20%.

a How many more miles has he driven this year?

b How many miles has he driven this year?

14 The Great Shoe Sale! 20% off all Ladies' Shoes.

Karen bought two pairs in the sale.

Before the sale they cost £39·95 and £49·95.

a How much did Karen pay for each pair?

b How much did Karen save altogether?

20% OFF

You may use a calculator for questions 15 and 16.

15 Find:

    a 35% of 620   **b** 45% of 825   **c** 18% of 500   **d** 61% of 300

    e 72% of 380   **f** 13% of 250   **g** 94% of 950   **h** 88% of 196.

16 The attendance at last year's Highland Games was 7850.

    This year's attendance was up 26%.

    What was this year's attendance?

Exercise 17.2B

 You should not use a calculator for questions 1−5.

1 Find 1% of:

    a £48   **b** £120   **c** £6·70   **d** £32·60.

2 Calculate these by finding 1% first:

    a 2% of 48 m   **b** 3% of 60 m   **c** 5% of 240 m   **d** 6% of 54 m.

3 Find the value of:

    a 50% of 416 g   **b** 25% of 932 g   **c** $33\frac{1}{3}$% of 87 g   **d** 20% of 175 g.

4 Over the season, Sheila's best time for the 400 metres improved by 10%.

    At the start of the season her best time was 58·0 seconds.

    a By how many seconds did Sheila's time improve?

    b What is her best time now?

5 There are 1278 students at Rosebank Academy.

    50% of the students go home for lunch.

    $33\frac{1}{3}$% have a school lunch.

    The rest bring a packed lunch.

    How many students:

    a go home   **b** have a school lunch   **c** bring a packed lunch?

 You may use a calculator for questions 6−10.

6 There are 1450 students at Greenhill Academy.

    52% of them are girls.

    a How many girls are there?

    b What percentage of the students are boys?

    c How many boys are there?

7 The population of the Isle of Arran was 5045 in 2001.

Over the next ten years its population decreased by 8%.

What was Arran's population in 2011?

8 In the football season which started in 2010, the total number of goals scored in the Scottish Premier League was 584.

In the 2011 season there was a percentage increase of 3% in the number of goals scored.

a How many goals were scored in the 2011 season?

b The goals in the 2012 season were 9·8% down on the 2011 figure.

How many goals were scored in the 2012 season?

Give your answers to **a** and **b** rounded to the nearest goal.

9 48 648 spectators attended the Cup Final.

48% of them were City supporters, 46% were United supporters and the rest supported neither team.

a How many of the spectators supported:
  i City   **ii** United?

b How many supported neither team?

Give your answers to **a** and **b** to the nearest whole number.

10 At the last election, four candidates stood for election in Tichfield.

The total votes cast was 27 875.

The table shows the percentage of votes each candidate received.

Candidate	Spence	Bloomer	Cringle	Belch
Share of the vote (%)	20	28	36	16

a Calculate the number of votes each candidate received, to the nearest whole number.

b **i** Who won the election?   **ii** By how many votes did they win?

Preparation for assessment

 You should not use a calculator for questions 1−4.

1 Find:

a $\frac{1}{2}$ of 38   **b** $\frac{1}{3}$ of 93   **c** $\frac{1}{5}$ of 125   **d** $\frac{1}{10}$ of 370   **e** $\frac{1}{8}$ of 3728.

2 Calculate:

a $\frac{1}{2} \times 3\cdot46$ **b** $\frac{1}{4} \times 5\cdot72$ **c** $\frac{1}{6} \times 49\cdot8$ **d** $\frac{1}{7} \times 36\cdot75$ **e** $\frac{1}{3} \times 82\cdot62$.

3 Find the value of:

   a   1% of £900   b   50% of £850   c $33\frac{1}{3}$% of £792   d   20% of £42·80.

4 Calculate:

   a   1% of 350   b   2% of 350   c   5% of 780   d   6% of 520.

 You may use a calculator for questions 5 − 10.

5 Find:

   a   28% of 560   b   62% of 854   c   36% of 61·25   d   82% of 47·50.

6 Maria has sent a total of 684 texts on her mobile phone.

   a $\frac{1}{2}$ of the texts were sent to her best friend Lisa.

      How many texts were sent to Lisa?

   b $\frac{1}{3}$ of them were sent to her sister Gemma.

      How many texts were sent to Gemma?

7 In Third Year of Grove High School there are 240 students.

   $\frac{1}{4}$ of the students have brown eyes, $\frac{1}{3}$ have blue eyes, $\frac{1}{5}$ have green eyes and the rest have hazel eyes.

   How many students have:

   a brown eyes   b   blue eyes   c   green eyes   d   hazel eyes?

8 At the flood damage sale, Janelle buys a dog basket usually costing £19·96.

   a   How much cheaper is the basket in the sale?

   b   She also buys a dog kennel, which usually costs £53·20.

      How much cheaper is it in the sale?

> **FLOOD DAMAGE SALE**
> 25% off all prices

 9 Remember the visitors to Edinburgh Castle in 2009. The number was 1 190 000.

   In 2010, the percentage increase in the number of visitors was 11%.

   a   How many visitors to the castle were there in 2010?

   b   Round your answer to nearest 1000.

18 Scale drawings

 ## Before we start...

Nicola is buying her first house.

She has been offered some secondhand furniture for the living room.

She has this rough sketch of the living room.

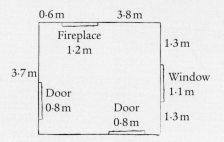

The measurements of the furniture are:

- yellow sofa 1·7 m by 0·9 m
- TV cabinet 1·5 m by 0·4 m
- wall cabinet 0·9 m by 0·4 m.
- red sofa 1·7 m by 0·9 m
- table 1·1 m by 0·5 m

How can Nicola check if the furniture will fit nicely into her room?

 ## What you need to know

1 Kirsty wanted to know the height of each standing stone.

First she measured their heights in the picture.

Measure the height of each stone in the picture.

Every centimetre on the picture stands for a metre. How high are the actual stones?

2 Draw lines that measure:

    a 4 cm   b 2·4 cm   c 32 mm   d 57 mm.

3 Convert these distances into metres:

    a 300 cm   b 742 cm   c 5·071 km   d 0·64 km.

4 Express each distance in centimetres:

    a 5 m   **b** 3·8 m   **c** 2·77 m   **d** 9·57 m.

5 Change these distances into kilometres:

    a 6000 m   **b** 9100 m   **c** 4750 m   **d** 7381 m   **e** 480 m.

6 Measure each angle marked in Figure 1.

Figure 1

7 Draw an angle of size: **a** 40°   **b** 167°.

8 Make an accurate drawing of the triangle in Figure 2.

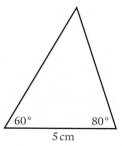

Figure 2

9 a In the map (Figure 3), which village is north of Innerleithen?

   b Which town is east of Innerleithen?

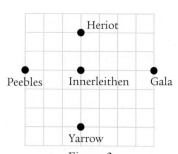

Figure 3

18.1 The mariner's compass

Mariners describe direction using north, south, east and west.

Halfway between north and east lies north-east.

Similarly, we describe directions south-east, south-west and north-west.

These eight directions are called the **cardinal points** of the compass.

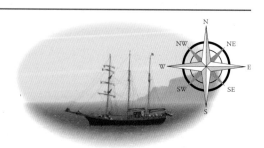

Example 1

Describe the direction travelled going from:

a Perth to Kirriemuir

b Kirriemuir to Perth.

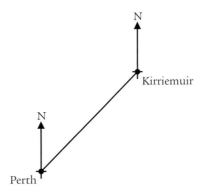

a Kirriemuir lies north-east of Perth.

b Perth lies south-west of Kirriemuir.

Exercise 18.1A

1

This plan shows the position of different breeds of cattle at a farm show.

a Which breed lies south-east of the White Parks?

b Which breed lies north-west of the Gloucesters?

c Which breed lies north-east of the Charolais?

d Which breeds lie south-west of the Holsteins?

e Which breeds lie north-east of the Aberdeen-Angus cattle?

f Archie is looking at the Galloways.
Describe a journey that will take him to see the Welsh Blacks.

2 **a** I flew north. What direction will I need to follow to get back to where I started?

b I travelled SE. In which direction will I need to travel to get back to where I started?

c I walked NE. What direction should I follow to retrace my steps?

Exercise 18.1B

1 The castle provides a map for visitors.

a What lies NE of the castle?

b What lies SW of the car park?

c I walked from the car park to the information point.
I then walked to the gardens.
Next, I visited the castle.
I then went to the gift shop.
Finally, I returned to the car park.
What directions did I follow?

d I walked N to a named point. I then headed SE to the pond. Where did I start?

e I walked N, SW, SE, NE, N and NW, ending up in the car park.
I always changed direction at a named point. Where did I start?

2 **a** Robert is in a microlite heading for Ben Dhu.

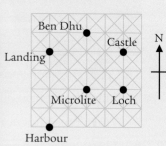

  i He looks clockwise to see over the loch.
  How many degrees has he turned his
  head through?

  ii How many degrees are there between
  N and E?

  iii How many degrees would he have turned
  if he had turned anticlockwise to look
  back at the harbour?

  iv How many degrees are there between N and SW?

b **i** Robert changes direction and heads for the landing.
He turns clockwise to look at the castle.
How many degrees has he turned through?

  ii How many degrees are there between NW and NE?

  iii How many degrees are there between NW and SE?

3 Always measuring clockwise, how many degrees are there between north and:

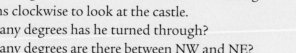

  a NE **b** E **c** SE **d** S **e** SW **f** W **g** NW?

18.2 Bearings

Ships use bearings to navigate safely at sea where there may be no features to help them.

A **bearing** is an angle, measured **clockwise** from **north**.

All bearings are given as **3 figures**.

86° becomes 086°.

5° becomes 005°.

Directions can be given more precisely using bearings than with the mariner's compass

Example 1

Describe the bearing of each ship from the harbour.

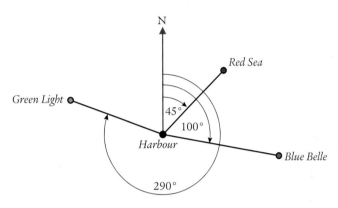

The *Red Sea* is on a bearing of 045°.

The *Blue Belle* is on a bearing of 100°.

The *Green Light* is on a bearing of 290°.

Exercise 18.2A

1   Six aircraft are spotted from an airport's control tower, T.

Each is recognised by its flight number.

Measure the bearing of each plane from the tower.

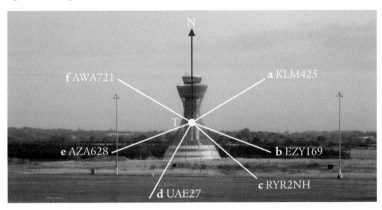

2 Six other planes are talking with the tower the next day.

Draw another diagram like the one in Question **1**, to show their bearings from the tower.

Remember to measure the angles clockwise from north.

a 040°   b 120°

c 155°   d 215°

e 330°   f 290°

Exercise 18.2B

1 Write down the bearings from north to:

a   south   b   east

c   south-east   d   north-west.

2 If you were walking on these bearings, what compass direction would you be following?

a 045°   b 270°

c 225°   d 000°

3 Measure the bearings of each leg in this boat's course.

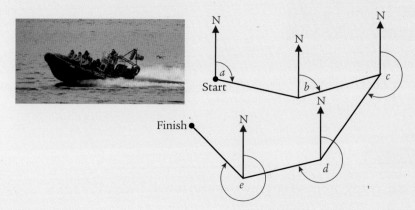

18.3 Scales

Here is a **scale drawing** of a caravan.

The scale on the diagram tells us **1 cm represents 1 metre**.

Each metre of the actual caravan is represented by 1 cm in the drawing.

The caravan is 5 metres long, so the scale drawing is 5 cm long.

The door in the drawing is 2·3 cm high. So the door in the caravan is 2·3 m tall.

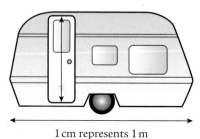

1 cm represents 1 m

Example 1

1 cm represents 3 m

2·5 cm

10 cm

This photo can be taken as a scale drawing of a ferry.

The scale is given as 1 cm represents 3 metres.

The length of the ferry in the photo is 10 cm.

The height of the ferry's bridge from the sea measures 2·5 cm.

a What is the actual length of the ferry?

b How high above the sea is the actual bridge?

c The top of the funnel is 6 m above the sea. What height will this be on the photo?

a 1 cm represents 3 m.
So 10 cm represents $10 \times 3 = 30$ m.
Actual length of ferry is 30 metres.

b 2·5 cm represents $2·5 \times 3 = 7·5$ m.
Actual bridge is 7·5 metres above the sea.

c 6 m in real life will be $6 \div 3 = 2$ cm.
The top of the funnel is 2 cm above the sea on the photo.

Exercise 18.3A

1 For each diagram:

   i measure the marked lengths   **ii** use the scales to calculate the actual lengths.

1 cm = 12 m

1 cm = 900 km

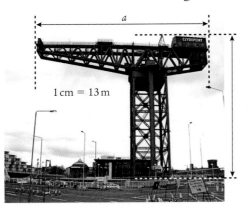

a

1 cm = 13 m

b

c

d

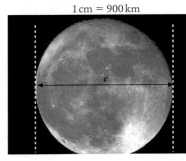

e

2 The map shows the route of an orienteering course.

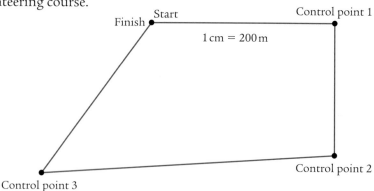

a Measure the length of each part of the course on the map.

b Calculate the actual distances between the control points.

c What is the difference in actual distance between the longest and shortest part?

3 Copy and complete the table.

	Scale of map	Actual distance	Distance on map
a	1 cm represents 200 m		4 cm
b	1 cm represents 300 m		2 cm
c	1 cm represents 500 m		4 cm
d	1 cm represents 2 km		5 cm
e	1 cm represents 3 km	18 km	
f	1 cm represents 50 km	600 km	
g	1 cm represents 100 km	450 km	

Exercise 18.3B

1 The ship, *Seafarer*, sailed from port to Seal Rock.

It then sailed on to Kittiwake Cliff before returning to port.

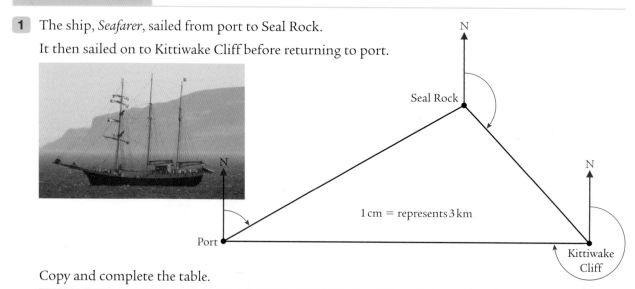

Copy and complete the table.

	Bearing followed	Distance on map	Actual distance
Port to Seal Rock			
Seal Rock to Kittiwake Cliff			
Kittiwake Cliff to port			

2 A garden centre has areas set aside for flowers and plants, a kitchen garden, and garden accessories. It also has a café. The plan below is drawn to scale.

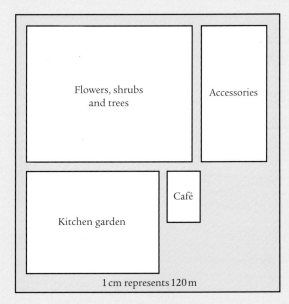

1 cm represents 120 m

a Measure the lengths and breadths of the four areas of the garden centre.

b Work out the real size of these areas.

c The owners plan to put in a car parking area that is 360 metres by 240 metres.
   i What size will this be in the scale drawing?
   ii Is there room on the site?

18.4 Scale drawings

The bigger the scale drawing is, the more accurate any measurement will be that is taken from it. Making a rough sketch will help you plan your steps.

Example 1

A stone mason needs to repair a large wall on a hill. To plan his job, he wants a scale drawing. First he makes a rough sketch showing the various sizes.

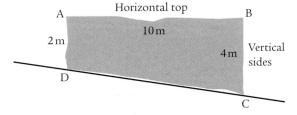

a Make an accurate scale drawing using 1 cm to represent 2 metres.

b How long is the wall along the ground, CD?

a 10 m in real life becomes 5 cm on the drawing.

2 m in real life becomes 1 cm on the drawing.

4 m in real life becomes 2 cm on the drawing.

- Draw a horizontal line 5 cm long to represent AB, the top of the wall.
- At a right angle to AB, draw a 1 cm line to represent the side AD.
- Again at a right angle to AB, draw a line 2 cm long to represent BC.
- Join D to C to complete the drawing.
- Add sizes and a scale: '1 cm represents 2 m'.

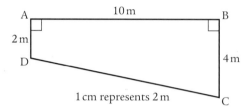

b Measuring DC, you will find it to be 5·2 cm long.

Actual length of wall CD is 5·2 × 2 = 10·4 metres.

Exercise 18.4A

1 Here are some stone mason's sketches.

Make accurate drawings of each, using the scales given.

a

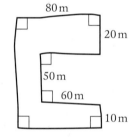

1 cm represents 10 metres

b

1 cm represents 10 metres

c

1 cm represents 2·5 metres

d

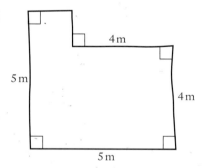

1 cm represents 50 cm

Example 2

The *Queen of the Sea* sailed on a bearing of 040° for 60 km.

Make an accurate scale drawing of the ship's route.

Use 1 cm to represent 10 km.

- Make a quick sketch.

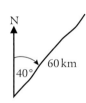

- Draw a north line.   You require this to measure the bearing
  accurately (... from north, clockwise).
- Measure an angle of 40° from north, clockwise.
- Using the scale, 6 cm represents 60 km.
  Draw a 6 cm line in the right direction.
- Include the scale on the drawing.

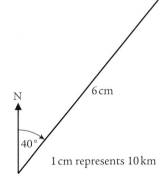

Exercise 18.4B

1 Make accurate scale drawings of each of the following journeys using the given scales.

    a A microlite flew 15 km on a bearing of 070°. Let 1 cm represent 3 km.

    b The ferry sailed 12 km on a bearing of 130°. Let 1 cm represent 2 km.

    c A hill walker travelled 16 km on a bearing of 240°. Let 1 cm represent 4 km.

2 These journeys have two stages.

  i Make an accurate scale drawing of each journey using the given scales.

  ii Find the distance, marked in red, between the start and finish of each journey.

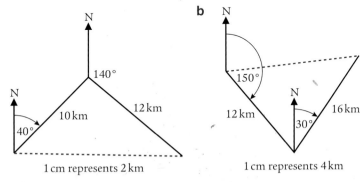

3 A plane flew on a bearing of 040° for 120 km.

  It then flew for a further 100 km on a bearing of 170°.

    a Using 1 cm to represent 20 km, make an accurate scale drawing of the plane's route.

    b Measure the distance between the starting and finishing points.

    c What is the actual distance between start and finish?

4 Two trawlers left a port.

One sailed on a bearing of 160° for 70 km.

The other sailed on a bearing of 240° for 100 km.

a Using 1 cm to represent 10 km, make an accurate drawing showing both routes on the one diagram.

b How far apart are the two trawlers in real life?

18.5 Giving directions

Maps can be used to give directions.

Example 1

Ian is in the travel agent.

How does he get to the café?

He turns right out of the travel agent on to Station Road.

He goes past Wee Lane and turns right into Fountainhall Drive.

After passing Blyth Street, he turns right into High Street.

The café is on his left.

```
┌─────────────────────────────────────────┐
│            Station Road                  │
│  ●┌──────────┐  ┌──┐  ┌──────────┐       │
│   │Travel     │ │Wee│ │          │       │
│   │agent      │ │Lane│ │         │       │
│   └──────────┘ └──┘  └──────────┘        │
│            Blyth Street                  │
│  ┌──────────────────────────────┐        │
│N │                              │ F       │
│o │                              │ o       │
│r └──────────────────────────────┘ u       │
│t          High Street            n        │
│h  ┌──────┐ ┌──┐ ┌──────────┐    t         │
│R  │      │ │Sk│ │     Café ●│    a         │
│o  │      │ │ip│ │          │    i         │
│a  └──────┘ │pe│ └──────────┘    n         │
│d           │rs│                 h         │
│          McLaren Road           a         │
│  ┌──────┐ ┌──┐ ┌──────────┐     l         │
│  │      │ │Ba│ │          │     l         │
│  │      │ │ke│ │          │     D         │
│  └──────┘ │rs│ └──────────┘     r         │
│          Lane                             │
│            School Road                    │
└─────────────────────────────────────────┘
```

This map of Greenby village will be used in both Exercise 18.5A and 18.5B.

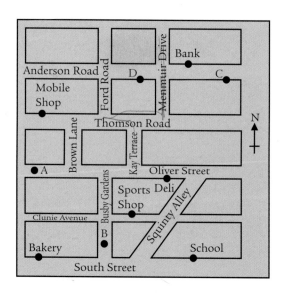

Exercise 18.5A

1 Sadiq is standing at A facing east.

   a What road is he on?

   b What road is first on his left?

   c What road is first on his right?

   d What road is second on his right?

2 Charlotte is at B cycling north.

   a What road is she on?

   b What is the first road on her right?

   c She takes the first road on her right and stops.

     i What shop is on her left?

     ii What road is next on her left?

3 June is walking north on Kay Terrace. She turns right then first left.

   a What road is she on now?

   b What road is next on her right?

Exercise 18.5B

1 David is standing at C looking west.

   a He takes the first road on his left.
     Then he turns right and first left.
     Write down the roads he has walked along.

   b Back at C, David now takes the second road on his left.
     Then he turns left and first right.
     What road is he now on?

2 Give directions for Jaz to get from D to:

   a the mobile shop   **b** the deli

   c the sports shop   **d** the bakery.

3 Give directions to get from:

   a the bakery to the bank

   b the school to the mobile shop

   c the bank to the sports shop.

18.6 Enlargements and reductions

These are two photos of the same swan and cygnets.

2 cm

3 cm

4 cm

6 cm

The second picture is an **enlargement** of the first.

It is twice the height and twice the width.

Each length in the second photo is double the size of that in the first.

The first picture is a **reduction** of the second.

Each length in the first photo is half the size of that in the second photo.

In the first photo, the swan is 1·5 cm tall. In the second, it is 2 × 1·5 = 3 cm tall.

Example 1

Enlarge this shape so that each side is doubled in size.

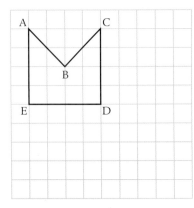

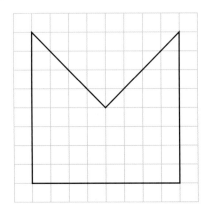

The shape is enlarged by counting squares and doubling all the lengths.

To walk from A to B we can go 2 squares right and 2 squares down.

We double this by going 4 squares right and 4 squares down.

Double the horizontal and vertical lines — the sloping ones should take care of themselves.

Exercise 18.6A

1 On squared paper: **i** copy each shape **ii** draw a shape with sides twice as long.

a

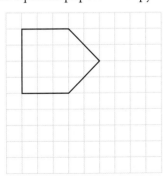

b

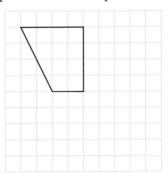

c

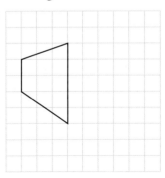

Exercise 18.6B

1 On squared paper: **i** copy each shape **ii** draw a shape with sides half the size.

a

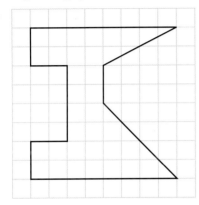

b

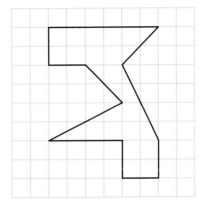

2 On squared paper: **i** copy each shape **ii** draw a shape with sides twice the size.

a

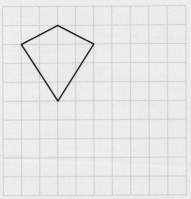

b

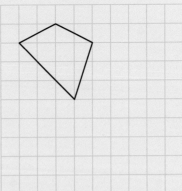

Preparation for assessment

1 On squared paper draw an enlargement of this shape.
Make each of its sides twice as long.

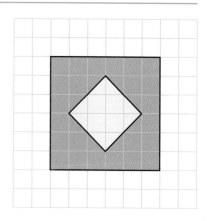

2 This map shows the positions of a fire station, a police station and the site of a new chemical factory.

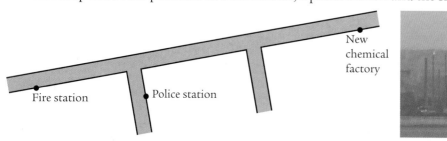

a Measure the direct distance between the police station and the fire station on the map.

b The scale of the map is 1 cm to 200 m.
What is the actual distance between the fire station and the police station?

c For safety reasons, the owners want the chemical factory to be within 2 km of a fire station.
Is the new chemical factory close enough to the fire station?

3 John and Norma are doing an orienteering course.
They must visit each of the control points in order. Here is a map of the course.

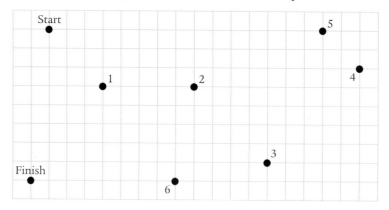

a Copy and complete this list of directions travelled as they complete the course.
South-east, east, _____, _____, _____, _____, _____.

b Copy and complete this list of the bearings followed.
135°, 090°, _____, _____, _____, _____, _____.

4   Remember Nicola is buying her first house.

She has been offered some secondhand furniture for the living room.

She has this rough sketch of the living room.

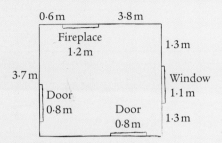

The measurements of the furniture are:
- yellow sofa 1·7 m by 0·9 m
- red sofa 1·7 m by 0·9 m
- TV cabinet 1·5 m by 0·4 m
- table 1·1 m by 0·5 m
- wall cabinet 0·9 m by 0·4 m.

How can Nicola check if the furniture will fit nicely into her room?

19 Patterns and formulae

❚❚ Before we start...

Mikey makes wristbands and belts.
One of his designs uses squares
and rectangles of leather.

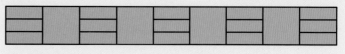

You can see from the picture that for 4 squares he needs 15 rectangles.

a How many rectangles does he need for 5 squares?

b How many rectangles does he need for 6 squares?

c Write a formula for working out the number of rectangles when you know the
number of squares.

d Use your formula to work out how many rectangles are needed for 61 squares.

▶ What you need to know

1 Draw the next two designs in each pattern.

a

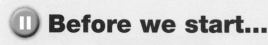

   1   2   3   ?   ?

                                 4   5

b

   1   2   3   4   5

2 Here are three patterns and three rules.

Match each pattern with a rule.

Patterns					
A	1	5	9	13	...
B	3	5	7	9	...
C	12	10	8	6	...

Rules	
1	Take away 2
2	Add 4
3	Add 2

3 Some patterns are formed by adding a fixed amount each time.

Continue each of the three patterns for two more terms:

  a 11, 10, 9, ..., ...   **b** 2, 5, 8, ..., ...   **c** 2, 7, 12, ..., ...

4 Copy and complete this table:

Number of pounds	1	2	3	4
Number of 20p coins	5	10		

19.1 Patterns

Simple **addition and subtraction rules** can be used to create patterns.

In this exercise all of the patterns are like this.

Example 1

For each pattern: **i** find the rule which turns each term into the next

                          ii continue the pattern for two more terms.

a 2, 9, 16, 23, ? , ?   **b** 48, 45, 42, 39, ? , ?

a In the pattern, the numbers are getting bigger.

   A quick check ... $9 - 2 = 7$, $16 - 9 = 7$, $23 - 16 = 7$

   ... to get the next term, we are adding 7 to the previous term.

   i The rule is $+7$.

   ii $23 + 7 = 30$ and $30 + 7 = 37$.

      So the next two terms are 30 and 37.

b In the pattern, the numbers are getting smaller.

   A similar check ... $48 - 45 = 3$, $45 - 42 = 3$, $42 - 39 = 3$

   ... to get the next term, we are subtracting 3 from the previous term.

   i The rule is -3

   ii $39 - 3 = 36$ and $36 - 3 = 33$.

      So the next two terms are 36 and 33.

Exercise 19.1A

1 In each case, use the given rule to continue the pattern for three more terms.

a $+4$ → | 1 | 5 | 9 | ? | ? | ? |

b -2 → | 15 | 13 | 11 | ? | ? | ? |

c $+6$ → | 2 | 8 | 14 | ? | ? | ? |

d -7 → | 55 | 48 | 41 | ? | ? | ? |

2 Match each pattern to a rule.

Patterns	Rules
A: 3, 4, 5, 6, ...	1: Add 3
B: 14, 11, 8, 5, ...	2: Add 1
C: 14, 17, 20, 23, ...	3: Take away 2
D: 22, 20, 18, 16, ...	4: Subtract 3

3 Malcolm works at the garden centre, laying slabs. As he builds paths he forms patterns.

For each pattern: **i** draw the next picture **ii** find how many slabs will be in the next two pictures.

a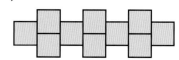

        4 slabs   7 slabs   10 slabs

b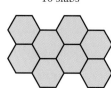

        4 slabs   6 slabs   8 slabs

c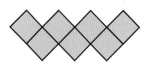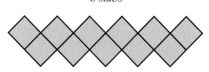

        3 slabs   7 slabs   11 slabs

4 For each of these patterns, find:
   i the rule for getting the next term   **ii** the next term.

     a 2, 8, 14, 20, ?   **b** 23, 20, 17, 14, ?   **c** 13, 16, 19, 22, ?

Simple **multiplication and division rules** can also be used to create patterns.

In this exercise all of the patterns are of this type.

Example 2

For each pattern: **i** find the rule for turning each term into the next **ii** find the next two terms.

a 3, 6, 12, 24, ?, ?   **b** 243, 81, 27, 9, ?, ?

a The numbers are increasing ... but not by the same amount.
  i Testing a few terms ... we can see that we are multiplying by 2 each time.
  ii So ... $24 \times 2 = 48$ and $48 \times 2 = 96$.
    So the next two terms are 48 and 96.

b The numbers are decreasing ... but not by the same amount.
  i Testing a few terms ... we can see that we are dividing by 3 each time.
  ii So ... $9 \div 3 = 3$ and $3 \div 3 = 1$.
    So the next two terms are 3 and 1.

Exercise 19.1B

1 Use the rules to continue each pattern for three more terms.

  a The rule is 'multiply by 3'. The pattern starts 2, 6, 18, ...

  b The rule is 'divide by 2'. The pattern starts 160, 80, 40, ...

  c The rule is 'multiply by 2'. The pattern starts 10, 20, 40, ...

  d The rule is 'divide by 3'. The pattern starts 486, 162, 54, ...

2 For each of these patterns find: **i** the rule for finding the next term **ii** the next two terms.

    a   6, 12, 24, 48, ...   **b**   324, 108, 36, ...   **c**   2, 8, 32, ...   **d**   96, 48, 24, ...

3 Mary had two towers made from toy bricks.

Tower A had 28 bricks. Tower B had 8 bricks.

Mary took three bricks from tower A.

She placed two of them on tower B and started a new tower, C, with the one brick left.

She repeated this time and time again until tower A and tower B were the same size.

    a   Write down the number pattern formed as:
- **i**   tower A shrinks
- **ii**   tower B grows.

    b   **i**   How many bricks will towers A and B have when they are the same size?
- **ii**   How high will tower C be when this happens?

4 On the first day of Christmas my true love gave to me ... a partridge in a pear tree!
         (1 present).

On the second day ... 2 turtle doves and a partridge in a pear tree
         (3 presents ... so 4 presents in total over the two days).

On the third day ... 3 French hens, 2 turtle doves and a partridge in a pear tree
         (6 presents ... so 10 presents in total over the three days).

On the fourth day ... 4 colly birds, 3 French hens, 2 turtle doves and a partridge in a pear tree
         (10 presents ... so 20 presents in total over the four days).

    a   How many presents will I get **on** the 12th day of Christmas?

    b   How many presents will I get in total?

19.2   Counting numbers

The **counting numbers** 1, 2, 3, 4, 5, ... form the simplest of patterns.

We can make up rules to turn the counting numbers into other patterns.

Example 1

a   What pattern do you get when you add 4 to the counting numbers?

b   What pattern do you get when you double the counting numbers?

a   The red counting numbers become the blue pattern by adding 4 to each.

Counting numbers (N)	1	2	3	4	5	...
Pattern ($N + 4$)	5	6	7	8	9	...

So you get: 5, 6, 7, 8, 9, ...

b The red counting numbers become the blue pattern by multiplying each by 2

Counting numbers (N)	1	2	3	4	5	...
Pattern (2 × N)	2	4	6	8	10	...

So you get: 2, 4, 6, 8, 10, ...

Exercise 19.2A

1 Work out the new pattern in each case.

a

Counting numbers	1	2	3	4	...	Rule
Pattern (N + 5)					...	+5

b

Counting numbers	1	2	3	4	...	Rule
Pattern (3 × N)				.	...	×3

c

Counting numbers	1	2	3	4	...	Rule
Pattern (N + 2)					...	+2

d

Counting numbers	1	2	3	4	...	Rule
Pattern (5 × N)					...	×5

2 Find the missing rule in each case.

a

Counting numbers	1	2	3	4	...	Rule
Pattern (rule?)	8	9	10	11	...	

b

Counting numbers	1	2	3	4	...	Rule
Pattern (rule?)	4	8	12	16	...	

c

Counting numbers	1	2	3	4	...	Rule
Pattern (rule?)	6	12	18	24	...	

d

Counting numbers	1	2	3	4	...	Rule
Pattern (rule?)	0	1	2	3	...	

3 Find the rule which changes:

a 1, 2, 3, 4, ... into 2, 3, 4, 5, ...

b 1, 2, 3, 4, ... into 10, 11, 12, 13, ...

c 1, 2, 3, 4, ... into 7, 14, 21, 28, ...

d 1, 2, 3, 4, ... into 10, 20, 30, 40, ...

4 There are 12 biscuits in a packet.

a Copy and complete the table.

Packets (N)	1	2	3	4
Biscuits (12 × N)	12			

b There will be 85 people at a tea party, each wanting a biscuit.

How many packets are needed?

5 Peter was born in 2000, just after the Olympic games were held in Sydney.

Knowing how many Olympic games he had lived through, he could work out his age.

a Copy and complete the table.

b How many sets of games will Peter have lived through when he is 32?

Olympic games (N)	1	2	3	4
Age (N × 4)	4			

c What age will Peter be when has watched the 5th games that occurred after he was born.

Example 2

Some patterns have **two-step** rules.

Look at how this fence is built from posts and crossbars.

No. of posts	1	2	3	4
No. of crossbars	0	4	8	12

The red row becomes the blue row in two steps

No. of posts	1	2	3	4
Step 1: ×4	4	8	12	16
Step 2: −4	0	4	8	12

To find the number of crossbars needed ... multiply the number of posts by 4 then take away 4.

Exercise 19.2B

1 Copy and complete each table.

a
Counting numbers	1	2	3	4	5
Step 1: ×2					
Step 2: +4					

b
Counting numbers	1	2	3	4	5
Step 1: ×9					
Step 2: −5					

c
Counting numbers	1	2	3	4	5
Step 1: ×3					
Step 2: −1					

d
Counting numbers	1	2	3	4	5
Step 1: ×10					
Step 2: −2					

2 For each rule:

  i use the two steps on the first five counting numbers: 1, 2, 3, 4, 5

  ii continue the new pattern for two more terms.

    a Multiply by 4 then subtract 2.   **b** Multiply by 5 then subtract 5.

    c Multiply by 8 then subtract 3.   **d** Multiply by 5 then add 1.

3 These three rules have been used on the counting numbers.

Match each two-step rule with one of the new patterns.

Rule A

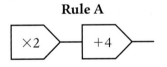

Pattern 1
4, 9, 14, 19, 24, ...

Rule B

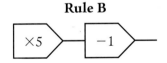

Pattern 2
6, 8, 10, 12, 14, ...

Rule C

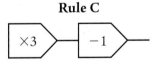

Pattern 3
2, 5, 8, 11, 14, ...

4 The Carrick-a-Rede rope bridge is in Northern Ireland.

The knots making each side form a pattern.

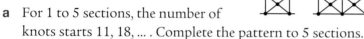

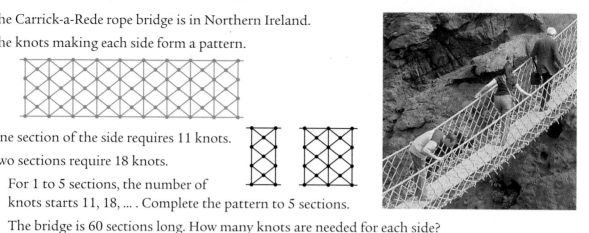

One section of the side requires 11 knots.

Two sections require 18 knots.

a For 1 to 5 sections, the number of knots starts 11, 18, ... Complete the pattern to 5 sections.

b The bridge is 60 sections long. How many knots are needed for each side?

5 It costs £10 to hire a cement mixer and then a further £5 for every day before it is returned.

a Copy and complete the table to show the costs.

Days	1	2	3	4	5
Step 1: ×5					
Step 2: +10					

> **For Hire**
> Only £10 and £5 for each day

b It cost £75 for Jamal to hire the mixer. For how many days did he take it?

19.3 Finding the rule

Find a two-step rule for changing the counting numbers 1, 2, 3, 4, 5, ... into the pattern 5, 7, 9, 11, 13, ...

Step 1:   We see that the pattern goes up in twos ... like the '2 times' table!

   5 (+2) 7 (+2) 9 (+2) 11 (+2) 13 (+2) ...

   This suggests that the first step is 'multiply by 2'

Step 2:   Compare the '2 times' table with the target pattern.

Counting numbers	1	2	3	4	5	...
×2	2	4	6	8	10	...
Target pattern	5	7	9	11	13	...

   It is easy to see that step 2 must be 'add 3'.

   So the rule is: multiply by 2 then add 3.

Counting numbers —— ×2 >—— +3 >—— target pattern

Exercise 19.3A

1 For each part:
  i copy and complete the table
  ii write the two-step rule for turning the counting numbers into the target pattern.

a

Counting numbers	1	2	3	4	5	...
Step 1: ×?						...
Step 2: +? pattern	5	9	13	17	21	...

b

Counting numbers	1	2	3	4	5	...
Step 1: ×?						...
Step 2: +? pattern	5	8	11	14	17	...

2 Start with 1, 2, 3, 4, 5, ...

Find the two-step — ⟨×?⟩ — ⟨+?⟩ — rule that makes the pattern:

  a 3, 5, 7, 9, 11, ...

  b 6, 10, 14, 18, 22, ...

  c 6, 11, 16, 21, 26, ...

  d 10, 18, 26, 32, 38, ...

  e 2, 5, 8, 11, 14, ...

  f 6, 13, 20, 27, 34, ...

(Hint: for parts **e** and **f**, the second step is a subtraction.)

3 Jeanie was taking a taxi. After each mile she noted the charge showing on the 'clock'.

Distance (miles)	1	2	3	4	5
Charge (£)	3·50	5·50	7·50	9·50	11·50

  a Find the rule for getting the charge from the distance.
  (Hint: it's a two-step rule.)

  b Jeanie's journey is 12 miles long. How much will it cost her?

Exercise 19.3B

1 a Find a two-step rule for turning the picture number into the number of matches.

Picture 1 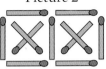   Picture 2   Picture 3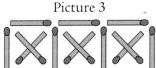

6 matches   11 matches   16 matches

  b How many matches make up the 10th picture?

2 a Hiring a hedge trimmer for 1 day costs £13.

For 2 days it costs £18.

For 3 days it costs £23, and for 4 days £28.

How do we find the cost when we know the number of days? (Hint: it's a two-step rule.)

  b How much would it cost to hire the trimmer for 7 days?

3 Margery laid a path of octagonal slabs.

Each time she added a slab, she counted the number of sides that made the perimeter of the path.

  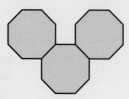 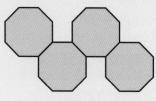

| 1 slab | 2 slabs | 3 slabs | 4 slabs |
| perimeter 8 | perimeter 14 | perimeter 20 | perimeter 26 |

a Write a two-step rule for finding the perimeter from the number of slabs.

b Can Margery make a path with a perimeter of: **i** 44 **ii** 60?

c What two-step rule for finding the perimeter from the number of slabs would work if you used:

i hexagons (6 sides) **ii** pentagons(5 sides) **iii** heptagons(7 sides).

19.4 Formulae

Example 1

Each white line in the middle of a road is 3 metres long.

The gaps between them are 1 metre long.

Write down a **formula** that lets us calculate the road length when we know the number of lines.

Make a table of the first few simple cases: 1 line, 2 lines, etc.

Number of white lines	1	2	3	4
Length of road (m)	3	7	11	15

From this we can work out a two-step rule for turning the number of lines into road length.

... 'multiply by 4 then subtract 1'.

This can be expressed as a **formula** for road length:

road length = (white lines) × 4 − 1.

Exercise 19.4A

1 Festival flags are strung evenly between posts.

The distance between the posts is 4 metres.

a Copy and complete the table.

(If there is only 1 post, no flags can be strung so the distance covered is 0 metres.)

Number of posts	1	2	3	4	5	6	7	...	12
Step 1	4	8	12	16				...	
Distance covered (m)	0	4	8	12	16			...	

b Write down a formula for finding the **distance covered** if you know the **number of posts**.

2 In the restaurant, tables can be rearranged to suit different groups.

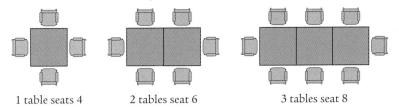

1 table seats 4   2 tables seat 6   3 tables seat 8

a Find a two-step rule for finding the **number of seats** when you know the **number of tables**.

b Write down a formula for the **number of seats**.

c How many tables and chairs will be needed for a party of: **i** 22 people   **ii** 24 people?

3 A builder charges £45 for a 1-hour job.

He charges £60 for a 2-hour job and £75 for a 3-hour job.

There is a simple two-step rule for finding the cost of the job when you know how long it will take.

a What is the two-step rule?

b Write down a formula for the **cost** when you know the **number of hours**.

c What is the cost of a 10-hour job?

Exercise 19.4B

1 The side of a bridge is made from girders.

 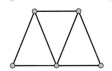 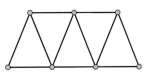

1 section   2 sections   3 sections
3 girders   7 girders   11 girders

a Find a formula for working out the number of girders when you know the number of sections.

b The bridge in the picture has 8 sections. How many girders makes up each side?

2 These designs are stitched on to a belt.

There is a rule connecting the number of stitches used and the number of the design.

Design 1   Design 2   Design 3   Design 4
8 stitches   13 stitches   18 stitches   23 stitches

a Find a formula for working out the number of stitches needed when you know the design number.

b How many stitches will be needed for design 12?

c Which design needs 53 stitches?

d A shop asked for designs with 38, 42 and 58 stitches.

Which of these orders is not possible?

3 Design 1 is the basis of a stitching pattern for a border.

It can be continued in different ways.
Here are two possible ways:

Design 1

i

ii

a Find a formula for each of these patterns.

b How many stitches would design 10 of each pattern have?

c Which one of the patterns could have 203 stitches?

Preparation for assessment

1 Here is a formula for changing **kilometres** into **miles**:

number of miles = 5 × number of kilometres ÷ 8

Anka is on holiday in France.

She is travelling to Le Mans.

A road sign tells her that the distance to Le Mans is 48 **kilometres.**

How many **miles** does she still have to travel?

2 Tommy uses old CDs to scare the birds from his cabbages.

He hangs the CDs on string from a wooden bar, as shown.

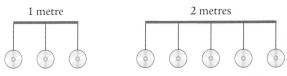 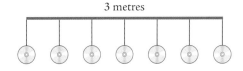

1 metre   2 metres   3 metres

a Copy and complete this table.

Length of wooden bar (m)	1	2	3	4	5	6
Step 1:						
Number of CDs	3	5				

b Write down the rule for finding the **number of CDs** when you know the **length of the wooden bar**.

3 Colin is a plumber.

If he is called out to a job on a weekday he charges a fee of £25 plus £20 for every hour that the job lasts.

This gives a formula:

weekday cost in £ = 25 + (20 × hours).

a Calculate the cost of a job lasting 3 hours on a Wednesday.

b If Colin is called out at the weekend he charges:
- £65 for a 1-hour job
- £95 for a 2-hour job
- £125 for a 3-hour job.

His weekend charges can be worked out using a simple two-step rule.

Complete this formula:

weekend cost in £ =

4 Remember Mikey makes wristbands and belts.
One of his designs uses squares and rectangles of leather.

You can see from the picture that for 4 squares he needs 15 rectangles.

a How many rectangles does he need for 5 squares?

b How many rectangles does he need for 6 squares?

c Write a formula for working out the number of rectangles when you know the number of squares.

d Use your formula to work out how many rectangles are needed for 61 squares.

Before we start...

Hannah is taking out a loan of £560.

She has to choose one of two offers.

OFFER 1	**OFFER 2**
APR of 15%	APR of 16%
+ a fee of £45	+ a fee of £45
which need not be paid	to be paid at the time
immediately.	of taking out the loan.
(It can be added to the loan)	

Which offer is cheaper?

Give your reasons and show your calculations.

 What you need to know

1 Look at these calculator displays. They are all results for money calculations.

> Remember to use £ or p when needed.

For each display, write down the sum of money shown: **i** in pounds   **ii** in pence.

a Display is in pounds.   **b** Display is in pounds.   **c** Display is in pence.

$$5.9 \qquad 0.34 \qquad 1200$$

2 Fill in the missing entries in this table.

Percentage	Decimal fraction	Common fraction
50%		
	0·01	
		$\frac{1}{4}$
	0·13	
6%		
		$\frac{99}{100}$

3 Do these calculations:

a £40 ÷ 5   **b** $\frac{1}{2}$ of £14   **c** £32 × 4   **d** $\frac{1}{5}$ of £135

e £140 ÷ 10   **f** £55 ÷ 2   **g** £85 ÷ 10   **h** $\frac{1}{10}$ of £2·20

i £125·10 ÷ 3   **j** £0·25 × 100   **k** £15·48 ÷ 2.

20.1 Calculating percentages

Facts you should remember

50% + 50% = 100%

$\frac{1}{2}$ + $\frac{1}{2}$ = 1

 $50\% = \frac{1}{2}$

$33\frac{1}{3}\%$ + $33\frac{1}{3}\%$ + $33\frac{1}{3}\%$ = 100%

$\frac{1}{3}$ + $\frac{1}{3}$ + $\frac{1}{3}$ = 1

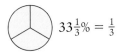 $33\frac{1}{3}\% = \frac{1}{3}$

 $20\% = \frac{1}{5}$

25% + 25% + 25% + 25% = 100%

$\frac{1}{4}$ + $\frac{1}{4}$ + $\frac{1}{4}$ + $\frac{1}{4}$ = 1

 $10\% = \frac{1}{10}$

 $25\% = \frac{1}{4}$

To find 1% of something, divide it by 100.

Example 1

Find $33\frac{1}{3}\%$ of £57.

$33\frac{1}{3}\%$ of £57 = $\frac{1}{3}$ of £57 = £57 ÷ 3 = £19.

> Check:
> £19 + £19 + £19 = £57

Example 2

Calculate 8% of £80.

First find 1% of £80.

1% of £80·00 = 80·00 ÷ 100 = £0·80.

So   8% = 8 × £0·80 = £6·40.

> To find 1% of something,
> divide by 100
> (move the decimal point 2 places left).

Exercise 20.1A

1 Calculate:

  a 10% of £30   **b** $33\frac{1}{3}\%$ of £600   **c** 25% of £490

  d 1% of £55   **e** 20% of £600   **f** 50% of £82.

2 Find:

  a 10% of 80p   **b** 20% of 50p   **c** 50% of £6·24

  d 25% of £5·20   **e** $33\frac{1}{3}\%$ of 99p   **f** 1% of £84·00.

3   **a** Find 1% of £450.

    b **Explain** how you now find 2% of £450

    c Find 2% of £450.

4 Calculate:

    a 3% of £400   **b** 7% of £800

    c 2% of £50   **d** 6% of £21.

5 A smartphone salesman earns 1% of the £65 selling price for each phone he sells.

    a How much does he earn if he sells one phone?

    b He sells 10 phones. How much does he earn?

6 Carol and Melanie wrote a successful App for smartphones. They earned £2500. They each took 50%.

    a How much did each take?

    b They joined a team to make Apps. The team earned £5200. Each member of the team took 25%.

       How much did Carol and Melanie each take this time?

Exercise 20.1B

1 Iain finds an online shop giving discounts on the normal prices of some video games.

Here is their list:

Game	Normal price	Discount
Super Kidz	£20	10%
Fate Fun	£30	20%
Sport Winner	£26	2%
Medal Gains	£22·50	$33\frac{1}{3}$%

    a For each game in the list, calculate the discount.

    b What would Iain pay for each game in the list?

2 In 2012 there were approximately 14 000 industrial robots in the UK.

By 2015 this number is expected to increase by 20%.

    a Find the size of this increase.

    b How many robots should there be in the UK in 2015?

3 Carbon dioxide levels in the atmosphere in 2000 were measured at 370 ppm (parts per million).

By 2013 this had increased by 7%.

    a What was the size of the increase?

    b What was the new level of carbon dioxide in 2013?

4 During 2011 the UK released 550 million tonnes of greenhouse gases into the atmosphere. During 2012 this amount had increased by 4%.

    a What was the size of the increase?

    b How many million tonnes did the UK release during 2012?

---

5 Steve asked Jennifer for a SMAC (Speed Mental Arithmetic Challenge).

One question she gave him was: What is 40% of 15?

He got the answer 6 almost immediately.

Jennifer was impressed. 'How did you do that?'

He said 'I found 20% by dividing by 5, then I doubled.'

Working in pairs, try to find quick ways of working out the following percentages of a number:

60%	5%	12½%	30%	75%
66⅔%	15%	35%	2½%	

Make a poster showing your discoveries.

Make up some questions and run some SMACs in the class!

Here's what you know:

50%: ÷2	33⅓%: ÷3
25%: ÷4	20%: ÷5
10%: ÷10	

20.2 Calculating percentages

Example 1

Calculate 23% of £4500.

First find 1% of £4500 by dividing by 100.

Then multiply by 23 to find 23% of £4500.

Here is the key sequence:

Check that your calculator gives 1035.

So   23% of £4500 is £1035.

Exercise 20.2A

1 Calculate:

    a 4% of £500   **b** 8% of £370   **c** 13% of £250   **d** 27% of £1200

    e 19% of £3800   **f** 37% of £70   **g** 92% of £750   **h** 61% of £122 000.

2 A virus infected 15% of the 360 computers in the offices of a large bank.

How many of their computers were infected?

3 A survey was done at a busy junction.

It was found that 13% of the 2300 cyclists observed went through a red light.

How many cyclists went through a red light?

4 A botanical gardens has a titan arum plant.

It is the world's smelliest plant when it flowers.

Sometimes it is called the corpse flower.

After twelve years it started to flower.

Its height suddenly increased by 28% from 95 cm in 4 days.

a How much did it increase in height?

b What was the new height?

5 Edwardo manufactures hearing aids.

It costs him £210 to produce one hearing aid.

He plans to make them using 3-D printing and would save 35% of this cost.

Using 3-D printing to make one hearing aid:

a how much would he save

b how much would it cost?

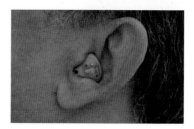

Exercise 20.2B

1 Calculate and round your answers to the nearest penny:

   a 17% of 40p   **b** 34% of 80p

   c 64% of 52p   **d** 4% of £59·15

   e 39% of £310·50   **f** 9% of £231·45.

Reminder for rounding	
24.6	Round this up to 25
24.5	Round this up to 25
24.4	Round this down to 24

2 The government may introduce a new tax on sugary drinks.

It would add 8% to the cost of the drinks.

Cola-Smart costs 93p a bottle.

a What would be the increase on a bottle? (Round your answer to the nearest penny.)

b What would the new price be?

3 WildWave Hair Stylists offer 'full head highlights' for £43·50.

They run an offer reducing this price by 17% for one day only.

Keira takes advantage of this offer.

a How much is her reduction?
(Round your answer to the nearest penny.)

b What is she charged?

4 An internet company offers printer cartridges at a reduction of 85% on the recommended price.

The recommended price is £2·88.

a Calculate the reduction (to the nearest penny).

b What is the reduced price?

5 Tess and Binh are travelling to France.

They keep an eye on the price of 1 euro.

January	**March**
starts at 84p	starts at 84p
falls 17%	falls 28%
then rises 28%	then rises 17%

Do you think the cost of a euro is the same at the end of January and the end of March?

Discuss in pairs without doing calculations.

Then do some calculations to find out if you were right.

Show all your calculations on a poster.

20.3 Simple interest

What is interest?

You can put some of your money in a savings account.

Savings accounts are offered by banks or building societies.

After a while, extra money, called **interest**, is added to your account.

Interest is calculated using a percentage called the **rate of interest**.

Example 1

Zain puts £400 into a savings account.

The rate of interest is 2% p.a.

Calculate his interest after one year.

p.a.
is short for 'per annum' and means 'yearly'

Interest = 2% of £400

= £400 ÷ 100 × 2

= £8

Zain's interest after one year is £8.

Exercise 20.3A

1 The **deposit** is the amount of money in a savings account.

Calculate the interest earned on each deposit in the table.

	Bank	Deposit	Rate of interest	Interest
a	Irish Allied	£200	3% p.a.	
b	Scottish Help	£1300	5% p.a.	
c	Secure Line	£850	6% p.a.	
d	FRSS	£98	2% p.a.	
e	India Invest	£12 000	4% p.a.	

2 Fergus puts £440 in a savings account for a year.

  a He thinks the interest rate is 5% p.a.

     How much interest can he expect to get?

  b However the bank changed the interest rate to 6% p.a.

     How much interest will he actually get?

  c How much more interest is this than he expects?

Exercise 20.3B

1 Yasmin has saved £845·37.

She keeps the money in a savings account with an interest rate of 4% p.a.

  a Calculate her interest for one year. (Round your answer to the nearest penny.)

  b How much will she have in her account after one year?

2 Calculate the interest on these deposits for one year:

	Bank	Deposit	Rate of interest	Interest
a	Midland Mutual	£355	2·5% p.a.	
b	UK Age	£1152	1·8% p.a.	
c	GRSB	£839	3·4% p.a.	
d	Ace Invest	£9817	5·1% p.a.	
e	Island Ltd	£28 513	6·2% p.a.	

Round all your answers to the nearest penny.

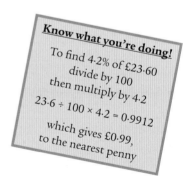

Know what you're doing!

To find 4.2% of £23·60 divide by 100 then multiply by 4.2

$23.6 ÷ 100 × 4.2 = 0.9912$

which gives £0.99, to the nearest penny

3 Shizu puts her savings of £2551·50 into a special savings account.

The interest rate is 6·4% p.a.

  a Calculate the interest after one year. (Round your answers to the nearest penny.)

  b How much does she have in the account now?

Shizu keeps all of this money in for another year.

The bank changes the rate of interest to 5·8% p.a.

  c How much interest does her money make after this second year?

  d How much does she have in her account now?

4 Work in pairs or a group.

Use the internet to find the best available rates of interest for savings accounts.

You will find some accounts have different rules about getting your money back!

Make a poster showing what you found out.

5 Work in pairs or a group.

Design a table showing a bank's yearly interest rates.

Your table will be used by customers at the bank. It will help them to calculate interest.

It must show different deposit amounts and three different rates of interest.

Make your table into a leaflet.

If you know how to make a spreadsheet you may wish to do it this way instead.

20.4 Loans

What does a loan cost?

When you borrow money it will cost you extra money.

Some of this extra cost is interest. Interest is calculated as a percentage of the loan.

You should look for a rate with the letters **APR**. This stands for **Annual Percentage Rate**.

The APR tells you the percentage of the loan you will be charged for one year.

You may also be charged a fee for setting up the loan.

Example 1

Hailey borrows £500 from a loan company.

They charge 12% APR for the loan and a £20 set up fee.

How much does she repay after one year?

Interest charged = 12% of £500 = £60.

Fee = £20.

Total cost = £60 + £20 = £80.

She will repay £500 + £80 = £580.

Exercise 20.4A

1 Calculate the cost of each of these loans.

	Loan Company	Loan	APR	Fee	Cost of loan
a	Pay Boost	£100	20%	None	
b	Sir Wallet	£1000	24%	£10	
c	Easy Money	£600	18%	£5	
d	Loan Pigeons	£230	40%	£30	

2 Elliot added a garage to his house.

He borrowed £3500 from a bank at an APR of 16% to help pay for it.

The bank charged a fee of £25.

a What was the cost of the loan for one year?

b How much is due to the bank after one year?

Exercise 20.4B

1 Aaron was refused a loan at the bank.

He read the Fast Finger Loan Company's advert.

It sounded cheap at 3·8% with no fees.

He borrowed £160 from them.

a What length of time does the 3·8% apply to?

b What is the APR rate? (Hint: 3·8 × 12.)

c What interest will Aaron be charged for a year?

d What is due to Fast Fingers after a year?

e The bank would have charged him 8% p.a. with no fees.

What would the same loan have cost him from the bank?

Fast Fingers

Only 3·8% Per month

up to £10 000

same day   APR 45·6%

Loans available now

NO FEES

2 Investigate payday loan companies on the internet.

What APR rates do they use for their customers?

How do their APR rates compare with bank interest rates?

You should work in pairs or a group and make a poster showing your discoveries.

Preparation for assessment

1 Work out mentally:

  a 25% of £37·20

  b 20% of £310·80

  c 50% of £1620·20

  d 10% of £7·20.

2 Work out mentally:

  a 1% of £850

  b 2% of £850

  c 10% of £55

  d 5% of £55

  e 15% of £55.

3 Lucas plays drums in a band.

One recent gig earned the band £3140.

Lucas received a 25% share.

How much was Lucas paid for the gig?

4 Calculate these percentages. You may need to round to the nearest penny.

   a   4% of £120   b   19% of £43

   c   78% of £130   d   31% of £932

   e   75% of £2   f   8% of £8·70

   g   18% of £294·61   h   5·6% of £48

5 Nicole runs an online games shop.

She recently sold three games for a total of £34·50.

Of this total, 23% is profit.

How much profit did she make?

6 Shona put £168 into a new savings account for a year.

The interest rate was 3% p.a.

   a   Calculate her interest.

   b   How much was in Shona's account after the year?

7 Craig takes out a loan of £600.

   a   What is the APR rate?

   b   What interest is he charged for a year?

   c   How much is due to Moneymen after a year?

Moneymen

Only 1·2% Per month

on your loan

100% guarenteed

NO extra FEES!!

APR 14·4%

8 Remember Hannah is taking out a loan of £560.

She has to choose one of two offers.

OFFER 1	OFFER 2
APR of 15% + a fee of £45 which need not be paid immediately. (It can be added to the loan)	APR of 16% + a fee of £45 to be paid at the time of taking out the loan.

Which offer is cheaper?

Give your reasons and show your calculations.

Before we start...

Rebecca started a tiling on this coordinate grid.
She used lots of V pentominoes.

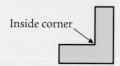

Inside corner

She thinks that if she continues with the tiling
then an inside corner will land on $(-5, -3)$.
Is she right? Show the reason for your answer.

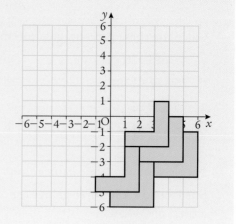

What you need to know

1 Which of these company logos have line symmetry?

a   b   c   d   e   f

2 Copy these shapes and draw in any lines of symmetry.

a   b 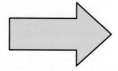 c

21.1 Mirror symmetry

What is mirror symmetry?

Place a mirror along the white dotted line.

The butterfly will look the same. Try it!

This is because the butterfly has **mirror symmetry**.

The white dotted line is the **axis (or line) of symmetry**.

Mirror symmetry is also called **line symmetry**.

Example 1

Copy and complete this symmetrical diagram.

The red dotted line is an axis of symmetry.

One way is to first find the mirror image of each corner …

… then join up the corners in the correct order …

… to get the final symmetrical shape.

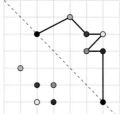

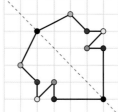

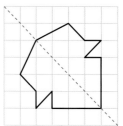

Exercise 21.1A

1 Copy and complete these diagrams.

The red line is an axis of symmetry of the completed shape.

a 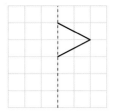   **b** 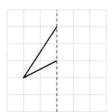   **c** 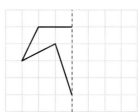   **d**

2 Here are the twelve pentominoes that can also be found in Chapter 15.

Some of them have an axis of symmetry.

One even has 4 axes of symmetry!

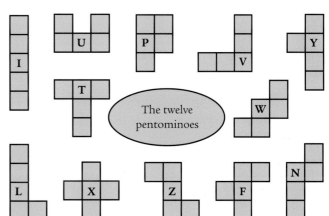

The twelve pentominoes

a Which pentominoes have exactly one axis of symmetry?

b One pentomino has exactly two axes of symmetry. Which one?

3 Dominic has found three ways of making symmetric shapes from pairs of pentominoes.

Neither of the two pentominoes he started with had any lines of symmetry.

Sketch each new shape and show the axis of symmetry.

a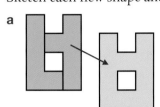

b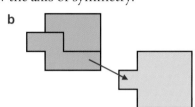

c His third shape combined the P and Y pentominoes. Can you find it?

4 For each diagram, imagine a mirror placed along the red line.

At which position, A, B or C would you see dot P?

a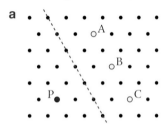

b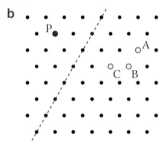

c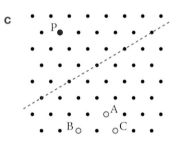

Exercise 21.1B

1 Copy and complete each diagram so that the red line is an axis of symmetry.

a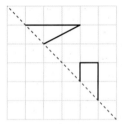

b

c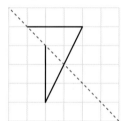

2 Is your face symmetrical?

The photographs on the right are all of the same face.

The original photograph is the top one.

The bottom left photograph uses the left half of the face and its mirror image.

The bottom right photograph uses the right half of the face and its mirror image.

Do you think the two faces at the bottom look like the same person or not?

Do a project in pairs or groups.

You might need help from the IT department.

Left half   Right half

1. Photograph your face.
2. Import it into a computer photo processing package.
3. Select the left half or right half of the photo.
4. Transform it by reflecting (flipping) horizontally.
5. Place the two halves together.
6. Print the result.

Make a poster or PowerPoint® display showing the results.

Is your face symmetrical?

21.2 Tilings

What is a tiling?

Take a shape (a tile). For example:

Now take lots of copies
of that shape:

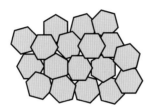

Try to fit them together with:

- no gaps
- no overlaps.

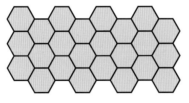

If you can do this you have made a tiling using the shape.

Sometimes two or more different shapes are used in a tiling.

Example 1

Eve says every one of the twelve pentominoes can make a tiling.

Harry thinks not and challenges her to tile with the U pentomino.
He says it's impossible to tile with it.

Can it tile?

Yes it can.

Here is Eve's tiling using the U pentomino.

Some of the shapes are turned over but that
is allowed!

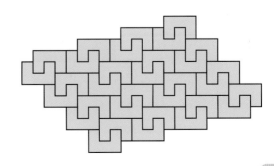

Exercise 21.2A

1 a Harry attempts to tile with the V pentomino.

The image shows his result.

Copy the tiling. Add another three tiles to make two rows.

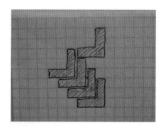

b Here is Harry's attempt to tile with the P pentomino.

Show how this tiling pattern will continue.

You should show how at least two rows fit together.

2 Choose at least three pentominoes (not U, V or P).

Show on squared paper how each one can tile.

You should always show how at least two rows fit together.

Exercise 21.2A

1 a How many different shapes are used to make this tiling?

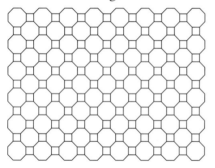

b How many different shapes are used to make this tiling?

c Do either of the tilings in **a** or **b** have axes of symmetry? Explain your answer clearly.

2 You might like to work in pairs or a group for this task.

These photos show tiling patterns using 2 by 1 bricks.

Rosie runs a garden landscaping business.

A customer wants a more unusual pattern for his brick drive than the ones shown.

Make up some unusual tiling designs. Each design should have a regular repeating pattern.
Produce a poster or design a leaflet advertising your new designs for Rosie's customer.

21.3 Coordinates with symmetry and tilings

What are coordinates?

Coordinates describe the position of a point.

You need a starting point: the **origin** O.

You need two **axes**: *x*-axis $\longrightarrow$ *x*

$\qquad\qquad\qquad$ *y*-axis $\; y\uparrow$

You need a **scale** on each axis: 1 2 3 4 5 6 7

The point P has **coordinates** (5, 3).

The *x*-**coordinate** is 5 and the *y*-**coordinate** is 3.

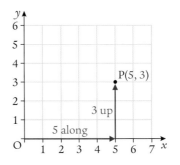

These two tiles form the start of a tiling pattern.

Find the coordinates of:

a the red point on the 1st tile

b the blue point on the 2nd tile

c the yellow point on the 1st tile.

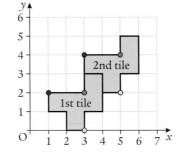

The coordinates are:

a (1, 2) $\qquad$ **b** (5, 4) $\qquad$ **c** (3, 0).

Example 2

Three more tiles are added to the row of the tiling pattern shown in Example 1.

Find the coordinates of the yellow points on all five tiles.

Here are the coordinates:

1st tile	2nd tile	3rd tile	4th tile	5th tile
(3, 0)	(5, 2)	(7, 4)	(9, 6)	(11, 8)

Exercise 21.3A

1 **a** Copy and complete the table to show the coordinates of the blue points.

1st tile	2nd tile	3rd tile	4th tile
	(1, 3)		

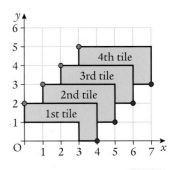

b Copy and complete the table to show the coordinates of the red points.

1st tile	2nd tile	3rd tile	4th tile
			(7, 3)

c A 5th tile is added to the pattern.

Write down the coordinates of the next blue and red dots.

2 a Copy and complete this table.

	1st tile	2nd tile	3rd tile
Yellow dot			
Purple dot			(4, 6)
Green dot			

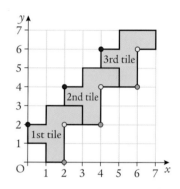

b More tiles are added to the row of the pattern.

Add a column headed '6th tile' to the table and complete it.

3

A mirror is placed on the red line.

Where would you see the image of:

a the blue dot

b the black dot

c the red dot?

To answer, give the coordinates.

4 The red line is a **mirror line** (axis of symmetry).

Copy and complete the table to show the coordinates of the images of the three dots.

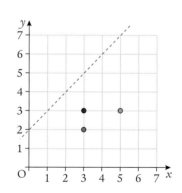

Red dot	Green dot	Blue dot

Exercise 21.3B

1

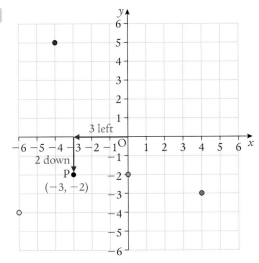

The coordinates of point P are $(-3, -2)$.

Find the coordinates of:

a the yellow dot

b the red dot

c the green dot

d the blue dot.

2 The red line is a **line of symmetry**.

Find the coordinates of the image of:

a the black dot

b the blue dot

c the yellow dot

d the green dot

e the red dot.

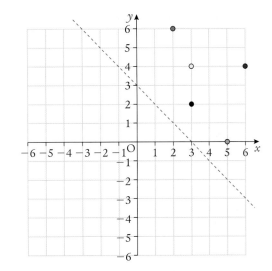

3

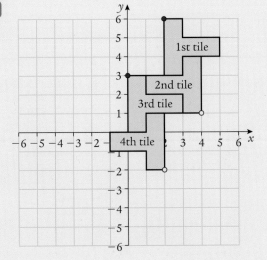

The diagram shows a pattern of tiles.

If the pattern is continued, find the coordinates of:

a the red dot on the 5th tile

b the yellow dot on the 6th tile

c the red dot on the 9th tile

d the yellow dot on the 12th tile.

Preparation for assessment

1   Complete the shape so that the red line is an axis of symmetry:

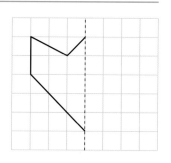

2      Look very closely at this parking sign.

Which letters and digits have mirror symmetry?

3   Tarun is making a tiling using the Z pentomino.

The image shows the start of his tiling

Draw a sketch on squared paper showing how the tiling continues.

Make sure your sketch shows at least two rows of tiles.

4   The diagram shows the start of a tiling pattern.

Give the coordinates of:

a   the red dot on the 3rd tile

b   the yellow dot on the 1st tile

c   the red dot on the 5th tile if the pattern continues

d   the yellow dot on the 7th tile if the pattern continues.

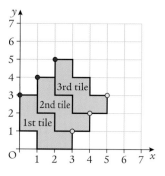

5   Remember Rebecca started a tiling on this coordinate grid.

She used lots of V pentominoes.

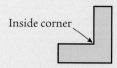

Inside corner

She thinks that if she continues with the tiling
then an inside corner will land on $(-5, -3)$.

Is she right? Show the reason for your answer.

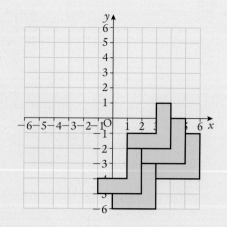

22 Statistics

⏸ Before we start...

Mr Paterson gives his class a test at the end of each topic.

Here are the scores of two students, Rose and Blair.

Rose	Test number	1	2	3	4	5	6	7	8	9	10
	Score	7	8	6	7	7	8	6	7	7	7

Blair	Test number	1	2	3	4	5	6	7	8	9	10
	Score	3	3	4	4	4	5	6	6	7	8

Mr Paterson couldn't decide which student was doing better.

a For each student's scores, calculate: **i** the mean **ii** the mode.

b For each student's scores: **i** draw a graph **ii** describe any trend.

c Can you decide who is doing better?

▶ What you need to know

1 Here is a pictogram to show the different meals which were served by a restaurant during one lunchtime.

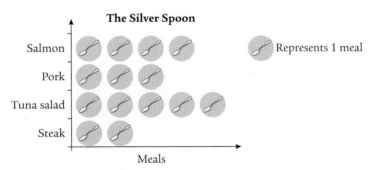

The Silver Spoon

Represents 1 meal

Salmon
Pork
Tuna salad
Steak

Meals

a What type of meal was served the most?

b How many pork meals were served by the restaurant?

c How many meals were sold in total?

d Would it have been possible to answer these questions without the key on the right?

2 Fletch was practising his archery. Here are his scores:

8, 6, 9, 5, 7, 8, 8, 5.

a How many arrows did he fire at the target?

b What was his total score?

c Calculate his mean score per arrow.

d What was the mode of these scores?

3 Jasmine counted the postcards she received one summer.

Country	France	Spain	Turkey	Greece	Italy
Number of postcards	9	8	5	2	4

The information is shown in this bar chart
... but the labels are missing.

a From which country did the most postcards come?

b The horizontal axis should be labelled, 'Countries'.
Which country name should be in place of:
i A   **ii** B   **iii** C?

c The vertical axis also needs a label.
What should it be?

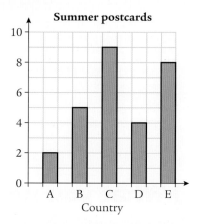

4 Sam and Mike are driving in France.

They make a ready reckoner to change kilometres into miles.

a How many miles are the same as 80 km?

b Estimate 20 km in miles.

c A road sign says that there are 60 km to go
to Saumur.
What (roughly) is this distance in miles?

d The distance between two towns is 40 km.
Estimate this distance in miles.

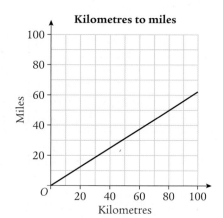

22.1 Pictograms

Example 1

Here is a pictogram which shows how many people attended a show at the Edinburgh Festival.

Write down the numbers attending on:

a   Saturday   b   Wednesday   c   Thursday.

Each icon stands for 6 people ... each icon is made from 6 parts ... so each part is worth 1 person.

a   Saturday ... 9 icons ... $9 \times 6 = 54$ ...   54 people attended.

b   Wednesday ... 3 icons and 5 parts ... $3 \times 6 + 5 = 23$ ...   23 people attended.

c   Thursday ... 4 icons and 2 parts ... $4 \times 6 + 2 = 26$ ...   26 people attended.

Exercise 22.1A

1   Jimmy counts the number of boats moored at Balmaha each day one week.

He records his findings in a pictogram.

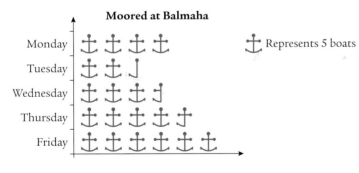

a   What was the busiest day?

b   How many boats were moored on :
   i Tuesday   ii Thursday?

c   How many more boats were moored on Friday than on Wednesday?

2 Ernesto charts the sale of trees in the lead up to Christmas.

In the diagram, each icon represents 10 sales.

Each branch represents 1 tree.

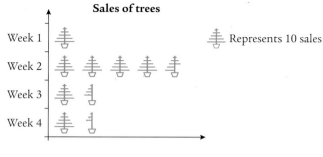

Sales of trees

Represents 10 sales

a Which week had the most sales?

b How many sales was this?

c What were the total sales over the four weeks?

d How many more trees were sold in week 2 than in week 1?

3 Caris counted the number of cars parked in the street in front of her house each hour.

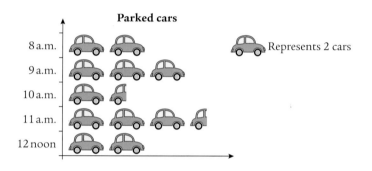

Parked cars

Represents 2 cars

a How many were parked at:
  i 8 a.m.   ii 9 a.m.?

b How many more were parked at 9 a.m. than at 10 a.m.?

c i What was the busiest time?
  ii How many cars were parked then?

Exercise 22.1B

1 Chris ran a concert during the week.

In the intervals, he sold CDs of the acts.

The table shows the sales.

Day	Mon	Tue	Wed	Thu	Fri
Sales	10	15	13	17	21

He is going to use the icon 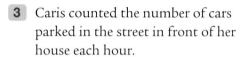 to represent 5 sales.

a How many icons are needed to represent Monday's sales?

b Draw how Wednesday's sales will be represented.

2 Miss Kaytoo sells replacement windows.

She uses a table and pictogram to record the different types of windows that she sells.

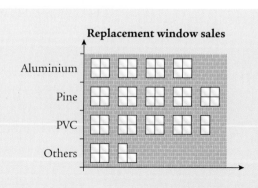

Replacement window sales

Aluminium

Pine

PVC

Others

Type	Aluminium	Pine	PVC	Others
Sales	16			

a The key is missing from the pictogram. Make a sketch of the key.

b Copy and complete the table.

3 Kat collects information on the number of coaches that turn up for the big match each Saturday over four weeks.

Week	1	2	3	4
Coaches	15	17	23	19

She decides to use 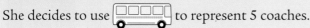 to represent 5 coaches.

 represents 4 coaches, and so on.

Draw a pictogram to show Kat's data.

22.2 Bar charts

Example 1

Rachel counts the weeds in her vegetable patch.

The bar graph shows her findings.

a Which was the most common weed?

b How many plantains did she count?

c How many more daisies than dandelions did she count?

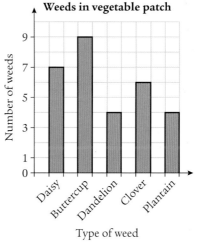

a Buttercup.

b 4 plantains.

c 7 daisies, 4 dandelions: $7 - 4 = 3$ more daisies.

Exercise 22.2A

1 Shani asked, 'How many mobile phones have you owned?'

From the answers, she made a bar chart.

a Who had owned the fewest mobile phones?

b Who had owned the most mobile phones?

c Who had owned twice as many as Ronnie?

d How many people had owned fewer than Zak?

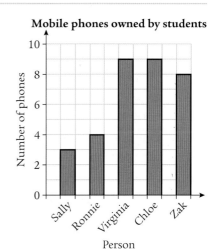

2 Five people are selling raffle tickets.

This bar chart shows the value of the tickets sold by each person.

a Who has sold the most tickets?

b Who has sold the least tickets?

c Who sold more tickets than G. Chandra?

d They were hoping to raise more than £300.

Have they succeeded?

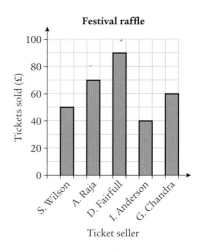

3 Walter kept a record of the birds that visited his bird table in one hour. Here are the results.

Bird	Blackbird	Chaffinch	Sparrow	Robin	Jackdaw	Blue Tit
Number	2	8	9	1	5	1

Draw a bar chart to illustrate this data.

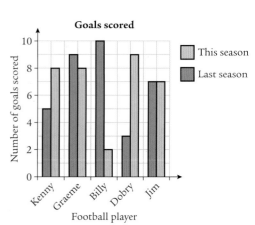

Exercise 22.2B

1 This bar chart shows the value of business made by the sales staff of a company.

a Who made sales to the value of £8000?

b What was the value of the sales made by Sonya?

c Who made the same amount of sales?

d The company set a sales target for the week of £6500. Who reached this target?

2 This bar chart shows the goals scored by five boys who have played in the same football team for the last two years.

a Who scored the same number of goals in both seasons?

b One player missed a lot of games this season through injury. Who do you think that was?

c One player changed his position from defence to attack. Who do you think that was?

d Who scored the most goals over the two seasons?

e How many more goals did Kenny score this season than last?

3 Lucy kept a record of the flavours of crisps sold in the school tuck shop over two weeks.

Flavour	Ready salted	Cheese & onion	Salt & vinegar	Prawn cocktail	Smokey bacon
This week	3	7	9	8	4
Last week	5	8	8	7	6

Draw a bar chart like the one in Question **2** to compare last week's sales with this week's.

22.3 Spotting trends and making comparisons

A line graph can be useful to see how a thing changes with time.
This is called a **trend**.

Example 1

This graph shows how the value of an antique chair has changed over time.

Describe the trend.

The graph shows that the value of the chair is increasing over time.

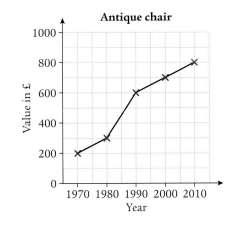

Exercise 22.3A

1 This graph shows Shelley's annual earnings from 2008 to 2012.

a How much did Shelley earn in 2009?

b In which year did Shelley's earnings stay the same ?

c Shelley had been working part time and then started working full time. In which year did she go full time?

d Is the trend rising, falling or remaining constant?

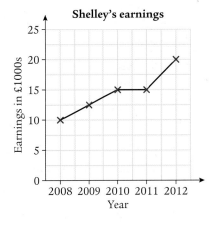

2 In science Esther does an experiment to see how quickly ice melts.

She makes a graph of her results.

   a How much did the ice cube weigh at the start?

   b How much did it weigh after 8 minutes?

   c When did it weigh 25 g?

   d Describe the trend.

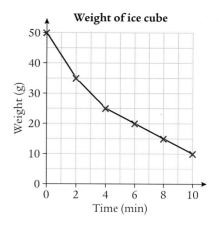

Weight of ice cube

3 Jacques has his weight checked every week.

The results are shown on this graph.

   a What was his weight at the start?

   b What is his weight in week 3?

   c When was his weight 40 kg?

   d Describe the trend.

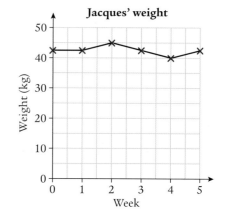

Jacques' weight

Comparing data sets

To compare sets of data it is best to sort them first.

This can be done by using frequency tables.

Example 2

Gordon keeps a record of his golf scores.

He wants to compare last year's scores with this year's.

Remember that in golf the lower the score, the better.

He has them displayed in frequency tables.

Last year	Score	75	76	77	78	79	80	81	82	83
	No. of times	1	2	4	5	8	6	5	4	2

This year	Score	72	73	74	75	76	77	78	79	80
	No. of times	1	3	9	7	6	6	3	2	2

a What was his lowest score: **i** this year   **ii** last year?

b What was his highest score: **i** this year   **ii** last year?

c What was the modal score for each year?

d Use his modal scores to complete the following sentence:

Generally, Gordon's scores were ...... this year than last year.

a i 72   **ii** 75.

b i 80   **ii** 83.

c This year ... modal score 74; last year ... modal score was 79.
The modal score is the score with the highest frequency.

d *Generally, Gordon's scores were **lower** this year than last year.*

Exercise 22.3B

1 This table shows the number of bales of hay that a farmer has in his barn on the first day of each month.

Month	Aug	Sept	Oct	Nov	Dec	Jan	Feb	Mar	Apr	May	Jun	Jul
No. of bales	510	508	498	470	425	360	305	203	122	76	51	47

a How many bales were there on:

    i 1st November   **ii** 1st February   **iii** 1st April?

b Was the number of bales increasing or decreasing?

c During which month did he have 450 bales in his barn?

d Copy and complete this sentence to describe the trend:

The longer it is after August, the ...... the number of bales in the barn.

2 George started up a business cleaning windows.

The table shows the number of customers he had in the weeks after he started his business.

Week	1	2	3	4	5	6	7	8	9
Customers	2	4	7	11	15	20	23	26	28

a How many customers did George have in week 4?

b How many customers did he have in week 7?

c Was the number of customers increasing or decreasing?

d Copy and complete this sentence:

The longer after George started his business, the ...... customers he has.

3 Simon worked in the Riverside Hotel.

When he carried the guests' bags to their rooms they sometimes gave him a tip.

Riverside	Tip in £	0	1	2	3	4	5
	No. of times	2	2	4	3	2	2

He later started working in the Palace Hotel.

Palace	Tip in £	0	1	2	3	4	5
	No. of times	0	1	2	2	6	4

a   How many times did Simon receive a tip of £5 at: i The Riverside Hotel   ii The Palace Hotel?

b   How many times did he receive no tip at: i The Riverside Hotel   ii The Palace Hotel?

c   What was the modal tip at: i The Riverside Hotel   ii The Palace Hotel?

d   Copy and complete the following:

In general, Simon received ...... tips at the Palace Hotel.

22.4 Probability

The **probability** of an event is a guide to the **likelihood** of that event occuring.

If an **incident** occurs and the number of **possible outcomes** is known then the probability of a particular outcome can be worked out.

If each outcome is equally likely then:

$$\text{probability of an event} = \frac{\text{number of ways the event can occur}}{\text{all the things that can occur}}.$$

Example 1

A dice is thrown.

a   How many different things can happen?

b   How many outcomes are even numbers?

c   What is the probability of an even number being thrown?

d   What is the probability of a number being thrown that can be divided by 3?

a   There are 6 possible outcomes: the dice could land on 1, 2, 3, 4, 5 or 6.

b   There are 3 possible even numbers: 2, 4, and 6.

c   'P(even)' is short for the probability that an even number will be thrown.

$$\text{So we have, P(even)} = \frac{\text{even outcomes}}{\text{all the possible outcomes}} = \frac{3}{6} = \frac{1}{2}.$$

d   Only 3 and 6 can be divided by 3.

$$\text{P(number can be divided by 3)} = \frac{\text{numbers divisible by 3}}{\text{all the possible outcomes}} = \frac{2}{6} = \frac{1}{3}.$$

Example 2

In Janet's class they did a short survey. They were each asked two questions:

Do you walk to school? and *Have you had any absences in the past month?*

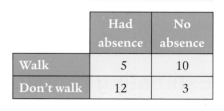

	Had absence	No absence
Walk	5	10
Don't walk	12	3

What is the probability that a person in Janet's class, picked at random, will:

a have walked to school

b have walked to school and had no absences

c have not walked to school and had no absences?

a Counting all the cells we see there are 30 students in the class.

15 of them walked to school.

$$P(\text{walk to school}) = \frac{15}{30} = \frac{1}{2}.$$

b $P(\text{walk to school and had no absences}) = \frac{10}{30} = \frac{1}{3}.$

c $P(\text{don't walk to school and had no absences}) = \frac{3}{30} = \frac{1}{10}.$

Exercise 22.4A

1 What is the probability of getting a head when you toss a coin?
Give your answer as a common fraction.

2 A school day is picked at random for an assembly. What is the probability that it will be a Monday?

3 You meet a stranger. What is the least likely month to contain his birthday?

4 The picture shows Michael's hand in a game of cards.

His opponent is about to pick one of Michael's cards at random.

a What is the probability that he will pick:
   i an 8   **ii** a spade   **iii** black?

b Which is more likely:
   i picking a jack or a heart
   ii picking a spade or not picking a spade?

5 This hand has 10 cards.

a Use this to help you fill in the table.

	Red	Black
Face		
Plain		

b What is the probability of picking: **i** a black plain card **ii** a red face card?

c Which is more likely:

   i you pick a red plain card or you pick a face card

   ii you pick a red card or you pick a plain card?

Estimating probability

If you assume the results of a survey are typical of a situation, you can estimate probabilities linked with that situation.

Example 3

A company making light bulbs takes a sample of 50 bulbs and measures their lifetimes.

Lifetime (months)	0	1	2	3	4	5
Frequency	2	8	10	15	10	5

Assuming the sample is typical of the product, estimate the probability that:

a a bulb will have a life of 3 months

b a bulb's lifetime will be less than 3 months.

a From 50 bulbs, 15 had a life of 3 months. So P(bulb has life of 3 months) $= \dfrac{15}{50} = \dfrac{3}{10}$.

b 20 bulbs had a life less than 3 months. So P(bulb has life less than 3 months) $= \dfrac{20}{50} = \dfrac{2}{5}$.

Exercise 22.4B

1 For the past four years, Tahir has kept an eye on the weather in November.

The table shows 120 days (four Novembers) of weather.

Assuming this is typical of November, what is the probability that 1st November next year will be:

Nov	Windy	Still
Rain	32	48
Dry	12	28

a a rainy windy day

b a rainy day

c dry but windy

d still and dry?

2 The vet logged his calls one morning. He noted the animal patients.

Animal	Cat	Dog	Horse	Cow	Sheep	Other
Calls	15	28	5	3	2	7

a If this is typical of his business, what is the probability that his next call will be:

   i about a cat   **ii** about a cat or a dog   **iii** not about a horse?

b Which is more likely: the next call will be about 'a cow or a sheep' or it will be about an animal in the 'other' category.

3 The local greengrocer made a chart of the damaged goods he had over a week.

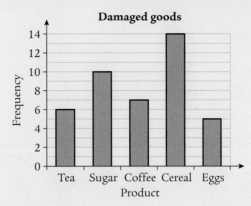

Damaged goods

If this is typical of the damaged goods he gets, what is the probability that the next damaged object will be:

a a cereal pack   **b** a sugar bag   **c** not an egg?

Preparation for assessment

1 Carrie counted the number of letters delivered in the post every morning for the week.

She recorded the numbers in this table, but forgot to fill it in on Saturday.

Day	Monday	Tuesday	Wednesday	Thursday	Friday	Saturday
Cars	4	6	5	2	7	

The total number of letters delivered in the week was 30.

There were no letters delivered on Sunday.

Using  to represent 2 letters, make a pictogram to illustrate the data.

2 The 2nd year girls at Valleyglen High School are raising money for new football strips.

They ask for donations from all the 2nd year classes. The bar chart shows the amount raised by each class.

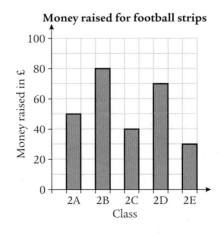

Money raised for football strips

a Which class raised the least money?

b Which class raised twice as much as 2C?

c What was the total amount of money raised?

3 This graph shows the number of motor cycles sold by a dealership between 2008 and 2013.

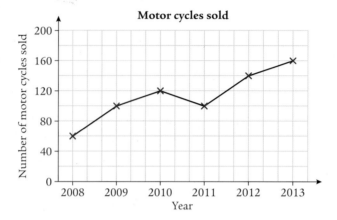

a How many motor cycles did the dealership sell in: **i** 2010 **ii** 2012?

b Describe the trend of the graph.

4 Jack has these 13 cards. His friend picks one at random.

What is the probability that the card is:

a red

b a face card

c worth less than 9 (an ace is worth 1)

d not a red face card?

5 Remember Mr Paterson gives his class a test at the end of each topic.

Here are the scores of two students, Rose and Blair.

Rose	Test number	1	2	3	4	5	6	7	8	9	10
	Score	7	8	6	7	7	8	6	7	7	7

Blair	Test number	1	2	3	4	5	6	7	8	9	10
	Score	3	3	4	4	4	5	6	6	7	8

Mr Paterson couldn't decide on which student was doing better.

a For each student's scores, calculate: **i** the mean **ii** the mode.

b For each student's scores: **i** draw a graph **ii** describe any trend.

c Can you decide who is doing better?